THE COMPLETE

STITCH DIRECTORY

◇

Knitting, Crochet, Embroidery and Needlepoint

THE COMPLETE
STITCH DIRECTORY

◇

Knitting, Crochet, Embroidery and Needlepoint

Crescent Books
New York

Executive Manager	Susan Egerton-Jones
Design Manager	Hans Verkroost
Editor	Patsy North
Designer	Sue Hall
Consultants	Linda Seward
	Penny Hill
	Marilyn Wilson
	Sue Hopper
	Margaret Tucker
Translation	Sheilagh Sainsbury Brown
Production	Peter Phillips
	Stewart Bowling

This 1989 edition published by Crescent Books,
distributed by Crown Publishers, Inc.,
225 Park Avenue South, New York, New York 10003.

Edited and designed by the Artists House
Division of Mitchell Beazley International Ltd
Artists House
14–15 Manette Street
London W1V 5LB

Text and illustrations from the work "Millepunti"
© 1982 Gruppo Editoriale Fabbri S.p.A. Milan
Additional pictures © 1988 Mitchell Beazley Publishers
Additional text and translation © 1988 Mitchell Beazley
Publishers
The work "The Complete Stitch Directory" © 1988
Mitchell Beazley Publishers

ISBN 0-517-67194-8

Typeset by Hourds Typographica, Stafford
Reproduction by M. & E. Reproduction, Fambridge
Printed in Milan by Gruppo Editoriale Fabbri S.p.A.

h g f e d c b a

CONTENTS

INTRODUCTION

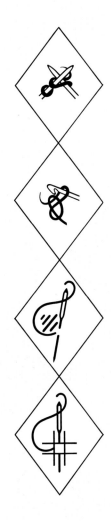

The Complete Stitch Directory is an invaluable reference book and source of inspiration for everyone interested in knitting, crochet and embroidery. These traditional crafts remain as popular today as they have ever been and they continue to attract new enthusiasts who appreciate the beautiful quality of hand-made items and would like to acquire the skills necessary to create them themselves. Manufacturers are responding to this enthusiasm by producing an ever-expanding range of yarns and threads, increasingly using unusual blends of colors and fibers, both natural and man-made, so that the possibilities for creating exciting designs in knitwear, crochet work and embroidery have never been better. It takes only one visit to a well-stocked yarn shop to make one's fingers start itching to begin a new piece of work.

The Complete Stitch Directory provides a wealth of material for those who wish to explore the crafts of knitting, crochet and embroidery more fully, whether to brush up on their technical knowledge or to pursue design ideas of their own. The book is divided into three main sections covering the basics as well as some of the more unusual techniques of each craft and each containing a comprehensive library of stitches, beautifully photographed in full color to show all the detail clearly. Full pattern instructions are given with each stitch.

The knitting and crochet sections begin with a thorough explanation of basic techniques with the aid of detailed diagrams, so that beginners can learn the groundwork while those with more expertise can refresh their memories about the various methods of increasing and decreasing, making neat edgings and borders and working in the round. In addition, traditional and more complicated techniques such as Aran knitting, filet crochet and Irish lace are included, with working diagrams and examples of the stitches and patterns which can be made.

The stitch collection in the knitting and crochet sections contains a wide range of patterns suitable for many different effects. For a delicate fabric, choose from the eyelet stitches or the lacy stitches or incorporate beads into the work, while for a chunky look, find inspiration from the knitted cables or the relief crochet. Some stunning effects can also be achieved by mixing shades of yarn and following one of the many multicolored patterns.

The collection of stitches will provide ideas for anyone interested in designing their own knit and crochet wear and can also be used to adapt a standard commercial pattern to create a completely original garment. To do this, select a new stitch that will suit the basic style of the garment and the type of yarn suggested for it: for example, a T-shaped sweater knitted in a chunky wool might look more interesting worked in one of the Aran patterns. Then experiment with the gauge of the new stitch to make sure that it will match the gauge of the original pattern. In this way, the garment will work up with the correct measurements. For beginners, it is best to use a simple shape so that the chosen stitch makes the impact rather than the detailed styling of the garment. Many of the knitting and crochet stitches can also be used for items around the home such as crib covers, blankets, travel rugs and pillows. Although size is not so critical here, select a stitch that is appropriate to the weight of yarn and the purpose for which it will be used.

The embroidery and needlepoint section of *The Complete Stitch Directory* encompasses a wide variety of stitches and methods from the basics of free embroidery to the more disciplined techniques of counted thread work such as Assisi work and Hardanger embroidery. It explains in detail how to work stem stitches, chain stitches, feather stitches and many more, with the aid of photographs showing the correct needle position. Other areas of embroidery covered are drawn thread work and smocking, with explanations of how to prepare the fabric and a selection of suitable stitches to use. Appliqué and beadwork are also

included and the section concludes with a colorful collection of needlepoint stitches, including some of the beautiful Florentine patterns.

In order to make *The Complete Stitch Directory* easy to use, each section is coded with the appropriate symbol for knitting, crochet, embroidery or needlepoint. This will be found at the top of each page, together with the type of technique or family of stitches and the name of each individual stitch on that page, making a useful reference when glancing through the book. In addition, there is a contents list for each section and a comprehensive index, so that any stitch or technique can be quickly located. For example, to find a selection of lacy stitches to use in a crochet design, look for this group of stitches in the contents list for the crochet section. This will refer you to six pages of lacy stitches to choose from.

So add *The Complete Stitch Directory* to your library – whether you are already a crafts enthusiast or a beginner about to embark on a new and rewarding pastime, you will refer to it again and again.

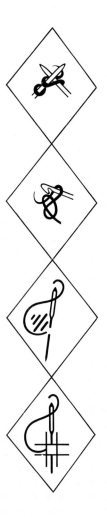

INTRODUCTION
TO
KNITTING

This knitting section presents a wealth of inspirational stitch patterns, ranging from delicate lacy stitches and multicolored designs full of visual impact to the heavily textured effects of cable knitting. It also explains all the basic techniques that a knitter may need to refer to when working a pattern.

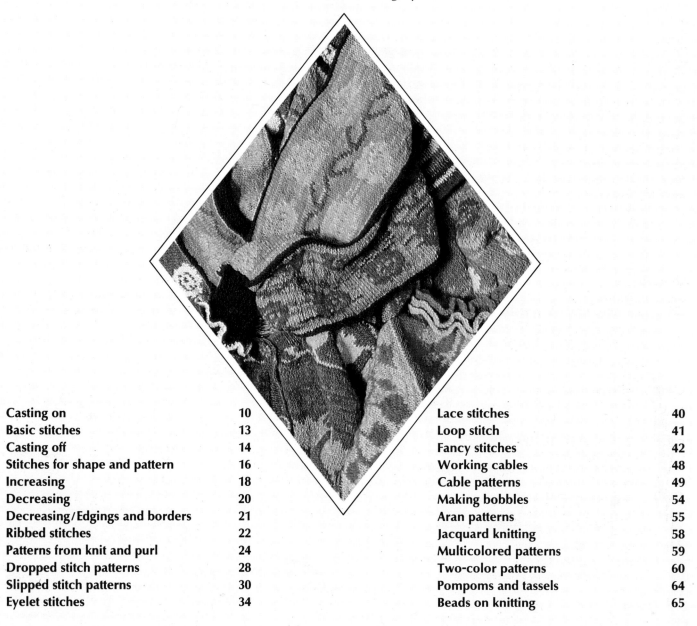

Materials

Needles Knitting needles are used in pairs or sets. They are machine-made of aluminum, steel, plastic or wood in varying lengths and are graded in sizes from 00 to 19.

Double-pointed needles are sold in sets of four or six, sized in the same way as ordinary needles. They are used for knitting in the round, either for tubular shapes such as socks, gloves or sweater sleeves or for flat rounds such as shawls.

Circular needles are a pair of pointed needles joined by a flexible length of wire or plastic. They are made in various sizes and lengths and are used for large tubular shapes such as sweaters or skirts.

Cable needles are very short double-pointed needles and come in just a few sizes. They are used for holding stitches while working a cable.

Yarns There are many types and weights of yarn, made of natural or man-made fibers or a mixture of both. However, you can knit with anything as long as it is flexible—even strips of fabric, ribbons and string.

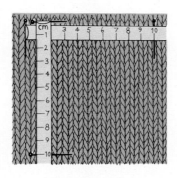

Gauge

Always work a stitch sample to check your gauge before making any garment. The gauge is given at the beginning of a pattern. Knit a sample at least 6in square, using the correct yarn, needles and pattern.

Measuring the stitches Lay the sample on a flat surface. Place pins vertically 4in apart and then count the stitches between them.

Measuring the rows Lay the sample on a flat surface. Place pins horizontally 4in apart and then count the rows between them.

If there are too many stitches and rows, try a size larger needle. If there are too few stitches and rows, try a size finer needle.

Abbreviations

beg	beginning
C2L	K second stitch through back of loop, then K first stitch and slip off needle together
C2R	K second stitch, then K first stitch and slip off needle together
C3B(P)	slip 1 stitch onto cable needle, hold at back of work, K2 then P1 from cable needle
C3F(K)	slip 2 stitches onto cable needle, hold at front of work, K1 then K2 from cable needle
C3F(P)	slip 2 stitches onto cable needle, hold at front of work, P1 then K2 from cable needle
C4B	slip 2 stitches onto cable needle, hold at back of work, K2 then K2 from cable needle
C4F	slip 2 stitches onto cable needle, hold at front of work, K2 then K2 from cable needle
dec	decrease

dpn	double pointed needle (cable needle)
inc	increase
K	knit
K-wise	knitwise
K1D	K into next stitch, 1 row down
P	purl
P-wise	purlwise
patt	pattern
PC2R	P second stitch, then P first stitch and slip off needle together
psso	pass slipped stitch over
p2sso	pass 2 slipped stitches over
rem	remaining
rep	repeat
RS	right side
sl1	slip 1 knitwise
sl1 P	slip 1 purlwise
sl1 yfwd	slip 1 purlwise keeping yarn at front of work
sl1 ybk	slip 1 purlwise keeping yarn at back of work
st st	stockinette stitch
T2L	P second stitch through back of loop, then K first stitch and slip off needle together

T2R	K second stitch, then P first stitch and slip off needle together
tbl	through back of loop(s)
tog	together
WS	wrong side
ybk	yarn back
yfwd	yarn forward
yo	yarn forward between K stitches
	yarn over needle between a P and a K stitch
	yarn around needle between P stitches or between a K and a P stitch
	yarn over to make a stitch
yo 2	yarn around needle twice
ytf	yarn to front

The instructions given between two asterisks * are repeated to the end of the row, or to the next instructions given.

Example 1: Row 1 *K1, P1*. This means repeat K1, P1 to the end of the row.

Example 2: Row 1 *K2, P3*, end with K2. This means repeat K2, P3 to the last 2 stitches, then K2.

Work instructions within brackets ( ) the number of times stated.

Casting on
Casting on with one needle
Casting on with two needles
Casting on with two needles: twisted method

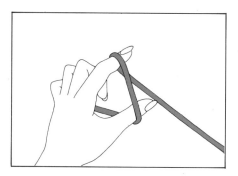

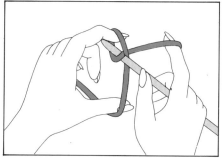

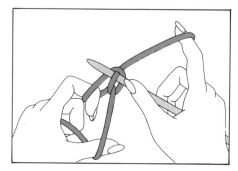

Casting on with one needle 1. Take the yarn in the left hand and pull a length three times longer than is needed to work with. With the thumb and first finger of the left hand, make a loop.

2. Holding the needle in the right hand, insert it through the loop from below. With the first finger of the right hand, wind the yarn from the ball under and over the needle from left to right.

3. With the first finger of the left hand slip the loop over the needle point, withdraw the finger and tighten the loop. The first stitch is made. Repeat for each stitch.

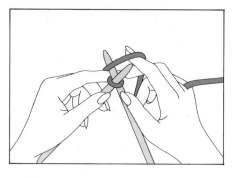

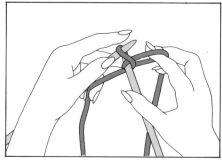

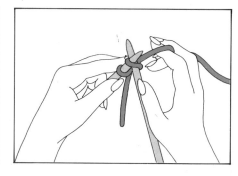

Casting on with two needles 1. Make the first stitch as in the previous method. Put it on the left-hand needle. Hold one needle in each hand. Insert the right-hand needle into the stitch and wind the yarn up and over the needle.

2. Draw the right-hand needle back a little and make the second stitch by pulling the left-hand needle up and drawing the yarn through the first stitch.

3. Put the second stitch onto the left-hand needle and continue making stitches with the right-hand needle and passing them onto the left-hand needle until the desired number of stitches are worked.

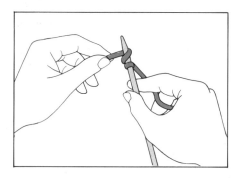

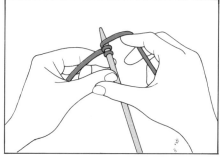

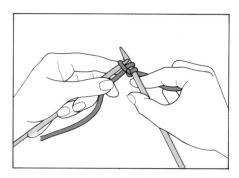

Casting on with two needles: twisted method 1. Pull a length of yarn to work with. Make a loop with the thumb and first finger of the left hand and insert the needle into it. Wind the working yarn over and under the needle from the left.

2. Hold the working yarn with the left hand, and the yarn coming from the ball in the right. Wind the latter under and over the needle from the right.

3. Lift the first loop over the second, using the left-hand needle. This makes the first stitch. Continue in this way until the desired number of stitches are worked.

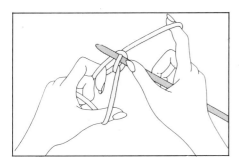

Double casting on: 1st method 1. This forms a casing through which ribbon or elastic may later be threaded. It requires a special method of casting on. Cast on half the number of stitches finally required, using a color different from that of the work.

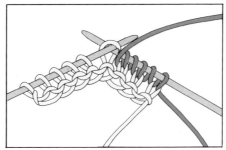

2. With the working yarn work the first row in the following way: Knit one stitch, bring the yarn to the front of the work, making a stitch (because the yarn will pass over the right-hand needle to work the next stitch).

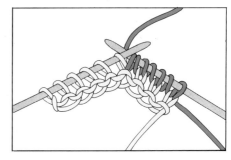

3. Knit into the next stitch and then yarn over to make a stitch. Repeat these two actions to the end of the row, ending up with double the number of stitches.

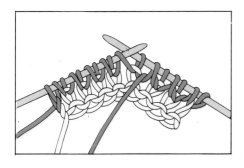

4. On the return row, slip the made stitches purlwise, without working them, holding the yarn to the back of the work. Purl the stitches which were previously knitted.

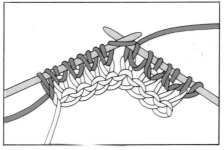

5. Now slip the purl stitches of the previous row, and taking the yarn to the back, knit the stitches slipped in the previous row.

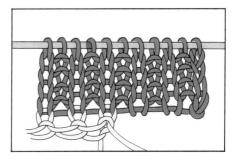

6. Work like this for four or five rows, then continue normally in 1/1 rib and the selected stitch. Finally unravel the different color cast-on edge.

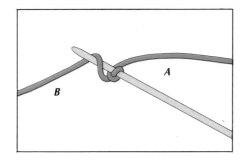

Double casting on: 2nd method 1. With the working yarn **A**, make the first stitch on the needle. Then take yarn **B** around the needle, passing it from the front, over the needle and back down.

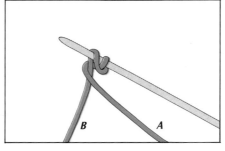

2. With the right hand, take yarn **A** under the needle from back to front, holding it firm. In this way the second stitch is made.

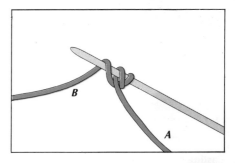

3. With the left hand, take yarn **B** over the needle again from front to back, as before.

Casting on
Double casting on, continued
Casting on with four needles
Casting on with a circular needle

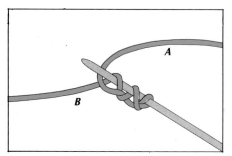

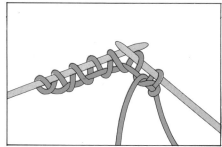

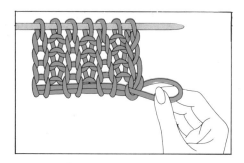

4. With the right hand, take yarn **A** from front to back under the needle, so making the third stitch. Continue in this way until the required number of stitches have been made.

5. On the following row knit into the knit stitches and slip the purl as set. Do not work the last stitch.

6. Work another four or five rows in this way, then start normal 1/1 ribbing. At the end of the work, carefully pull the loop made by the unworked stitch and draw out the starting yarn.

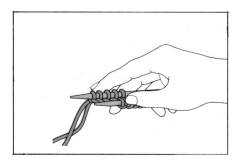

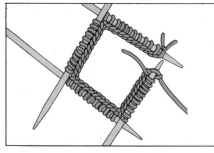

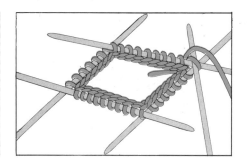

Casting on with four needles: 1st method
1. On each of the four double-pointed needles, cast on a quarter of the total stitches. Having completed one needle, lay the second alongside the first, with the point slightly protruding. Continue in this way with the other needles.

2. Having cast on the last stitch, mark this point with a marker thread of a different color knotted through the stitch. Each round will start here.

3. Start working with a fifth needle taking care at the first and last stitches, pulling the yarn tight to avoid a hole forming at the start or end of the work. At the end of the first round, the marker thread shows the start of the second.

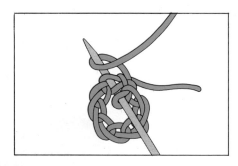

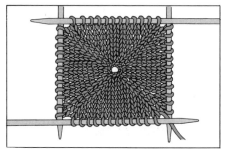

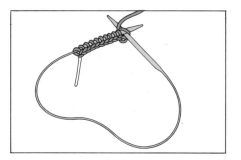

Casting on with four needles: 2nd method
1. This is used to work a flat piece of work starting at the center. With a crochet hook make a chain of eight stitches (or a number divisible by four) and pick these up with the needles.

2. Slip two stitches onto each needle. Continue working, increasing one stitch between each group of two on the first round, and increasing two stitches at the center of each section on the following rounds.

Casting on with a circular needle Cast on the number of stitches required for the work, then at the start of the work knot a marker thread of a contrasting color through the stitch. Each round starts here. Keep the last stitch on the right-hand point and work the round from the left.

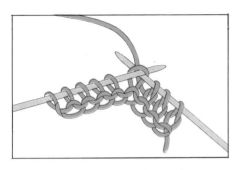

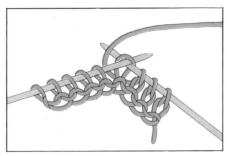

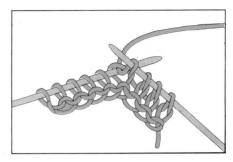

Knit or plain stitch 1. Keep the needle holding the stitches in the left hand and with the yarn held firmly behind the needle, insert the right-hand needle into the next stitch from front to back.

2. With the first finger of the right hand take the yarn around the point of the right-hand needle as shown.

3. Withdraw the right-hand needle a little, lifting the yarn through and letting the worked stitch fall from the left-hand needle.

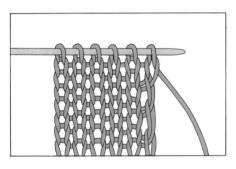

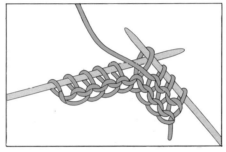

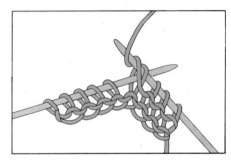

4. Finish the row in this way. The result will be a line of knit stitches on one side of the work and a line of purl on the other. Working alternate rows of knit and purl makes stockinette stitch, as shown above.

Purl stitch 1. Keeping the needle holding the stitches in the left hand, insert the needle from back to front, with the yarn in front of the needle.

2. Take the working yarn around the needle, coming back to the front under the needle.

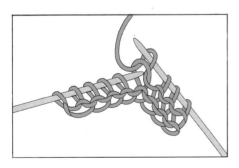

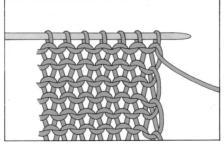

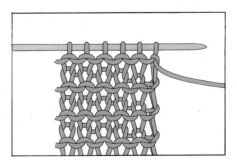

3. Lift the yarn through, letting the worked stitch fall from the left-hand needle.

4. Continue in this way to the end of the row. This produces purl stitches on one side of the work and knit on the other. The purl side of stockinette stitch can be used as the right side, as shown above. It is then called reverse stockinette stitch.

Garter stitch This basic stitch is worked with all rows the same, either all knit or all purl without alternating.

Casting off

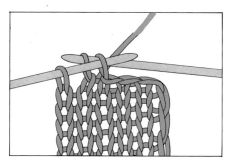

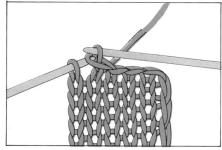

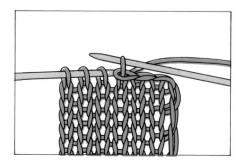

Casting off: simple method 1. Work two stitches then *pass the point of the left-hand needle into the first of these stitches.

2. Lift the first stitch over the second, carefully lengthening it*.

3. Work another stitch normally and repeat from * to *.

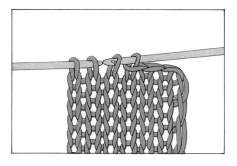

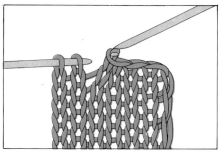

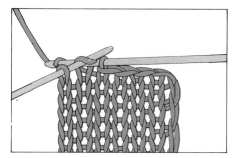

Casting off with a crochet hook: 1st method 1. This method results in a tighter finish. Leave the stitches on the left-hand needle and insert the crochet hook into the first two stitches.

2. *Draw the second stitch through the first. Insert the crochet hook into the next stitch, and repeat from *. In this method the working yarn is not used.

Casting off with a crochet hook: 2nd method This method uses the working yarn, and the tension of the work can be regulated. Insert the crochet hook into the first two stitches, *wind the yarn around the crochet hook, pull it through the stitches. Insert the crochet hook into the next stitch and repeat from *.

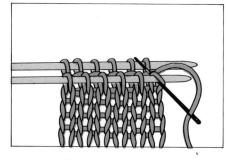

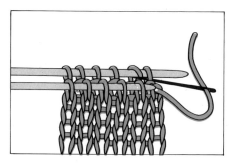

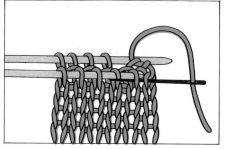

Casting off double stitches 1. Insert a needle through the stitches so that they are divided into two groups, slipping the second group alternately onto the second needle. Thread a sewing needle. Thread this through a stitch on the front needle, letting the stitch drop.

2. Thread through the first two stitches on the back needle: enter into the first stitch from behind and come out through the next stitch from the inside. Let them both drop.

3. *Return to the front needle, re-entering the first stitch (the one just dropped) and coming out through the next stitch as shown, letting it drop.

Casting off

Casting off double stitches, continued   Finishing the work
Casting off joining two pieces   Darning in vertically
                                          Darning in horizontally

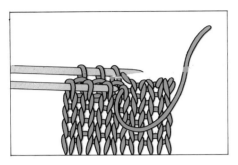

4. Return to the back needle, re-enter from behind the stitch previously dropped, come out through the next stitch and let it drop*. Repeat from * to *.

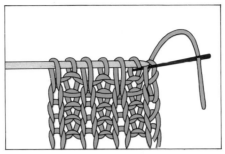

Casting off double stitches from one needle 1. The previous method can be worked leaving the stitches on one needle. Insert the threaded sewing needle into the first stitch from behind, then through the second, letting them drop.

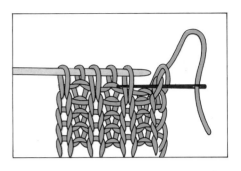

2. *Re-enter the first stitch from behind and out through the third stitch. Enter the second stitch from behind and out through the fourth*. Continue in this way, always taking two stitches.

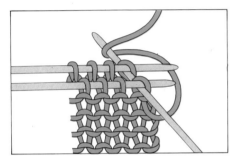

Casting off joining two pieces 1. This is worked on the wrong side. Keep the pieces to be joined on two needles, right sides together. With a third needle knit together the first stitch from each needle, making a single stitch.

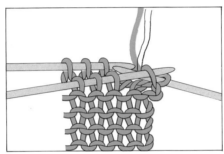

2. *Knit together the next two stitches, one from each needle, making a second stitch. Slip the first stitch over the second*.

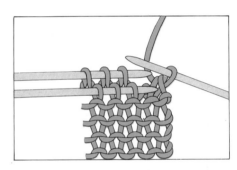

3. Repeat from * to * to the end of the row. This method achieves two sections of work cast off with one seam. It is widely used to finish shoulder seams.

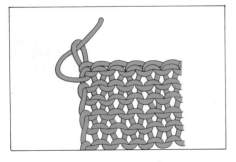

Finishing the work At the end of the last row cut the yarn, passing it through the last stitch to prevent unravelling.

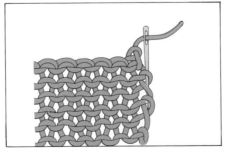

Darning in vertically Thread a sewing needle with the working yarn and weave in and out of the row ends for about 4cm (1½in).

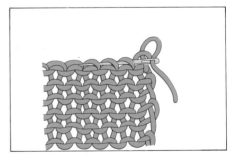

Darning in horizontally Work as explained for vertical darning in, weaving through the nearest edge, usually the seam edge.

Stitches for shape and pattern
Twisted stitches   Making a stitch
Slipped stitches   Slipped stitch decreasing

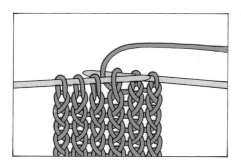

Twisted knit or plain stitch Make a knit stitch in the normal way, but knit into the back of the stitch making the work less elastic as the stitches are twisted.

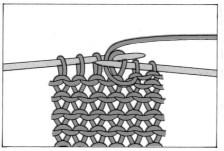

Twisted purl stitch Work a purl stitch, bringing the needle through the back of the loop to the front, twisting the stitch.

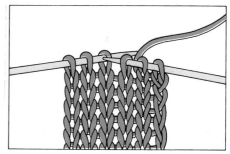

Slip stitch knitwise With the yarn to the back of the work, enter a stitch as though to knit it and slip it onto the right-hand needle without doing so.

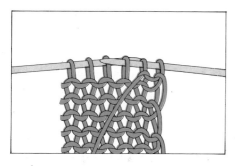

Slip stitch purlwise With the yarn to the front, enter the stitch as though to purl it and slip it onto the right-hand needle without doing so.

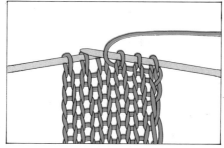

Making a yarn over between knit stitches Bring the yarn to the front, then over the needle to the back and continue working. On the return row work the yarn over as a normal stitch.

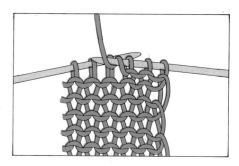

Making a yarn over between purl stitches Take the yarn to the back of the work over the needle, then to the front again, and continue working. On the return row work the yarn over as a normal stitch.

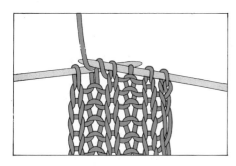

Making a yarn over between a knit and a purl stitch Having worked a knit stitch, bring the yarn forward under the right-hand needle, then wind it over the needle and back to the front. Purl the next stitch.

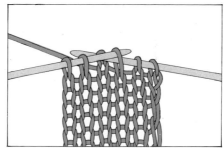

Slipped stitches, single decrease Slip one stitch and work the following. With the left-hand needle lift the unworked stitch over the worked stitch, letting it drop.

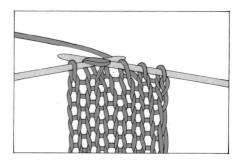

Slipped stitches, double decrease Slip one stitch without working it, work the next two together and pass the slipped stitch over, letting it drop.

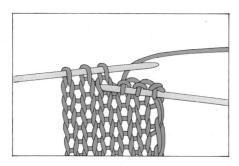

Single elongated stitch Insert the needle into the stitch in the row below the one that should be worked next. Knit the stitch.

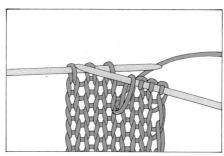

Double elongated stitch Insert the needle into the stitch four or more rows below the one that should be worked next, letting the stitch on the needle drop and run down. Knit it. This is used in stitches with a honeycomb effect.

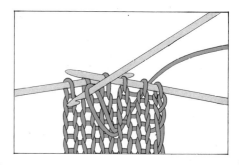

Elongated stitch using a crochet hook This is a variation of the previous example. Instead of using the needle, insert the crochet hook several rows below and draw through a loop, which is then knitted with the next stitch.

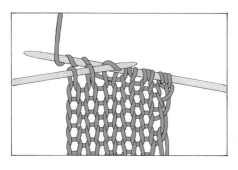

Elongated stitches: alternative method 1. Wind the yarn around the needle at least three times for each stitch. Then knit into the next stitch.

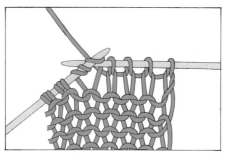

2. On the next row, on either the right or wrong side of the work, work the stitches normally letting the extra loops drop off the needle. Long stitches formed in this way are generally used in lacy bands between solid areas.

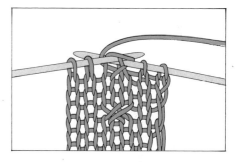

Cross two stitches right, knitting Knit into the front of the second stitch on the left-hand needle, but do not drop the stitch off. Then knit into the front of the first stitch and let them drop off the needle together.

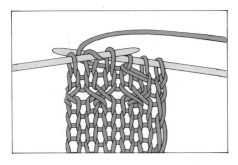

Cross two stitches left, knitting Knit into the back of the second stitch on the left-hand needle but do not drop the stitch off. Then knit into the back of the first stitch and allow both stitches to drop off the needle together.

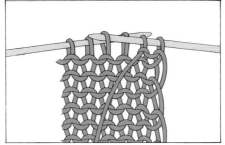

Cross two stitches right, purling Purl into the front of the second stitch on the left-hand needle, but do not drop the stitch off. Then purl into the front of the first stitch and let both stitches drop off the needle together.

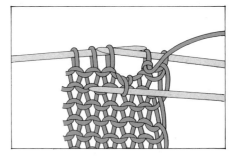

Cross two stitches left, purling Purl into the front of the second stitch on the left-hand needle from behind the first stitch (held on a cable needle). Then purl into the front of the first stitch and allow to drop off the needle.

Increasing

Knitting into the same stitch twice   Yarn forward method
Invisible increasing   Extending a row
Raised increasing   Increasing at edges

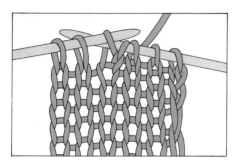

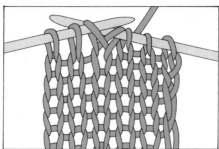

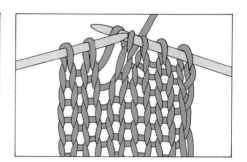

Knitting into the same stitch twice This method of increasing can be worked in several ways. On a knit row, knit into the same stitch twice, first into the front of the stitch and then into the back, letting it drop from the left-hand needle. On a purl row, purl first into the front and then into the back of the stitch.

Invisible increasing Before working the stitch on the needle, work the one below in the previous row, then work into the back of the first one. This method can also be used on a purl row.

Raised increasing 1. In this method the horizontal bar between two stitches is worked.

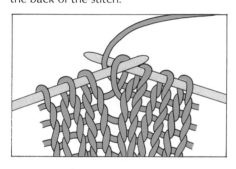

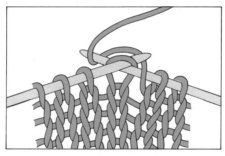

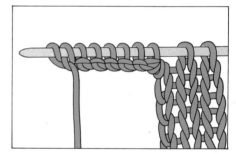

2. Pick up this bar with the right-hand needle and slip it onto the left, twisting it as you do so, This method can also be used on a purl row and is almost invisible if the stitch is worked into the back.

Yarn over method This is the simplest way of increasing a stitch in the work. Bring the yarn over between the needles on a knit row and then knit into the next stitch. On the return row work this stitch normally. For increasing on a purl row, see page 16.

Extending a row Cast on the required number of stitches at the start or end of a row by the method normally used.

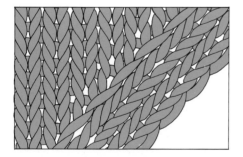

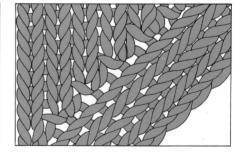

Simple increasing at edges Use the first method described above for increasing within a row, ie. knit twice into the same stitch. In paired increasing, when increasing is worked three stitches from the start of the row, it must be made four stitches from the end of the row.

Invisible increasing at edges Use the invisible increasing method described above, ie. work an increase by inserting the needle into the stitch in the previous row and working into it. Paired increasing is achieved by working into the stitch below the third stitch from the beginning and the end of a row.

Simple moss increasing at edges Work a knit stitch normally, but without letting it drop from the needle. Bring the yarn to the front and purl into the same stitch. For paired increasing, increase three stitches in from the start of the row and on the fourth stitch from the end of the row.

18

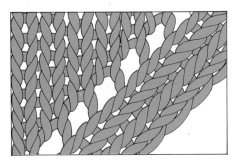

Simple raised increasing at edges Lift the horizontal bar between the right and left-hand needles and knit into the back of it. Paired increasing is achieved by working into the horizontal bar after the third stitch from the start of the row and before the third stitch from the end of the row.

Simple barred increasing at edges Work into the back loop of the stitch from the previous row and then into the stitch on the needle. Paired increasing is achieved by increasing into the stitch below the third stitch from the start of the row and into the stitch below the third stitch from the end of the row.

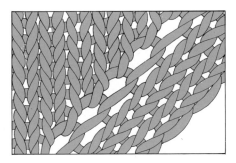

Lace increasing at edges Increase by taking the yarn forward and over the needle and working it on the following row, making a small hole. Paired increasing is achieved by taking the yarn over the needle after the third stitch from the start of the row and before the third stitch from the end of the row.

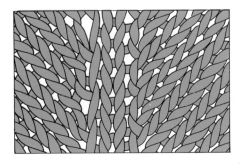

Double bar increasing Knit into the front and back of the stitch before a center stitch, then knit into the front and back of the center stitch.

Double invisible increasing In the stitch before the center stitch, make an invisible increasing stitch left. Knit the center stitch and then make an invisible increasing stitch right.

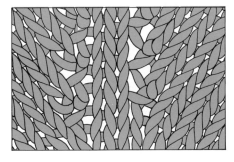

Double moss increasing Knit and purl into the stitch before the center stitch, knit the center stitch, and then knit and purl into the next stitch.

Double raised increasing Knit into the horizontal thread before the center stitch, knit the center stitch and then knit into the next horizontal thread.

Double invisible increasing into one stitch Knit into the loop below the center stitch, then knit into the back of the center stitch and knit again into the loop below the center stitch.

Double lace increasing Take the yarn over the needle, knit the center stitch and take the yarn over the needle again. Work the loops normally on the next row.

Decreasing

Knit decreasing | Slip stitch decreasing
Purl decreasing | Decreasing at edges

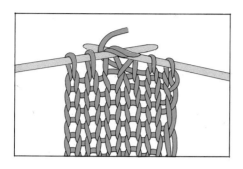

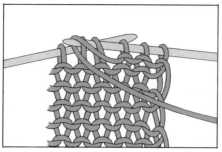

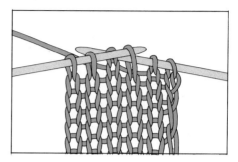

Knit decreasing This is the simplest and most commonly used method. Knit two stitches together, making one.

Purl decreasing Purl next two stitches together, making one.

Slip stitch decreasing Slip a stitch from the left-hand needle onto the right-hand needle. Knit normally into the next stitch and pass the slipped stitch over it.

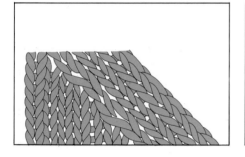

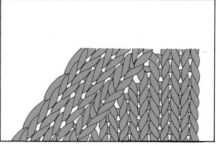

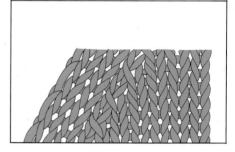

Knit decreasing inside a border of two stitches, sloping to the left Using the slip stitch decreasing described above, slip the third stitch over the fourth.

Knit decreasing inside a border of two stitches, sloping to the right Using the knit decreasing method described above, knit the fourth and third stitches from the end together.

Alternative method With a left slope use purl decreasing on the wrong side of work. With a right slope use knit decreasing on the right side of work, working into the back of the stitch. Symmetry is achieved by working together the fourth and third stitches at the end of either the knit or purl rows.

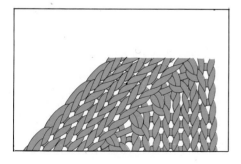

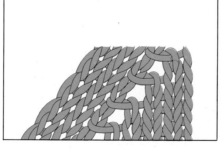

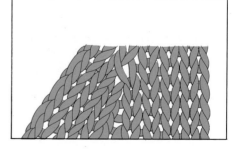

Decorative decreasing Whether the slope is to the left or to the right, purl the stitches. Symmetry is achieved by working together the third and fourth stitches at either end of a row.

Lacy decreasing Work a left slope on the wrong side of the work and a right slope on the right side of the work in the following way: work until there are five stitches left on the needle. Slip two stitches onto right-hand needle, lift second stitch over first. Slip stitch back onto left-hand needle and work to end.

Double slip stitch decreasing Slip one stitch, knit the next two together and pass the slipped stitch over the resulting stitch.

20

Decreasing/Edgings and borders
Double decreasing
Plain, purled and cabled edgings
Garter stitch, moss stitch and 1/1 ribbed borders

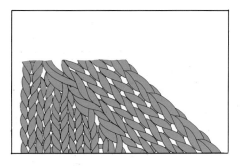

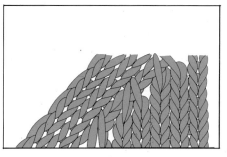

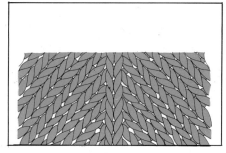

Double knit decreasing, sloping left On the right side of the work, knit three stitches together through the back of the loops.

Double knit decreasing, sloping right On the right side of the work, knit three stitches together normally.

Decreasing on a central line Slip two stitches knitwise, passing the needle first through the second and then through the first, from left to right. Knit into the next stitch, and then pass the two slipped stitches over the knitted stitch.

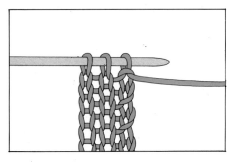

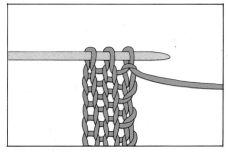

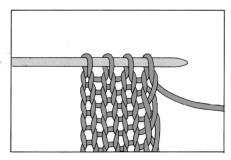

Plain edging Use this method for making an invisible seam. With right side of work facing, knit into the back of the first and last stitch. On the wrong side of work, purl the first stitch and slip the last stitch without working it.

Purled edging Use this method for normal seams. On either a purl or a knit row, slip the first stitch knitwise without working it and knit into the last stitch.

Cabled edging Use this method when stitches are to be picked up later. With right side facing, slip the first stitch knitwise without working it and knit into the last stitch. On wrong side, slip the first stitch purlwise without working it and purl into the last stitch.

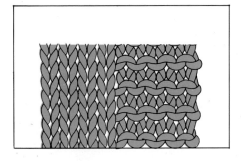

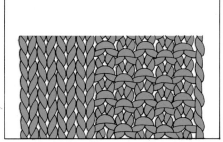

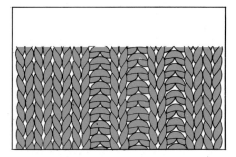

Garter stitch border This is used to finish sections of work done in stockinette stitch. Work into the back of the knit stitches forming the border, making the border a firm, integral part of the work.

Moss stitch border This is also used to finish the edge of a section of work done in stockinette stitch and is an integral part of the work. Work the border stitches in moss stitch.

1/1 ribbed border This is another example of a worked-in border. Work the border in 1/1 rib over an odd number of stitches, working two knit stitches at the edge.

Ribbed stitches

Simple 1/1 rib	Twisted 1/1 rib
2/2 rib	7/3 flat rib
Simple purled rib	Double purled rib

Simple 1/1 rib This is the simplest and most widely used of the rib stitches, and is worked over an even number of sts. *Row 1* *K1, P1*. *Row 2* *K1, P1*. Rep these 2 rows.

Twisted 1/1 rib This a variation of simple 1/1 rib, the only difference being that the knit stitches are worked into the back of the stitch, resulting in a firmer fabric.

2/2 rib Work over a number of sts divisible by 4. *Row 1* *K2, P2*. *Row 2* *K2, P2*. Rep these 2 rows.

7/3 flat rib Work over a number of sts divisible by 10. *Row 1* *K7, P3*. *Row 2* *K3, P7*. Rep these 2 rows. The width of this type of rib can be varied.

Simple purled rib Work over a number of sts divisible by 5 + 2. *Row 1* *P2, K1, P1, K1*, end with P2. Row 2 *K2, P3*, end with K2. Rep these 2 rows.

Double purled rib Work over a number of sts divisible by 7 + 3. *Row 1 (RS)* P3, *K1, P1, K2, P3*. *Row 2* K3, *P2, K1, P1, K3*. *Row 3* P3, *K2, P1, K1, P3*. *Row 4* K3, *P1, K1, P2, K3*. Rep these 4 rows.

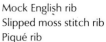

Ribbed stitches

English rib	Mock English rib
Slip stitch rib	Slipped moss stitch rib
Irish rib	Piqué rib

English rib Work over an even number of sts. *Row 1* *Make 1, sl1 ybk, K1*. *Row 2* *Make 1, sl1, K2 tog (work tog made and slipped stitch of previous row)*. Rep these 2 rows.

Mock English rib Work over a number of sts divisible by 4. *Row 1* *K3, P1*. *Row 2* *K2, P1, K1*. Rep these 2 rows.

Slip stitch rib Work over a number of sts divisible by 5 + 2. *Row 1* *P2, K1, sl1 P ybk, K1*, end with P2. *Row 2* *K2, P3*, end with K2. Rep these 2 rows.

Slipped moss stitch rib Work on a number of sts divisible by 5. *Row 1* *K1, P1, K1, P1, K1*. *Row 2* *Sl1 P yfwd, P1, K1, P1, K1*. Rep these 2 rows.

Irish rib Work over a number of sts divisible by 3. *Row 1* P. *Row 2 (RS)* *K1, K2tog*. *Row 3* *Sl1 P yfwd (the K2tog of previous row), K1*. Rep the last 2 rows.

Piqué rib Work over a number of sts divisible by 10. *Row 1* *P3, K1, P3, K3*. *Rows 2 and 3* Work the stitches as set. *Row 4* K. Rep these 4 rows.

Patterns from knit and purl

Moss stitch Double moss stitch
Elongated moss stitch Single seed stitch
Half triple seed stitch Half quadruple seed stitch

Moss stitch Work over an even number of sts. *Row 1* *K1, P1*. *Row 2* *P1, K1*. Rep these 2 rows. This stitch has the same appearance on both sides of the work.

Double moss stitch Work over an even number of sts. *Row 1* *K1, P1*. *Row 2* *K1, P1*. *Row 3* *P1, K1*. *Row 4* *P1, K1*. Rep these 4 rows.

Elongated moss stitch Work over an even number of sts. *Rows 1, 2, 5 and 6* K. *Row 3* *K1, P1*. *Rows 4 and 8* Work the stitches as set. *Row 7* *P1, K1*. Rep these 8 rows.

Single seed stitch Work over a number of sts divisible by 4. *Row 1* *K3, P1*. *Row 2 and all even rows* P. *Rows 3 and 7* K. *Row 5* K1, *P1, K3*, end with P1, K2. *Row 9* Rep from row 1.

Half triple seed stitch Work over a number of sts divisible by 7. *Row 1* *P3, K4*. *Row 2* P2, *K3, P4*, end with P2. *Rows 3 and 7* K. *Rows 4 and 8* P. *Row 5* K2, *P3, K4*, end with K2. *Row 6* K3, *P4, K3*, end with P4. *Row 9* Rep from row 1.

Half quadruple seed stitch Work over a number of sts divisible by 6. *Rows 1 and 3* K1, *P1, K5*, end with P1, K4. *Row 2* *P3, K3*. *Rows 4 and 8* P. *Rows 5 and 7* K4, *P1, K5*, end with P1, K1. *Row 6* *K3, P3*. *Row 9* Rep from row 1.

Patterns from knit and purl

Reverse ridge stitch	Ripple stitch
Chequered stitch	Basket stitch
Square stitch	Triangle stitch

Reverse ridge stitch   Work over any number of sts. *Row 1* K. *Row 2* P. *Rows 3 and 4* K. *Row 5* P. *Row 6* K. This stitch appears the same on both sides of the work. The bands can be varied in height according to the number of rows left between the knit rows.

Ripple stitch   Work over a number of sts divisible by 4 + 1. *Row 1* P. *Row 2* *K1, P3*, end with K1. *Row 3* *P1, K3*, end with P1. *Row 4* As row 2. *Row 5* Rep from row 1.

Chequered stitch   Work over a number of sts divisible by 14. *Rows 1 to 10* *K7, P7*. *Rows 11 to 20* *P7, K7*. Rep from row 1.

Basket stitch   Work over a number of sts divisible by 14. *Rows 1 and 9* K. *Rows 2 and 10* P. *Rows 3, 5 and 7* *P10, K4*. *Rows 4, 6, and 8* *P4, K10*. *Rows 11, 13 and 15* P3, *K4, P10*, end with K4, P7. *Rows 12, 14 and 16* K7, *P4, K10*, end with P4, K3. *Row 17* Rep from row 1.

Square stitch   Work over a number of sts divisible by 10 + 1. *Rows 1 and 7* K. *Rows 2 and 6* P. *Rows 3 and 5* K4, *P3, K7*, end with K4. *Row 4* P4, *K3, P7*, end with P4. *Rows 8 and 10* K2, *P7, K3*, end with K2. *Row 9* P2, *K7, P3*, end with P2. Rep from row 1.

Triangle stitch   Work over a number of sts divisible by 12. *Row 1* K1, *P9, K3*, end K2. *Row 2* P3, *K7, P5*, end with P2. *Row 3* K3, *P5, K7*, end K4. *Row 4* P5, *K3, P9*, end with P4. *Row 5* K5, *P1, K11*, end K6. *Rows 6 and 12* P. *Row 7* P4, *K3, P9*, end P5. *Row 8* K4, *P5, K7*, end K3. *Row 9* P2, *K7, P5*, end P3. *Row 10* K2, *P9, K3*, end K1. *Row 11* *K11, P1*. Rep from row 1.

Patterns from knit and purl

Simple diagonal stitch   Double diagonal stitch
Large dot stitch   Diamond pattern

Simple diagonal stitch Work over a number of sts divisible by 5. *Row 1* *P1, K4*. *Row 2* P3, *K1, P4*, end with K1, P1. *Row 3* K2, *P1, K4*, end with P1, K2. *Row 4* P1, *K1, P4*, end with K1, P3. *Row 5* *K4, P1*. *Row 6* *P4, K1*. *Row 7* K1, *P1, K4*, end with P1, K3. *Row 8* P2, *K1, P4*, end with K1, P2. *Row 9* K3, *P1, K4*, end with P1, K1. *Row 10* *K1, P4*. *Row 11* Rep from row 1.

Double diagonal stitch Work over a number of sts divisible by 7. *Row 1* *P3, K4*. *Row 2* P3, *K3, P4*, end with K3, P1. *Row 3* K2, *P3, K4*, end with P3, K2. *Row 4* P1, *K3, P4*, end with K3, P3. *Row 5* *K4, P3*. *Row 6* K2, *P4, K3*, end with P4, K1. *Row 7* P2, *K4, P3*, end with K4, P1. *Row 8* *P4, K3*. *Row 9* K1, *P3, K4*, end with P3, K3. *Row 10* P2, *K3, P4*, end with K3, P2. *Row 11* K3, *P3, K4*, end with P3, K1. *Row 12* *K3, P4*. *Row 13* P1, *K4, P3*, end with K4, P2. *Row 14* K1, *P4, K3*, end with P4, K2. *Row 15* Rep from row 1.

Large dot stitch Work over a number of sts divisible by 10. *Row 1* *K7, P3*. *Row 2* K4, *P5, K5*, end with P5, K1. *Row 3* P2, *K3, P7*, end with K3, P5. *Row 4* As row 2. *Row 5* As row 1. *Rows 6 to 10* Work in st st. *Row 11* K2, *P3, K7*, end with P3, K5. *Row 12* P4, *K5, P5*, end with K5, P1. *Row 13* *P7, K3*. *Row 14* P4, *K5, P5*, end with K5, P1. *Row 15* K2, *P3, K7*, end with P3, K5. *Rows 16 to 20* Work in st st. *Row 21* Rep from row 1.

Diamond pattern Work over a number of sts divisible by 14. *Row 1* *(P1, K1) 4 times, K6*. *Row 2* On this and all even rows, work the sts as set. *Rows 3 and 15* *(K1, P1) 3 times, K4, P1, K3*. *Rows 5 and 13* *K2, P1, K1, P1, K4, P1, K1, P1, K2*. *Rows 7 and 11* *K3, P1, K4, (P1, K1) 3 times*. *Row 9* *K6, (K1, P1) 4 times*. *Row 17* Rep from row 1. With this stitch the wrong side of the work can also be used.

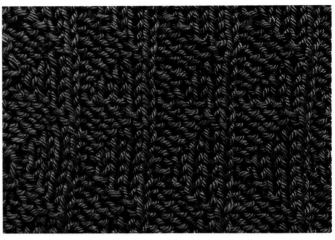

Brocade stitch Work over a number of sts divisible by 12 + 1. *Row 1 (RS)* K1, *P1, K9, P1, K1*. *Row 2* K1, *P1, K1, P7, K1, P1, K1*. *Row 3* K1, *P1, K1, P1, K5, (P1, K1) twice*. *Row 4* P1, *(P1, K1) twice, P3, K1, P1, K1, P2*. *Row 5* K1, *K2, (P1, K1) 3 times, P1, K3*. *Row 6* P1, *P3, (K1, P1) twice, K1, P4*. *Row 7* K1, *K4, P1, K1, P1, K5*. *Row 8* As row 6. *Row 9* As row 5. *Row 10* As row 4. *Row 11* As row 3. *Row 12* As row 2. Rep these 12 rows.

Pennant stitch Work over a number of sts divisible by 6. *Row 1* *K1, P5*. *Row 2* *K4, P2*. *Row 3* *K3, P3*. *Row 4* *K2, P4*. *Row 5* *K5, P1*. *Row 6* As row 4. *Row 7* As row 3. *Row 8* As row 2. Rep these 8 rows.

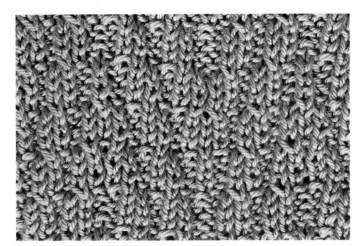

Pinnacle crepe stitch Work over a number of sts divisible by 18 + 1. *Rows 1 and 3* P1, *(K2, P2) twice, K1, (P2, K2) twice, P1*. *Rows 2 and 4* K1, *(P2, K2) twice, P1, (K2, P2) twice, K1*. *Rows 5 and 7* P1, *P1, K2, P2, K2, P3, (K2, P2) twice*. *Rows 6 and 8* K1, *K1, P2, K2, P2, K3, (P2, K2) twice*. *Rows 9 and 11* As rows 2 and 4. *Rows 10 and 12* As rows 1 and 3. *Rows 13 and 15* As rows 6 and 8. *Rows 14 and 16* As rows 5 and 7. Rep these 16 rows.

Pyramid stitch Work over a number of sts divisible by 8 + 1. *Rows 1 and 3 (RS)* *P1, K1*, end with P1. *Rows 2 and 4* *K1, P1*, end with K1. *Rows 5 and 7* *P2, (K1, P1) 3 times*, end with P1. *Rows 6 and 8* *K2, (P1, K1) 3 times*, end with K1. *Rows 9 and 11* *P3, K1, P1, K1, P2*, end with P1. *Rows 10 and 12* *K3, P1, K1, P1, K2*, end with K1. *Rows 13 and 15* *P4, K1, P3*, end with P1. *Rows 14 and 16* *K4, P1, K3*, end with K1. Rep these 16 rows.

Dropped stitch patterns

Large honeycomb stitch   Bee stitch
Twin bee stitch   Diamond bee stitch

Large honeycomb stitch   Work over a number of sts divisible by 2 + 1. *Row 1* K1, *P1, K1*. *Row 2* P1, *K1, P1*. *Row 3* K1, *P1, K1*. *Row 4* P1, *K1, P1*. *Row 5* *K1, work a bee (K into next st on left-hand needle 4 rows down, letting the st drop off left-hand needle and unravel)*, end with K1. *Row 6* As row 2. *Row 7* As row 1. *Row 8* As row 2. *Row 9* K1, P1, *work a bee, P1*, end with K1. *Row 10* Rep from row 2.

Bee stitch   Work over a number of sts divisible by 6 + 5. *Row 1 and all odd rows (WS)* K. *Rows 2 and 4* P. *Row 6* *P5, work a bee (K into next st on left-hand needle 5 rows down, letting the st drop off the left-hand needle and unravel)*, rep from * to *, end with P5. *Rows 8 and 10* P. *Row 12* P2, *work a bee, P5*, end with P2. *Row 14* Rep from row 2.

Twin bee stitch   Work over a number of sts divisible by 7 + 4. *Rows 1, 3, 5, 7 and 9* P. *Rows 2, 4, 6, 8 and 10* K. *Row 11* *P4, work a bee (K into next st on left-hand needle 4 rows down, letting the st drop off left-hand needle and unravel), P1, work a bee*, end with P4. *Row 12* Rep from row 2.

Diamond bee stitch   Work over a number of sts divisible by 4 + 3. *Row 1 (RS)* P3, *K1, P3*. *Row 2* K. *Row 3* P. *Row 4* K3, *work a bee (K into next st on left-hand needle 3 rows down, letting st drop off left-hand needle and unravel), K3*. *Row 5* P1, *K1, P3*, end with K1, P1. *Row 6* K. *Row 7* P. *Row 8* K1, *work a bee, K3*, end with work a bee, K1. Rep these 8 rows.

Honeycomb stitch   Work over an even number of sts. *Rows 1 and 3* K.   *Row 2* *K1, K1d (K into next st, 1 row down)*.   *Row 4* *K1d, K1*. Rep these 4 rows.

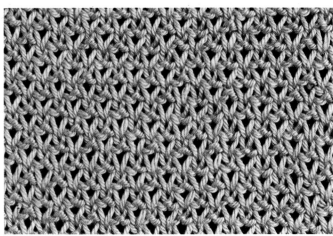

Dust stitch   Work over an even number of sts. *Row 1* *P1, ybk, sl1 P yfwd*. *Row 2 and all even rows* P. *Row 3* *Ybk, sl1 P yfwd, P1*. *Row 5* Rep from row 1.

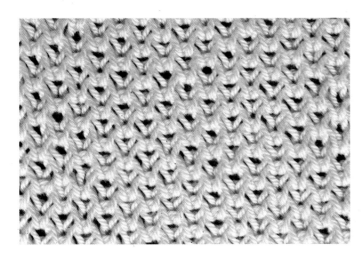

Sand stitch   Work over an even number of sts. *Rows 1 and 2* K. *Row 3* *K1, K1d (K into next st, 1 row down)*. *Row 4* *With the right-hand needle lift the floating horizontal thread from K1d of previous row and K it tog with the st above it, K1*. *Row 5* *K1d, K1*. *Row 6* *K1, then work as for row 4*. *Row 7* Rep from row 3.

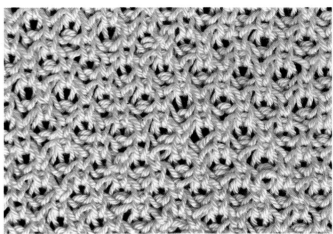

Alternating honeycomb stitch   Work over an even number of sts. *Row 1* K. *Rows 2, 3, 4 and 5* *K1, K1d (K into next st, 1 row down)*, end with K2. *Rows 6, 7, 8 and 9* K2, *K1d, K1*. *Row 10* Rep from row 2.

Slipped stitch patterns

Slipped stockinette stitch   Slipped granite stitch
False 1/1 rib   Tunisian rib

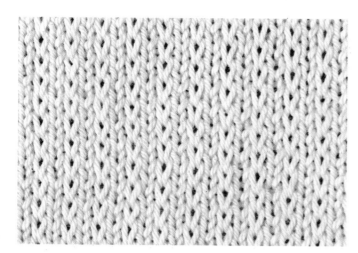

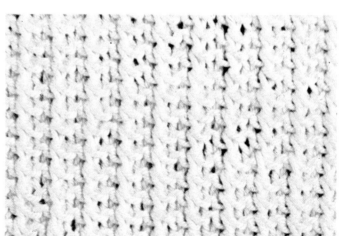

Slipped stockinette stitch   Work over an odd number of sts. *Row 1 (WS)* P. *Row 2* K1, *sl1 ybk, K1*. Rep these 2 rows.

Slipped granite stitch   Work over a number of sts divisible by 4. *Row 1* *K2, sl2 P ybk*. *Row 2* *P2, K2*. *Row 3* *Sl2 P ybk, K2*. *Row 4* *K2, P2*. Rep these 4 rows.

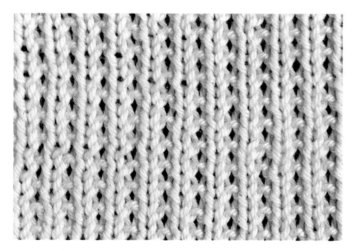

Mock 1/1 rib   This stitch is less elastic than rib as the slipped stitches prevent it from stretching. It may also be worked as a 2/2 version. Work over an odd number of sts. *Row 1 (WS)* K1, *P1, K1*. *Row 2* P1, *sl1 P yfwd, P1*. Rep these 2 rows.

Tunisian rib   Work over an even number of sts. *Row 1 (RS)* K. *Row 2 and all even rows* *Sl1 P yfwd, yo, K1, making a st*, end with K1. *Row 3 and all odd rows* *K1, K2tog tbl (the sl st and made st of previous row)*. Rep last 2 rows.

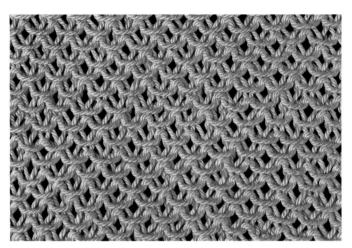

Stamen stitch This is a firm horizontal stitch, giving a honeycomb effect, and can be worked on either large or small gauge needles. In this example large needles are used, so that the weave appears more open. Work over an even number of sts. *Row 1 and all odd rows* P. *Row 2 (RS)* *Sl1 P yfwd, P1*. *Row 4* *P1, sl1 P yfwd*. Rep from row 1.

Slipped moss stitch Work over an even number of sts. *Row 1* *K1, sl1 yfwd*. *Row 2* *P1, sl1 ybk*. *Row 3* As row 2. *Row 4* As row 1. Rep these 4 rows.

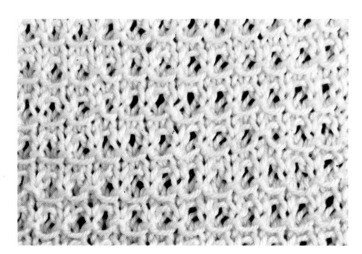

Garland stitch Work over an odd number of sts. *Row 1* K. *Row 2* P. *Row 3* *P1, sl1 P yfwd*. *Row 4* *P1, K sl st on previous row*, end with P1. Rep these 4 rows.

3/1 stitch Work over a number of sts divisible by 4 + 3. *Row 1 (RS)* K3, *sl1 ybk, K3*. *Row 2* K3, *sl1 yfwd, K3*. *Row 3* K1, *sl1 ybk, K3*, end with sl1 ybk, K1. *Row 4* K1, *sl1 P yfwd, K3*, end with sl1 P yfwd, K1. Rep these 4 rows.

Slipped stitch patterns

Link stitch   Zip stitch
Diagonal slip stitch   Mock 2/2 rib

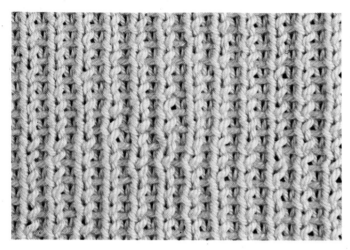

Link stitch Work over an odd number of sts. *Row 1* *K1, sl1 P yfwd*. *Row 2* P. Rep these 2 rows.

Zip stitch Work over a number of sts divisible by 3 + 1. *Row 1 (WS)* K. *Row 2* *K1, sl2 P yfwd*, end with K1. Rep these 2 rows.

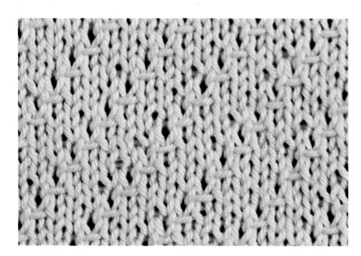

Diagonal slip stitch Work over a number of sts divisible by 4. *Row 1* *K3, sl1 P yfwd*. *Row 2 and all even rows* P. *Row 3* *K2, sl1 P yfwd, K1*. *Row 5* *K1, sl1 P yfwd, K2*. *Row 7* *Sl1 P yfwd, K3*. *Row 9* Rep from row 1.

Mock 2/2 rib stitch This has the appearance of normal rib, but has only slight elasticity, as the slipped stitch prevents stretching. Work over a number of sts divisible by 4 + 2. *Row 1 (WS)* K2, *P2, K2*. *Row 2* P2, *sl2 P yfwd, P2*. Rep these 2 rows.

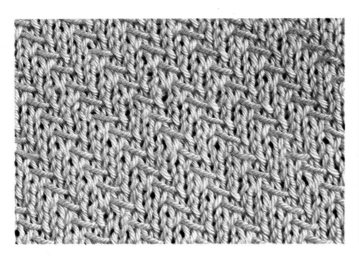

Diagonal cloth stitch Work over a number of sts divisible by 4 + 2. *Row 1* *K2, sl2 P yfwd*, end with K2. *Row 2 and all even rows* P. *Row 3* Sl1 P yfwd, *K2, sl2 P yfwd*, end with K1. *Row 5* Sl2 P yfwd, *K2, sl2 P yfwd*. *Row 7* K1, *sl2 P yfwd, K2*, end with sl1 P yfwd. *Row 8* P. Rep these 8 rows.

Zigzag stitch Work over a number of sts divisible by 4 + 1. *Row 1* P. *Row 2* K1, *sl1 P ybk, K3. *Row 3* *P3, sl1 P yfwd*, end with P1. *Row 4* K1, *drop sl st to front of work, K2, pick up sl st and K it, K1*. *Row 5* P. *Row 6* K5, *sl1 P ybk, K3*. *Row 7* *P3, sl1 P yfwd*, end with P5. *Row 8* K3, *sl2 P ybk, let sl st drop as above, sl same 2 sts to left-hand needle, pick up dropped st and K into it, K3*, end with K2. Rep these 8 rows.

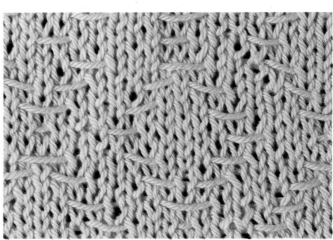

Box stitch Work over a number of sts divisible by 12. *Rows 1, 3, 5, 7 and 9* *K9, sl3 P yfwd*. *Row 2 and all even rows* P. *Rows 11, 13 and 15* *K1, sl3 P yfwd*. *Row 17* Rep from row 1.

Slipped diamond stitch Work over a number of sts divisible by 16 + 2. (Slip all sts purlwise with yfwd.) *Row 1 and all odd rows (WS)* P. *Row 2* K1, *K3, sl2, K3, sl1, K3, sl2, K2*, end with K1. *Row 4* K1, *K2, sl2, K3, sl3, K3, sl2, K1*, end with K1. *Row 6* K1, *(K1, sl2, K3, sl2) twice*, end with K1. *Row 8* K1, sl2, *(K3, sl2) twice, K3, sl3*, end with sl1, K1. *Row 10* K1, *sl1, K3, sl2, K5, sl2, K3*, end with K1. *Row 12* As row 8. *Row 14* As row 6. *Row 16* As row 4. Rep these 16 rows.

Eyelet stitches

Parallel eyelet stitch   Triple eyelet stitch
Slipped eyelet stitch   Embroidered eyelet stitch

Parallel eyelet stitch   Work over a number of sts divisible by 7. *Row 1* *K2, P2tog, yo, K3*. *Row 2 and all even rows* P. *Rows 3 and 7* K. *Row 5* *K3, yo, P2tog, K2*. *Row 8* P. Rep these 8 rows.

Triple eyelet stitch   Work over a number of sts divisible by 8 + 7. *Row 1 and all odd rows (WS)* P. *Row 2* K. *Row 4* K2, yo, sl1, K2tog, psso, yo *K5, yo, sl1, K2tog, psso, yo*, end with K2. *Row 6* K3, yo, sl1, K1, psso, *K6, yo, sl1, K1, psso*, end with K2. *Row 8* K. *Row 10* K1, *K5, yo, sl1, K2tog, psso, yo*, end with K6. *Row 12* K7, *yo, sl1, K1, psso, K6*. Rep these 12 rows.

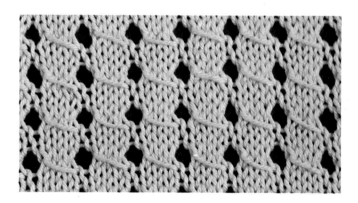

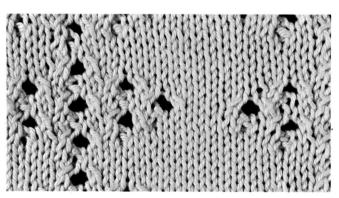

Slipped eyelet stitch   Work over a number of sts divisible by 4. *Row 1* K. *Row 2* *P4, yo*. *Row 3* *Make 1, drop made st from previous row, sl1 K-wise, K3, pass sl st over last 3 sts*. *Row 4* P. Rep these 4 rows.

Embroidered eyelet stitch   Work over a number of sts divisible by 21 + 3. *Row 1 and all odd rows (WS)* P, working P1, K1 into any yo's of previous row. *Row 2* K. *Row 4* K10, *K2tog, yo, sl1, K1, psso, K17*, end with K10. *Row 6* K6, *K2tog, yo, sl1, K1, psso, K4, K2tog, yo, sl1, K1, psso, K9*, end with K6. *Row 8* K3, *K2tog, yo, sl1, K1, psso, K3*. *Row 10* As row 6. *Row 12* As row 4. Rep these 12 rows.

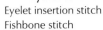

Polka eyelet stitch   Work over an even number of sts. *Row 1 (RS)* K. *Row 2* P. *Row 3* P1, *yo, P2tog*, P1. *Row 4* P. *Rows 5 and 6* As rows 1 and 2. *Row 7* P2, *yo, P2tog*. *Row 8* As row 4. Rep these 8 rows.

Eyelet insertion stitch   Work over an odd number of sts. *Row 1 (RS)* K. *Row 2* P. *Rows 3 and 4* K. *Row 5* *K2tog, yo*, end with K1. *Row 6* K. Rep these 6 rows.

Eyelet rib   Work over a number of sts divisible by 6 + 2. *Row 1* *P2, K2tog, yo twice, sl1, K1, psso*, end with P2. *Row 2* K2, *P1, work (K1, P1) into yo's of previous row, P1, K2*. *Row 3* *P2, K4*, end with P2. *Row 4* P2, *K4, P2*. Rep these 4 rows.

Fishbone stitch   Work over a number of sts divisible by 9. *Row 1* *(K2tog, yo) twice, K1, (yo, K2tog tbl) twice*. *Row 2* P. Rep these 2 rows.

Eyelet stitches

Purled calyx stitch   Eyelet trellis
Peacock stitch   Lace eyelet stitch

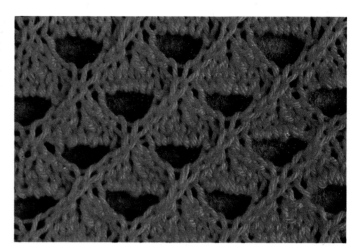

Purled calyx stitch   Work over a number of sts divisible by 5 + 3. *Row 1* K3, *P2, K3*. *Row 2* *P3, K1, yo, K1*, end with P3. *Row 3* K3, *P1, K1, P1, K3*. *Row 4* *P3tog, K1, yo, K1, yo, K1*, end with P3tog. *Row 5* Work (K1, yo, K1) into next st, *P1, P3tog, P1, work (K1, yo, K1) into next st. *Row 6* *P3, ybk, sl1, K1 tbl but do not drop st from needle, lift sl st over loop on right needle, Ktog loop on left-hand needle with next st*, end with P3. Rep these 6 rows.

Eyelet trellis   Work over a number of sts divisible by 8. *Rows 1 and 5* P. *Row 2* *(K2tog) twice, yo twice, (sl1, K1, psso) twice*. *Row 3* *P2tog tbl into yo's, work (P1, K1) 3 times, P2tog*. *Row 4* K1, *K6, K2tog without letting sts drop, K first st again and let both drop from needle*, end with K7. *Row 6* K4, *(K2tog) twice, yo twice, (sl1, K1, psso) twice*, end with K4. *Row 7* P4, rep from * to *, as in row 3, P4. *Row 8* K3, *K2tog, K again into first st as in row 4, K6*, end with K3. Rep these 8 rows.

Peacock stitch   Work over a number of sts divisible by 18. *Row 1 (RS)* K. *Row 2* P. *Row 3* (K2tog) 3 times, (yo, K1) 6 times, (K2tog) 3 times*. *Row 4* K. Rep these 4 rows.

Lace eyelet stitch   Both sides of work look the same. Work over a number of sts divisible by 4 + 4 for the selvedge. (NOTE: The 3rd row should be worked loosely, using a needle three or four sizes larger than for the rest of the work.) *Row 1* P2, *yo, P4tog*, end with P2. *Row 2* K2, *K1, (K1, P1, K1) into st made on previous row*, end with K2. *Row 3* K. Rep these 3 rows.

Zigzag eyelet stitch Work over a number of sts divisible by 11 + 2. *Row 1 (WS) and all odd rows* P. *Row 2* K6, *yo, sl1, K1, psso, K9*, end with K5. *Row 4* K7, *yo, sl1, K1, psso, K9*, end with K4. *Row 6* K3, *K2tog, yo, K3, yo, sl1, K1, psso, K4*, end with K3. *Row 8* *K2, K2tog, yo, K5, yo, sl1, K1, psso*, end with K2. *Row 10* K1, *K2tog, yo, K7, yo, sl1, K1, psso*, end with K1. *Row 12* *K2tog, yo, K9*, end with K2. Rep these 12 rows.

Divided lozenge stitch Work over a number of sts divisible by 10 + 6. *Row 1* K1, yo, *K3, sl2 K-wise, K1, p2sso, K3, yo, K1, yo*, end with K3, sl1, K1, psso. *Row 2 and all even rows* P. *Row 3* K2, yo, *K2, sl2 K-wise, K1, p2sso, K2, yo, K3, yo*, end with K2, sl1, K1, psso. *Row 5* K3, yo, *K1, sl2 K-wise, K1, p2sso, K1, yo, K5, yo*, end with yo, K1, sl1, K1, psso. *Row 7* K4, yo, *sl2, K1, p2sso, yo, K7, yo*, end with sl1, K1, psso. *Row 9* Sl1, K1, psso, K3, yo, *K1, yo, K3, sl2 K-wise, K1, p2sso, K3, yo*, end with K1. *Row 11* Sl1, K1, psso, K2, yo *K3, yo, K2, sl2 K-wise, K1, p2sso, K2, yo*, end with K2. *Row 13* Sl1, K1, psso, K1, yo, *K5, yo, K1, sl2 K-wise, K1, p2sso, K1, yo*, end with K3. *Row 15* Sl1, K1, psso, yo, *K7, yo, sl2 K-wise, K1, p2sso, yo*, end with K4. *Row 16* P. Rep these 16 rows.

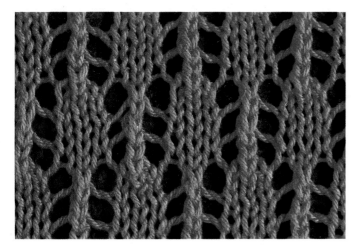

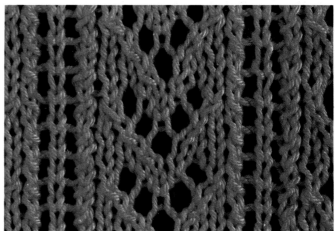

Tadpole stitch Work over a number of sts divisible by 6 + 1. *Rows 1, 3, and 5* K1, *yo, sl2 K-wise, K1, p2sso, yo, K3*. *Row 2 and all even rows* P. *Rows 7, 9 and 11* K1, *K3, yo, sl2 K-wise, K1, p2sso, yo*, end with sl1, K1, psso, K1. *Row 13* Rep from row 1.

'V' panel stitch Work over a number of sts divisible by 12. *Row 1* *K3, yo, sl1, K1, psso, K2, K2tog, yo, K1, yo, psso*. *Row 2 and all even rows* P. *Row 3* *K1, K2tog, yo, K1, yo, sl1, K1, psso, K1, K2tog, yo, K1, yo, sl1, K1, psso*. *Row 5* *K2tog, yo, K3, yo, sl1, K1, psso, K2tog, yo, K1, yo, sl1, K1, psso*. *Row 6* P. Rep these 6 rows.

Bunches of roses Work over a number of sts divisible by 16 + 9. *Row 1 and all odd rows* P. *Row 2* K10, *K2tog, yo, K1, yo, sl1, K1, psso, K11*, end with K10. *Row 4* K9, *K2tog, yo, K3, yo, sl1, K1, psso, K9*. *Row 6* K10, *yo, sl1, K1, psso, yo, K3tog, yo, K11*, end with K10. *Row 8* K11, *yo, sl1, K2tog, psso, yo, K13*, end with K11. *Row 10* K2, *K2tog, yo, K1, yo, sl1, K1, psso, K11*, end with K2. *Row 12* K1, rep from * to * as in row 4, and end with K1. *Row 14* K2, rep from * to * as in row 6, and end with K2. *Row 16* K3, *yo, sl1, K2tog, psso, yo, K13*, end with K3. Rep these 16 rows.

Peacock's tail pattern Work over 28 sts. *Rows 1 and 3 (RS)* K. *Rows 2 and 4* P. *Row 5* K12, K2tog, yo twice, sl1, K1, psso, K12. *Row 6 and all even rows (WS)* P to end, working P1, K1 into 2 yo's of previous row if necessary. *Rows 7, 11, 15, 19, 23 and yo's 27* K. *Row 9* K10 (K2tog, yo twice, sl1, K1, psso) twice, K10. *Row 13* K8, (K2tog, yo twice, sl1, K1, psso) 3 times, K8. *Row 17* K6, (K2tog, yo twice, sl1, K1, psso) 4 times, K6. *Row 21* K4 (K2tog, yo twice, sl1, K1, psso) 5 times, K4. *Row 25* K2 (K2tog, yo twice, sl1, K1, psso) 6 times, K2. *Row 29* As row 13. *Row 30* As row 6. Rep these 30 rows.

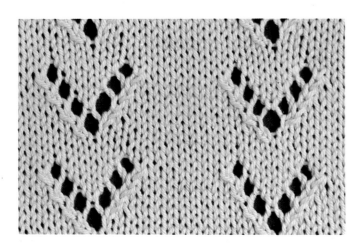

Swallow eyelet pattern The eyelet pattern is worked over 9 sts and is spaced with 1 or more sts in st st. In the sample the spacing is 6 sts. *Row 1* *K4, yo, sl1, K1, psso, K3*. *Row 2 and all even rows* P. *Row 3* *K2, K2tog, yo, K1, yo, sl1, K1, psso, K2. *Row 5* *K1, K2tog, yo, K3, yo, sl1, K1, psso, K1*. *Row 7* *K2tog, yo, K5, yo, sl1, K1, psso*. *Row 8* P. Rep these 8 rows.

Shetland eyelet pattern Work over 9 sts. *Row 1 and all odd rows (WS)* P. *Row 2* K2, K2tog, yo, K1, yo, sl1, K1, psso, K2. *Row 4* K1, K2tog, yo, K3, yo, sl1, K1, psso, K1. *Row 6* K1, yo, sl1, K1, psso, yo, sl2, K1, p2sso, yo, K2tog, yo, K1. *Row 8* K3, yo, sl2, K1, p2sso, yo, K3. Rep these 8 rows.

Raised leaf pattern Work over a number of sts divisible by 7 + 6. *Row 1* P6, *yo, K1, yo, P6*. *Rows 2 and 14* *K6, P3*, K6. *Row 3* P6, *K1, yo, K1, yo, K1, P6*. *Rows 4 and 12* *K6, P5*, K6. *Row 5* P6, *K2, yo, K1, yo, K2, P6*. *Rows 6 and 10* *K6, P7*, K6. *Row 7* P6, *K3, yo, K1, yo, K3, P6*. *Row 8* *K6, P9*, K6. *Row 9* P6, *sl1, K1, psso, K5, K2tog, P6*. *Row 11* P6, *sl1, K1, psso, K3, K2tog, P6*. *Row 13* P6, *sl1, K1, psso, K1, K2tog, P6*. *Row 15* K6, *sl1, K2tog, psso, K6*. *Rows 16, 18 and 20* K. *Rows 17 and 19* P. Rep these 20 rows.

Eyelet fantasy stitch Work over a number of sts divisible by 13. *Row 1* *K4, K2tog, yo, K1, yo, sl1, K1, psso, K4*. *Row 2 and all even rows* P. *Row 3* *K3, K2tog, K1, yo, K1, yo, K1, sl1, K1, psso, K3*. *Row 5* *K2, K2tog, K2, yo, K1, yo, K2, sl1, K1, psso, K2*. *Row 7* *K1, K2tog, K3, yo, K1, yo, K3, sl1, K1, psso, K1*. *Row 9* *K1, yo, K2tog, K7, sl1, K1, psso, yo, K1*. *Row 11* *K2, yo, sl1, K1, psso, K5, K2tog, yo, K2*. *Row 13* *K3, yo, sl1, K1, psso, K3, K2tog, yo, K3*. *Row 15* *K4, yo, sl1, K1, psso, K1, K2tog, yo, K4*. *Row 17* *K5, yo, sl1, K2tog, psso, yo, K5*. *Row 19* Rep from row 1.

Candelabra stitch Work over a number of sts divisible by 8 + 1. *Row 1* *K1, yo, K2, sl1, K2tog, psso, K2, yo*, end with K1. *Row 2 and all even rows* P. *Rows 3, 5 and 7* As row 1. *Row 9* K2, *K2tog, yo, K1, yo, sl1, K1, psso, K3*, end with K2. *Row 11* *K1, K2tog, yo, K3, yo, sl1, K1, psso*, end with K1. *Row 13* K2tog, *yo, K5, yo, sl2, K1, p2sso*, end with sl1, K1, psso. *Row 15* Rep from row 1.

Eyelet pyramids Work over a number of sts divisible by 11 + 5. *Row 1* *K3, (yo, sl1, K1, psso) 4 times*, end with K5. *Row 2 and all even rows* P. *Row 3* *K4, (yo, sl1, K1, psso) 3 times, K1*, end with K5. *Row 5* *K5, (yo, sl1, K1, psso) twice, K2*, end with K5. *Row 7* *K6, yo, sl1, K1, psso, K3*, end with K5. *Row 9* K5, rep from * to * as row 1. *Row 11* K5, rep from * to * as row 3. *Row 13* K5, rep from * to * as row 5. *Row 15* K5, rep from * to * as row 7. *Row 16* P. Rep these 16 rows.

Lace stitches

Lace stitch   Turkish stitch   Fantasy lace stitch
Lace rib stitch   Lace stockinette stitch   Undulating stitch

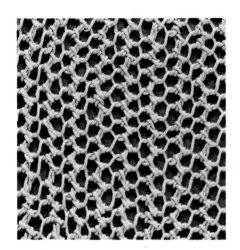

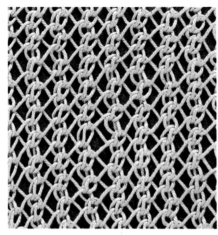

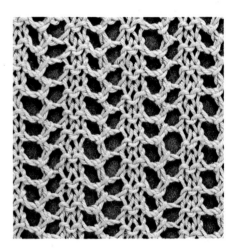

Lace stitch Work over an even number of sts. *Row 1 and all following rows* K1, *yo, sl1, K1, psso*, end with K1.

Turkish stitch Work over an even number of sts. *Row 1 and all following rows* K1, *yo, K2tog*, end with K1.

Fantasy lace stitch Work over a number of sts divisible by 4. *Row 1 and all following rows* *K1, yo, P2tog, K1*.

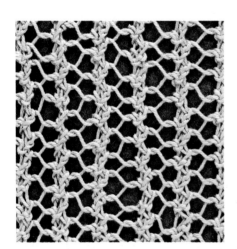

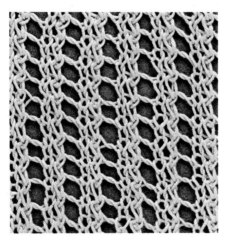

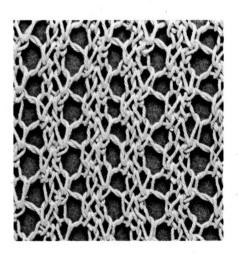

Lace rib stitch Work over a number of sts divisible by 3. *Row 1 and all following rows* *K1, yo, K2tog*.

Lace stockinette stitch Work over a number of sts divisible by 3. *Row 1 (RS)* *K1, yo twice, K2tog*. *Row 2* P to end, working the first yo and dropping the second. Rep these 2 rows.

Undulating lace stitch Work over a number of sts divisible by 3. *Row 1 (RS)* *K1, yo twice, K2tog*. *Row 2* P to end, working the first yo and dropping the second. *Row 3* *K2tog, yo twice, K1*. *Row 4* As row 2. Rep these 4 rows.

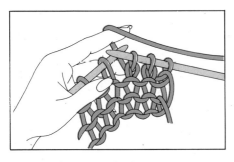

Loop stitch: 1st method 1. This method results in rows of looped fringing and over many rows a fluffy, fur-like effect is achieved. Use a soft yarn. *Rows 1, 2, 3 and 4* K. *Row 5 (WS)* *Lift the yarn at the back of the work with the left index finger.

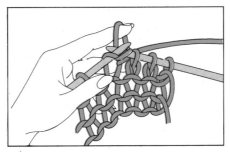

2. K into the first st, making a loop and without letting the stitch drop.

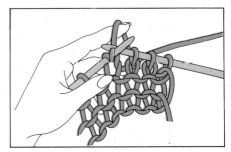

3. With the right-hand needle transfer the loop to the left-hand needle, so making two stitches, still holding the yarn on the left index finger.

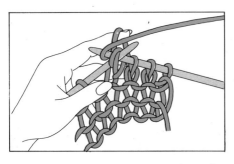

4. K2tog tbl, withdraw the finger from the loop ready to make another on the following stitch*. Rep from * to * in each stitch. *Row 6* K tbl to end. Rep these 6 rows.

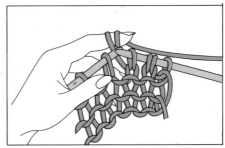

2nd method 1. This requires a heavier yarn, and results in long wide loops. Work over an even number of sts. *Rows 1 and 2* K. *Row 3* K1, *wind the yarn two or three times around the left index finger.

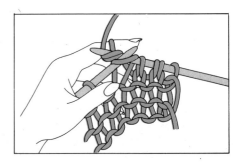

2. Pass the right-hand needle into the following stitch and the loops on the finger.

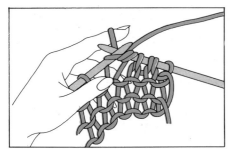

3. Using the right-hand needle, draw the loops on the finger through the stitch on the left-hand needle.

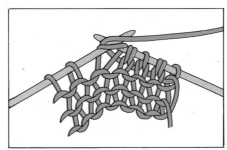

4. K into next stitch, pulling it tight*. Rep from * to * to the end of the row, ending K1.

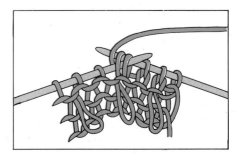

5. *Row 4* K, working the two loops as K2tog tbl. *Rows 5 to 8* K. Start again at row 3. The number of rows between the looped rows can be varied according to the effect required.

Fancy stitches

Rope stitch   Zigzag columns
Undulating rib   Crossed lacing stitch
Crossed thorn stitch   Crossed thorn ribbing

Rope stitch Work over a number of sts divisible by 6 + 4. *Row 1* P4, *K2, P4*. *Row 2* *K4, PC2R (P second st, then P first st)*, end with K4. Rep these 2 rows.

Zigzag columns Work over a number of sts divisible by 8 + 2. *Row 1 (WS)* K1, *K7, P1*, end with K1. *Row 2* P1, *C2L, P6*, end with P1. *Row 3* K1, *K6, P1, K1*, end with K1. *Row 4* P1, *P1, C2L, P5*, end with P1. *Rows 5 to 8* Rep these 4 rows. *Rows 9 to 16* Rep rows 1 to 8 working C2R instead of C2L.

Undulating rib Work over a number of sts divisible by 9 + 5. *Row 1* *P5, C2R, C2L*, end with P5. *Row 2* Work sts as set. *Row 3* *P5, C2L, C2R*, end with P5. *Row 4* As row 2. Rep these 4 rows.

Crossed lacing stitch Work over a number of sts divisible by 4. *Row 1 (RS)* K1, *C2L, K2*, end with K1. *Row 2* K1, *P into second st, then P into first st, slipping both from needle tog, K2*, end with K1. Rep these 2 rows.

Crossed thorn stitch Work over a number of sts divisible by 4. *Row 1* *C2R, C2L*. *Row 2* P. Rep these 2 rows.

Crossed thorn ribbing Work over a number of sts divisible by 12 + 4. *Row 1* *K4, (C2R, C2L) twice*, end with K4. *Row 2* P. Rep these 2 rows.

Fancy stitches

Diagonal crossed stitch Crossed purl stitch
Crater stitch Crossed granite stitch
Zigzag rib Wave stitch

Diagonal crossed stitch Work over an even number of sts. *Rows 1 and 3 (WS)* P. *Row 2* *K2tog without letting sts drop from needle, and K into first st again, letting both sts drop from needle*. *Row 4* K1, rep 2nd row from * to *, end with K1. Rep these 4 rows.

Crossed purl stitch Work over an even number of sts. *Rows 1 and 3* K. *Row 2 (WS)* *P2tog without letting sts drop, P again into first st letting both sts drop off needle*. *Row 4* P1, rep 2nd row from * to *, end with P1. Rep these 4 rows.

Crater stitch Work over a number of sts divisible by 8 + 1. *Row 1* K. *Row 2 and all even rows* P. *Row 3* K1, *C2R, C2L, K4*. *Row 5* K1, *C2L, C2R, K4*. *Row 7* K. *Row 9* K5, *C2R, C2L, K4*, end C2R, C2L. *Row 11* K5, *C2L, C2R, K4*, end with C2L, C2R. *Row 12* P. Rep these 12 rows.

Crossed granite stitch Work over a number of sts divisible by 8 + 2. *Row 1* *K2, (C2R) 3 times*, end with K2. *Row 2* P. *Row 3* *K2, (K into third st on left-hand needle, then into second, then into first and let the 3 sts drop off needle tog) twice*, end with K2. *Row 4* P. Rep these 4 rows.

Zigzag rib Work over a number of sts divisible by 6. *Row 1* *P2, (T2R) twice*. *Row 2* *(T2L) twice, K2*. Rep these 2 rows.

Wave stitch Work over a number of sts divisible by 4 + 2. *Row 1* P2, *P3, K1*. *Row 2 and all even rows* Work the sts as set. *Row 3* P2, *K fourth st on left-hand needle, P into each of the 3 P sts, letting 4 sts drop tog*. *Row 5* P2, *K1, P3*. *Row 7* P2, *sl next st onto cable needle and hold at front of work, P3, then K1 from cable needle*. *Row 8* As row 2. Rep these 8 rows.

Fancy stitches

Acorn stitch   Bow stitch
Pebble stitch   Peppercorn stitch

Acorn stitch   Work over a number of sts divisible by 4 + 3. *Rows 1 to 4* Work in st st. *Row 5* P3, *(K1, P1, K1) all in next st, P3*. *Row 6* K3, *P3, K3*. *Row 7* P3, *K3, P3*. *Rows 8 and 9* As rows 6 and 7. *Row 10* P5, *K3tog, P3*. Rep these 10 rows.

Bow stitch   Work over a number of sts divisible by 18 + 9. *Rows 1 and 7 (RS)* K9, *P9, K9*. *Rows 2 and 8* P9, *K9, P9*. *Rows 3, 5, 13 and 15* K. *Rows 4, 6, 10, 14, 16 and 20* P. *Row 9* K13, *insert right-hand needle into the front of the next st, 9 rows down, draw through a loop and sl it onto left-hand needle and K it tog with first st on needle, K17*, end with K13. *Rows 11 and 17* P9, *K9, P9*. *Rows 12 and 18* K9, *P9, K9*. *Row 19* K4, *draw through a loop from the 9th row down and K it tog with first st on left-hand needle, as in row 9, K17*, end with K4. Rep these 20 rows.

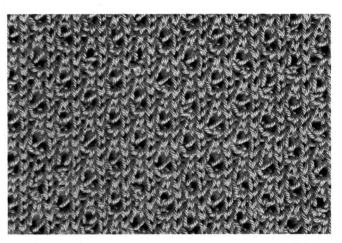

Pebble stitch   Work over a number of sts divisible by 4. *Row 1 (RS)* P. *Row 2* K2, *work (K1, P1, K1) into next st, P3tog*, end with K2. *Row 3* P. *Row 4* K2, *P3tog, work (K1, P1, K1) into next st*, end with K2. Rep these 4 rows.

Peppercorn stitch   Work over a number of sts divisible by 4 + 3. *Rows 1 and 3 (WS)* P. *Row 2* K3, *(K next st and sl back on left-hand needle) 3 times, K st again, called wk4, K3*. *Row 4* K1*, wk4, K3*, end with K1. Rep these 4 rows.

Elongated rhombus stitch Work over a number of sts divisible by 12 + 1. *Row 1 (WS)* P2, *K4, P1, K4, P3*, end with K4, P1, K4, P2. *Row 2* K1, *T2L, P3, K1, P3, T2R, K1*. *Row 3* P1, *K1, P1, (K3, P1) twice, K1, P1*. *Row 4* K1, *P1, T2L, P2, K1, P2, T2R, P1, K1*. *Row 5* P1, *K2, P1*. *Row 6* K1, *P2, T2L, P1, K1, P1, T2R, P2, K1*. *Row 7* P1, *K3, (P1, K1) twice, P1, K3, P1*. *Row 8* K1, *P3, T2L, K1, T2R, P3, K1*. *Rows 9 and 11* P1, *K4, P3, K4, P1*. *Row 10* K1, *P4, ytf, sl next 3 sts onto right-hand needle, ybk, sl same 3 sts onto left-hand needle, ytf, sl 3 sts onto right-hand needle – called wrap 3, P4, K1*. *Row 12* K1, *P3, T2R, K1, T2L, P3, K1*. *Rows 13, 15, 17 and 19* As rows 7, 5, 3 and 1. *Row 14* K1, *P2, T2R, P1, K1, P1, T2L, P2, K1*. *Row 16* K1, *P1, T2R, P2, K1, P2, T2L, P1, K1*. *Row 18* K1, *T2R, P3, K1, P3, T2L, K1*. *Row 20* K2, *P4, K1, P4, wrap 3*, end with P4, K1, P4, K2. Rep these 20 rows.

Vertical zigzag stitch Work over a number of sts divisible by 9. *Row 1* *K3, (T2R) 3 times*. *Row 2 and every alt row* P to end. *Row 3* *K2, (T2R) 3 times, K1*. *Row 5* *K1, (T2R) 3 times, K2*. *Row 7* *(T2R) 3 times, K3*. *Row 9* *(T2L) 3 times, K3*. *Row 11* *K1, (T2L) 3 times, K2*. *Row 13* *K2, (T2L) 3 times, K1*. *Row 15* *K3, (T2L) 3 times*. *Row 17* Rep from row 1.

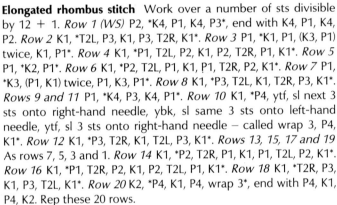

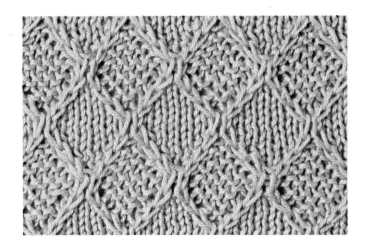

Purled rhombus stitch Work over a number of sts divisible by 8. *Row 1* *K2, C2R, C2L, K2*. *Row 2* *K2, sl1 P yfwd, P2, sl1 P yfwd, K2*. *Row 3* *K1, C2R, K2, C2L, K1*. *Row 4* *K1, sl1 P yfwd, P4, sl1 P yfwd, K1*. *Row 5* *C2R, K4, C2L*. *Row 6* *Sl1 P yfwd, P6, sl1 P yfwd*. *Row 7* K. *Row 8* As row 6. *Rows 9 to 13* As rows 5 to 1, reading C2L for C2R and vice versa. *Rows 14 and 16* *K3, sl2 P yfwd, K3*. *Row 15* K. *Row 17* Rep from row 1.

Sycamore stitch Work over a number of sts divisible by 8. *Row 1* *C2L, K6*. *Row 2* *P6, sl1 P yfwd, K1*. *Row 3* *K1, C2L, K5*. *Row 4* *P5, sl1 P yfwd, K2*. *Row 5* *K2, C2L, K4*. *Row 6* P4, sl1 P yfwd, K3*. *Row 7* K. *Row 8* P. *Row 9* *K6, C2R*. *Row 10* *K1, sl1 P yfwd, P6*. *Row 11* *K5, C2R, K1*. *Row 12* *K2, sl1 P yfwd, P5*. *Row 13* *K4, C2R, K2*. *Row 14* *K3, sl1 P yfwd, P4*. *Row 15* K. *Row 16* P. *Row 17* Rep from row 1.

Fancy stitches

Popcorn   Alternating bobbles
Hazelnut stitch   Pineapple stitch

Popcorn Work over a number of sts divisible by 6 + 5. *Rows 1 to 4* K. *Row 5* K5, *work (K1, P1, K1, P1) all into next st, K5*. *Row 6* K5, *ytf, sl3, K1, sl third, second and first sts separately over the last st worked, completing the 'popcorn', K5*. *Rows 7 to 10* K. *Row 11* K2, *(K1, P1, K1, P1) all into next st, K5*, end with K2. *Row 12* K2, *ytf, sl3, K1, complete the 'popcorn' as in row 6, K5*, end with K2. Rep these 12 rows.

Alternating bobbles Work over a number of sts divisible by 6 + 5. *Rows 1 to 5* K. *Row 6* K5, *(yo and K1) 3 times into next st to make 6 sts for the bobble, turn the work, sl1, P5, turn the work again and sl1, K5, turn the work again and (P2tog) 3 times, turn again and complete the bobble with sl1, K2tog, psso, K5*. *Row 7* K5, *P1 tbl, K5*. *Rows 8 to 11* K. *Row 12* K8, *work a bobble as in row 6, K5*, end with K3. *Row 13* K8, *P1 tbl, K5*, end with K3. Rep rows 2 to 13. If a larger bobble is required, turn the work twice more on the 6 sts.

Hazelnut stitch Work over a number of sts divisible by 6 + 2. *Row 1* *P2, K1*, end with P2. *Row 2* *K2, P1, K2 (K1, P1, K1, P1) all in next st*, end with K2. *Row 3* *P8, K1*, end with P2. *Row 4* K2, *P1, K8*. *Row 5* As row 3. *Row 6* K2, *P1, P4tog, P1*. *Row 7* As row 1. *Row 8* *K2, (K1, P1, K1, P1) all in next st, K2, P1*, end with K2. *Row 9* P2, *K1, P8*. *Row 10* *K8, P1*, end with K2. *Row 11* As row 9. *Row 12* K2*, P1, P4tog, P1*. Rep these 12 rows.

Pineapple stitch Work over a number of sts divisible by 6 + 2. *Row 1 (RS)* K1, *sl3 ybk, K2tog, pass the 3 slipped sts over, one at a time, loosely P (into the back, then into the front) twice and then into the back again of next st*, end with K1. *Row 2* P1, *K5, P1*, end with P1. *Rows 3 and 5* K1, *K1, P5*, end with K1. *Rows 4 and 6* As row 2. *Row 7* K1, *loosely P (into the back, then into the front) twice and then into the back again of next st, sl3 ybk, K2tog, pass the 3 slipped sts over one at a time*, end with K1. *Row 8* P1, *P1, K5*, end with P1. *Rows 9 and 11* K1, *P5, K1*, end with K1. *Rows 10 and 12* As row 8. Rep these 12 rows.

Shutter stitch Work over a number of sts divisible by 4. *Row 1* *Yo, K4*. *Row 2* P. *Row 3* *Yo, K into the third st on left-hand needle, then knit the second and first tog, C2L*. Rep rows 2 to 3.

Crossed link stitch Work over a number of sts divisible by 4. *Rows 1 and 3 (RS)* K1, *P2, K2*, end with P2, K1. *Row 2* P1, K1, *miss the next 3 sts, insert needle into fourth st and pull through a loop, then K first st on left-hand needle, P next 2 sts, drop the fourth (the st from which the loop was drawn)*, end with K1, P1. *Row 4* P1, *K2, P2*, end with K2, P1. Rep these 4 rows.

Crossed square stitch Work over a number of sts divisible by 18 + 10. *Rows 1, 3, 5, 7 and 9 (RS)* *(P1, C2R) 3 times, P1, K8 tbl*, end with (P1, C2R) 3 times, P1. *Rows 2, 4, 6, 8 and 10* *(K1, P2) 3 times, K1, P8 tbl*, end with (K1, P2) 3 times, K1. *Rows 11, 13, 15, 17 and 18* P1, *K8 tbl, (P1, C2R) 3 times, P1*, end with K8 tbl, P1. *Rows 12, 14, 16, 19 and 20* K1, *P8 tbl, (K1, P2) 3 times, K1*, end with P8 tbl, K1. Rep these 20 rows.

Brick stitch Work over a number of sts divisible by 14 + 4. *Rows 1 and 2* P. *Rows 3, 5 and 7* *K1, PC2R, K1, P10*, end with K1, PC2R, K1. *Rows 4, 6 and 8* *P1, K2, P1, K10*, end with P1, K2, P1. *Rows 9 and 10* P. *Rows 11, 13 and 15* *P7, K1, PC2R, K1, P3*, end with P4. *Rows 12, 14 and 16* *K7, P1, K2, P1, K3*, end with K4. Rep these 16 rows.

Working cables
Simple cable from right to left
Simple cable from left to right
Double cable with two double pointed needles

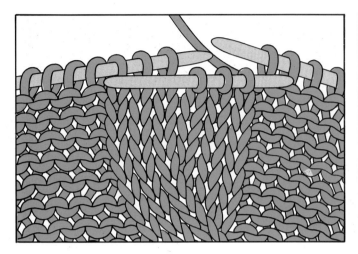

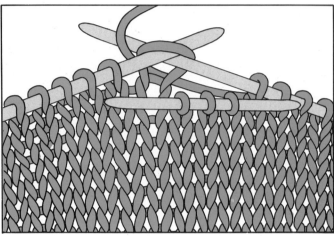

Simple cable from right to left 1. The number of stitches in the cable must be even. Work to the cable position, then put the first group of stitches to be cabled (the first 3 of a cable of 6 stitches) on a double pointed needle and hold at the front of the work.

2. Knit the following 3 stitches, then return to the double pointed needle and knit the stitches from it. When working the first stitch from the double pointed needle, take care that the yarn is pulled firmly to avoid a loose stitch at the back of the work.

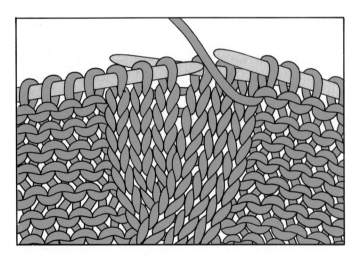

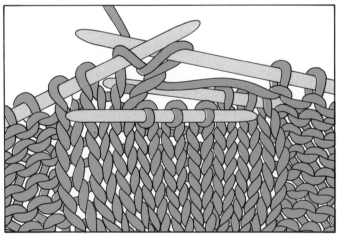

Simple cable from left to right Put the first group of stitches to be cabled on the double pointed needle and hold at the back of the work. Work the following 3 stitches, then return to the double pointed needle and knit the stitches from it.

Double cable with two needles Work on 9 stitches. Put the first 3 stitches on a double pointed needle and hold at the back of the work. Then put the following 3 stitches on a double pointed needle and hold at the front of the work. Knit the following 3 stitches, then work the stitches from the back needle and then from the front needle. The result is a double cable crossed at the center.

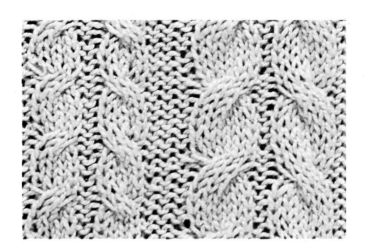

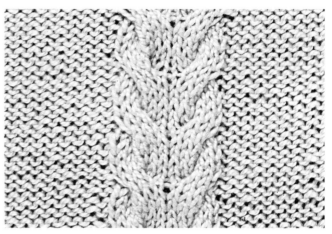

Simple cable   For a 4 st cable moving to left (or to right) every 4 rows. *Rows 1 and 3 (WS)* *K2, P4*, end with K2. *Row 2* P2, *K4, P2*. *Row 4* *P2, put next 2 sts on dpn to the front (or back), K2, K2 from dpn*, end with P2. Rep these 4 rows. For a 6 st cable moving to left (or to right) every 6 rows: *Rows 1, 3, 5* *K2, P6*, end with K2. *Rows 2 and 4* *P2, K6*, end with P2. *Row 6* *P2, put next 3 sts on dpn to the front (or back), K3, K3 from dpn needle*, end with P2. Rep these 6 rows.

Ear of grain cable   This sample shows a cable of 13 sts on a background of reverse st st. *Row 1 (RS)* K13. *Row 2* P13. *Row 3* Put 3 sts on dpn, and hold at back of work, K3, K3 from dpn, K1, put 3 sts on dpn, and hold at front of work, K3, K3 from dpn. *Row 4* P13. Rep these 4 rows.

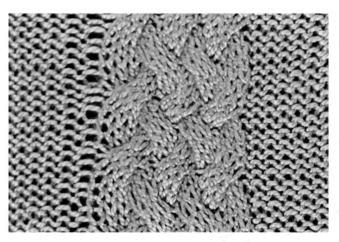

Triple cable   This cable is worked over 9 sts. This sample shows 3 reverse st sts between each cable. *Rows 1 and 3 (WS)* *K3, P9*, end with K3. *Row 2* P3, *K9, P3*. *Row 4* *P3, put 3 sts on dpn and hold at front of work, K3, K3 from dpn, K3*, end with P3. *Rows 5 and 7* As rows 1 and 3. *Row 6* As row 2. *Row 8* *P3, K3, put 3 sts on dpn and hold at back of work, K3, K3 from dpn*, end with P3. Rep these 8 rows.

Composite cable   This 18 st cable can be worked on a background of garter stitch or flanked by 5 reverse st sts, as in this example. *Rows 1, 5 and 9* *P5, K18*, end with P5. *Row 2 and all even rows* Work the sts as set. *Row 3* *P5, (put 3 sts on dpn and hold at back of work, K3, K3 from dpn) 3 times*, end with P5. *Row 7* *P5, K3, (put 3 sts on dpn and hold at front of work, K3, K3 from dpn) twice, K3*, end with P5. *Row 11* Rep from row 3.

Cable patterns

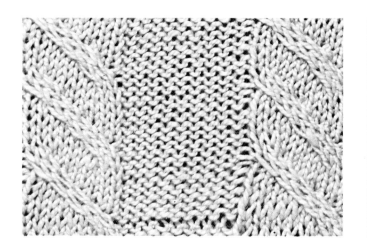

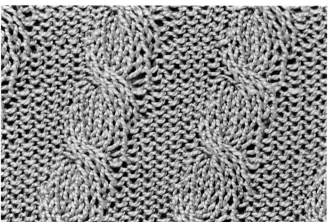

Cross banded cable   This is a 10 st cable. This sample shows it on a reverse st st background. *Row 1* Make a left cross thus: place 2 sts on dpn and hold at front of work, K2, K2 from dpn, K5. *Row 2* P6, sl2 P-wise, P2. *Row 3* K2, make a left cross as above, K4. *Row 4* P4, sl2 P-wise, P4. *Row 5* K4, make a left cross as above, K2. *Row 6* P2, sl2 P-wise, P6. *Row 7* K6, make a cross as above. *Row 8* P10. Rep these 8 rows.

Slanting cable   Work over a number of sts divisible by 12 + 6. *Rows 1 and 3* *P6, K6*, end with P6. *Row 2 and all even rows* Work the sts as set. *Row 5* As for row 1, shifting the patt 1 st to the right; start, therefore, with P5, *K6, P6*, end with K1. *Row 7* Work the sts as set, and work a cable. *Row 9* Shift the patt again 1 st to the right and start with P4. Continue in this way, shifting the patt every 4 rows; *at the same time,* work a cable on 7th and every foll 6th row, working on 6 sts in st st. Place 3 sts on dpn and hold at front of work, K3, K3 from dpn.

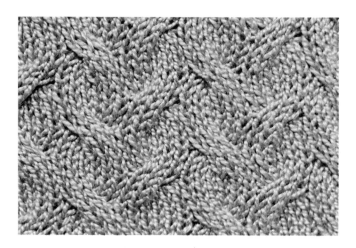

Wind on the sand   Work over a number of sts divisible by 12. *Row 1* K. *Row 2 and all even rows* P. *Row 3* *Place 3 sts on dpn and hold at front of work, K3, K3 from dpn, K6*. *Row 5* K. *Row 7* *K6, place 3 sts on dpn and hold at back of work, K3, K3 from dpn*. *Row 8* P. *Row 9* Rep from row 3.

Twisted cable   Work over a number of sts divisible by 9 + 3. *Row 1* *P3, K6*, end with P3. *Row 2 and all even rows* Work sts as set. *Row 3* *P3, place 2 sts on dpn and hold at back of work, K2, K2 from dpn, K2*, end with P3. *Row 5* *P3, K2, place 2 sts on dpn and hold at front of work, K2, K2 from dpn*, end with P3. *Row 7* Rep from row 3.

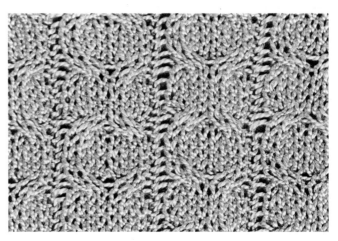

Open cable This needs 2 dpns. Work over a number of sts divisible by 16. *Row 1* *P2, K2*. *Rows 2 to 6* Work the sts as set. *Row 7* *P2, (work the first cable over next 6 sts), place 2 K sts on dpn and hold at front of work, place 2 P sts on second dpn and hold at back of work, K2, P2 from dpn, K2 from dpn, P2, K2, P2, K2*. *Rows 8 to 12* Work as rows 2 to 6. *Row 13* Shifting the cable in the foll way: *P2, K2, P2, K2, P2, work the cable on the 6 foll sts*. *Row 14* Rep from row 2.

Medallion cable Work over a number of sts divisible by 10 + 2. *Row 1* P2, *K8, P2*. *Row 2* K2, *P8, K2*. *Row 3* P2, *C4B, C4F, P2*. *Row 4* As row 2. *Rows 5 to 8* Rep rows 1 and 2 twice. *Row 9* P2, *C4F, C4B, P2*. *Row 10* As row 2. *Rows 11 and 12* As rows 1 and 2. Rep these 12 rows.

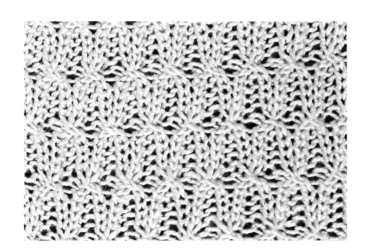

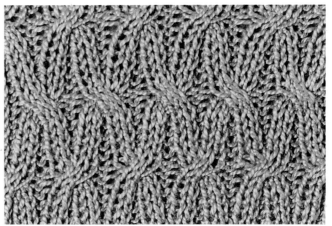

Simple chalice stitch Work over a number of sts divisible by 4 + 2. *Rows 1, 3 and 5* P2, *K2, P2*. *Rows 2 and 4* K2, *P2, K2*. *Row 6* K1, *place 1 st on dpn and hold at front of work, P1, skip 1, K into next st, sl it over skipped st, K1 from dpn, P skipped st*, end with K1. *Rows 7, 9 and 11* K2, *P2, K2*. *Rows 8 and 10* P2, *K2, P2*. *Row 12* K1, skip 1, K into next st, sl it over skipped st as before, P skipped st, rep from * to * as in row 6, and end with place 1 st on dpn and hold at front of work, P1, K1 from dpn, K1. Rep these 12 rows.

Double chalice stitch Work over a number of sts divisible by 8 + 2. *Rows 1, 3, 5 and 7 (WS)* K2, *K2, K2*. *Rows 2, 4 and 6* P2, *K2, P2*. *Row 8* P2, *place 4 sts on dpn and hold at back of work, K2, sl 2 P sts from dpn onto left-hand needle and P them, K2 rem sts from dpn, P2*. *Rows 9 to 15* As for rows 1 to 7. *Row 16* P2, K2, *P2, place next 4 sts on dpn and hold at front of work, K2, sl 2 P sts from dpn to left-hand needle, and P them, K2 rem sts from dpn*, end with P2, K2, P2. Rep these 16 rows.

Cable patterns

Horseshoe cable   Twisted cable
Ribbed cable   Chain cable

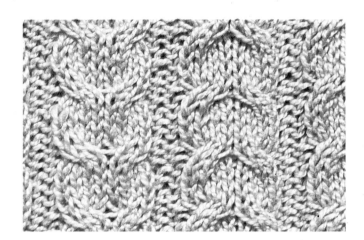

Horseshoe cable Work over 8 sts. These samples are shown on a reverse st st background. Plain horseshoe cable (on right): *On 5th then on every 6th row* Place 2 sts on a dpn in front of the work, K2, then K2 from dpn; place 2 sts on dpn behind work, K2, then K2 from dpn. Reversed horseshoe cable (on left): *On 5th then on every 6th row* Place 2 sts on dpn at back of work, K2, K2 from dpn; place 2 sts on dpn at front of work, K2, K2 from dpn.

Twisted cable Work over a number of sts divisible by 9 + 3. This sample is shown on a reverse st st background. *Rows 1 and 3* *P3, K6*, end with P3. *Row 2 and all even rows* Work the sts as set. *Row 5* *P3, place 3 sts on dpn at front of work, K3, K3 from dpn*, end with P3. *Row 7* As row 1. *Row 9* *P3, place 3 sts on dpn at back of work, K3, K3 from dpn*, end with P3. *Row 10* As row 2. Rep these 10 rows.

Ribbed cable Work over 7 sts. This sample is shown on a reverse st st background. *Row 1 (WS)* *P1 tbl, K1*, 3 times, end with P1 tbl. *Row 2* Place 3 sts on dpn at front of work, K1 tbl, P1, K1 tbl, P1, work sts from dpn as follows: K1 tbl, P1, K1 tbl. *Rows 3, 5 7 and 9* Work as row 1. *Rows 4, 6, 8 and 10* *K1 tbl, P1*, 3 times, end with K1 tbl. Rep these 10 rows.

Chain cable Work over a number of sts divisible by 10 + 4. Two dpns are needed. *Rows 1, 3 and 5* *P4, K2, P2, K2*, end with P4. *Row 2 and all even rows* Work the sts as set. *Row 7* *P4, place the first of the following 6 sts on a dpn at front of work, place next 2 sts on other dpn at back of work, K2, K st from dpn at front of work, K1, K sts from dpn at back of work*, end with P4. *Row 9* Rep from row 1.

Cable patterns
Looped chain cable   Irregular chain cable
Chessmen cable   Butterfly wings

Looped chain cable This needs 2 dpns. Work over a number of sts divisible by 24 + 4. *Rows 1, 3, 5, and 7* *P4, K2*, end with P4. *Row 2 and all even rows* Work the sts as set. *Row 9* *P4, work the cable on 8 foll sts: place 2 K sts on dpn and hold at front of work, place 4 P sts on dpn and hold at back of work, K2, P4 from back dpn, K2 from front dpn, P4, K2, P4, K2*, end with P4. Continue to work sts as set. *Row 17* As row 9. *Rows 18 to 22* Continue to work sts as set. *Row 23* *P4, K2, P4, K2, P4, work cable on 8 foll sts, as above, end with P4. *Rows 24 to 30* Continue to work sts as set. *Row 31* As row 23. *Row 33* Rep from row 9.

Irregular chain cable This needs 2 dpns. Work over a number of sts divisible by 14 + 2. *Row 1* *P2, K5*, end with P2. *Rows 2, 3 and 4* Work sts as set. *Row 5* *P2, work the cable on next 5 sts: place next st on dpn and hold at front of work, place next 3 sts on dpn and hold at back of work, K1, K3 from dpn, then K1 from 2nd dpn, P2, K5*, end with P2. *Rows 6, 7 and 8* As row 2. *Row 9* *P2, K5, P2, work cable on next 5 sts*, end with P2. *Rows 10 to 16* As row 2. *Row 17* As row 9. *Rows 18, 19 and 20* As row 2. *Row 21* As row 5. *Rows 22 to 28* As row 2. *Row 29* Rep from row 5.

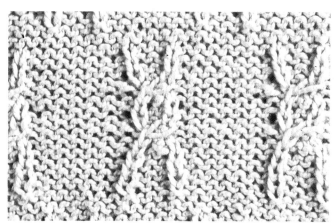

Chessmen cable Work over a number of sts divisible by 12 + 6. *Rows 1 and 3 (RS)* P6, *K6, P6*. *Rows 2 and 4* K6, *P6, K6*. *Row 5* P6, *place 3 sts on dpn and hold at back of work, K3, K3 from dpn, P6*. *Rows 6 and 8* K6, *P6, K6*. *Row 7* P6, *K6, P6*. *Rows 9 and 11* K6, *P6, K6*. *Rows 10 and 12* P6, *K6, P6*. *Row 13* *Place 3 sts on dpn and hold at back of work, K3, K3 from dpn, P6*, end with placing 3 sts on dpn and hold at back of work, K3, K3 from dpn. *Rows 14 and 16* P6, *K6, P6*. *Row 15* K6, *P6, K6*. Rep these 16 rows.

Butterfly wings Work over a number of sts divisible by 12 + 7. *Row 1 (WS)* K. *Rows 2, 4, 8 and 12* P1, *K1, P3, K1, P7*, end with K1, P3, K1, P1. *Rows 3, 5, 7, 9, 11 and 13* K1, *P1, K3, P1, K7*, end with P1, K3, P1, K1. *Rows 6 and 10* P1, *place 4 sts on dpn and hold at back of work, K1, place the 3 P sts on left-hand needle and P them, K last st on dpn, P7*, end with P1 instead of 7. *Row 14* P. *Row 15* K. *Rows 16, 18, 22 and 26* P7 *K1, P3, K1, P7*. *Rows 17, 19, 21, 23, 25 and 27* K7, *P1, K3, P1, K7*. *Rows 20 and 24* P7, rep from * to * as in row 6. *Row 28* P. Rep these 28 rows.

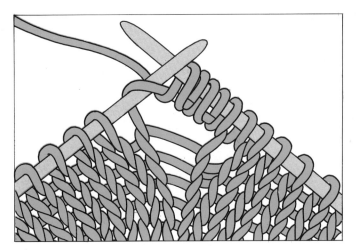

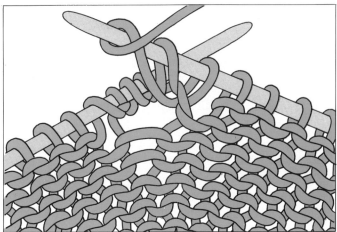

Making bobbles 1. This is one method of making bobbles and is usually worked in stockinette stitch or reverse stockinette stitch. *Row 1* Into the bobble st work (yo, K1) 3 times; there are now 6 sts on the needle, all made from the same st. Turn the work.

2. *Row 2 (WS)* Sl1 P, K rem 5 sts. Turn the work. *Row 3* Sl1, K rem 5 sts. Turn the work. *Row 4 (WS)* (P2tog) 3 times. 3 sts rem. Turn the work.

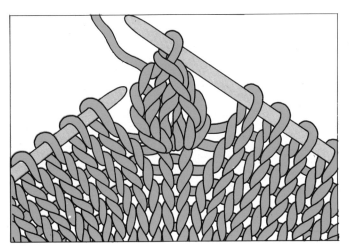

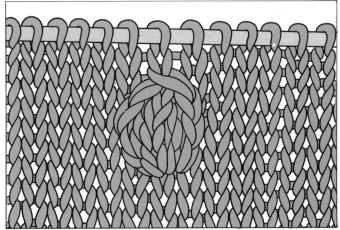

3. *Row 5 (RS)* Sl1, K2tog, psso. 1 rem st. Continue row normally.

4. These 5 rows, worked on 6 sts, make a bobble which stands out from the knitted background. For a larger bobble work on 8 sts, for a smaller bobble work on 4 sts, depending on the thickness of the yarn.

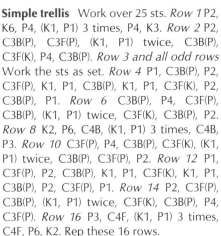

Simple trellis Work over 25 sts. *Row 1* P2, K6, P4, (K1, P1) 3 times, P4, K3. *Row 2* P2, C3B(P), C3F(P), (K1, P1) twice, C3B(P), C3F(K), P4, C3B(P). *Row 3 and all odd rows* Work the sts as set. *Row 4* P1, C3B(P), P2, C3F(P), K1, P1, C3B(P), K1, P1, C3F(K), P2, C3B(P), P1. *Row 6* C3B(P), P4, C3F(P), C3B(P), (K1, P1) twice, C3F(K), C3B(P), P2. *Row 8* K2, P6, C4B, (K1, P1) 3 times, C4B, P3. *Row 10* C3F(P), P4, C3B(P), C3F(K), (K1, P1) twice, C3B(P), C3F(P), P2. *Row 12* P1, C3F(P), P2, C3B(P), K1, P1, C3F(K), K1, P1, C3B(P), P2, C3F(P), P1. *Row 14* P2, C3F(P), C3B(P), (K1, P1) twice, C3F(K), C3B(P), P4, C3F(P). *Row 16* P3, C4F, (K1, P1) 3 times, C4F, P6, K2. Rep these 16 rows.

Mossy trellis Work over 28 sts. *Row 1 (RS)* P5, C4F, P10, C4F, P5. *Row 2 and all even rows* Work sts as set. *Row 3* P4, C3B(P), C3F(K), P8, C3B(P), C3F(K), P4. *Row 5* P3, *C3B(P), K1, P1, C3F(K)*, P6, rep from * to *, end with P3. *Row 7* P2, *C3B(P), (K1, P1) twice, C3F(K)*, P4, rep from * to *, end with P2. *Row 9* P1, *C3B(P), (K1, P1) 3 times, C3F(K)*, P2, rep from * to *, end with P1. *Row 11* *C3B(P), (K1, P1) 4 times, C3F(K)*, rep from * to *. *Row 13* K2 tbl, (K1, P1) 5 times, C4F, (K1, P1) 5 times, K2 tbl. *Row 15* *C3F(P), (K1, P1) 4 times, C3B(P)*, rep from * to *. *Row 17* P1, *C3F(P), (K1, P1) 3 times, C3B(P)*, P2, rep from * to *, end with P1. *Row 19* P2, *C3F(P), (K1, P1) twice, C3B(P)*, P4, rep from * to *, end with P2. *Row 21* P3, *C3F(P), K1, P1, C3B(P)*, P6, rep from * to *, end with P3. *Row 23* P4, C3F(P), C3B(P), P8, C3F(P), C3B(P), P4. *Row 24* As row 2. Rep these 24 rows.

Diamonds with bobbles *Row 1 (WS)* P1, K3, make bobble thus: K into front, back, front, back, front of next st – called wk bobble – then let it drop from needle, K2, P2, K1, P2, K2, wk bobble, K3, P1. *Row 2* K1, P3, K5tog tbl to complete bobble, P2, sl next 3 sts onto dpn and hold at front of work, K2, sl P st from dpn onto left-hand needle and purl it, K2 tbl from dpn, P2, K5tog tbl, P3, K1. *Row 3* P1, K6, P2, K1, P2, K6, P1. *Row 4* K1, P5, C3B(P), P1, C3F(P), P5, K1. *Row 5* P1, K5, P2, K3, P2, K5, P1. *Row 6* K1, P4, C3B(P), P3, C3F(P), P4, K1. *Row 7* P1, K4, P2, K2, wk bobble, K2, P2, K4, P1. *Row 8* K1, P3, C3B(P), P2, K5tog tbl, P2, C3F(P), P3, K1. *Row 9* P1, K3, P2, K7, P2, K3, P1. *Row 10* K1, P2, C3B(P), P7, C3F(P), P2, K1. *Row 11* P1, K2, P2, K2, wk bobble, K3, wk bobble, K2, P2, K2, P1. *Row 12* K1, P1, C3B(P), P2, K5tog tbl, P3, K5tog tbl, P2, C3F(P), P1, K1. *Row 13* P1, K1, P2, K11, P2, K1, P1. *Row 14* K1, P1, K2, P11, K2, P1, K1. *Row 15* P1, K1, P2, K3, wk bobble, K3, wk bobble, K3, P2, K1, P1. *Row 16* K1, P1, C3F(P), P2, K5tog tbl, P3, K5tog tbl, P2, C3B(P), P1, K1. *Row 17* P1, K2, P2, K9, P2, K2, P1. *Row 18* K1, P2, C3F(P), P7, C3B(P), P2, K1. *Row 19* P1, K3, P2, K3, wk bobble, K3, P2, K3, P1. *Row 20* K1, P3, C3F(P), P2, K5tog tbl, P2, C3B(P), P3, K1. *Row 21* P1, K4, P2, K5, P2, K4, P1. *Row 22* K1, P4, C3F(P), P3, C3B(P), P4, K1. *Row 23* P1, K5, P2, K3, P2, K5, P1. *Row 24* K1, P5, C3F(P), P1, C3B(P), P5, K1. Rep these 24 rows.

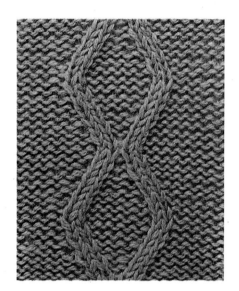

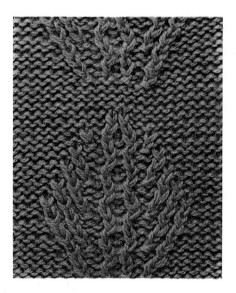

Simple lozenge pattern Work over 14 sts. *Row 1* P5, K4, P5. *Row 2 and all even rows* Work sts as set. *Row 3* P4, C3B(P), C3F(P), P4. *Row 5* P3, C3B(P), P2, C3F(P), P3. *Row 7* P2, C3B(P), P4, C3F(P), P2. *Row 9* P1, C3B(P), P6, C3F(P), P1. *Row 11* P1, C3F(P), P6, C3B(P), P1. *Row 13* P2, C3F(P), P4, C3B(P), P2. *Row 15* P3, C3F(P), P2, C3B(P), P3. *Row 17* P4, C3F(P), C3B(P), P4. *Row 18* As row 2. Rep these 18 rows.

Trees Work over 33 sts. *Rows 1, 3, 5 and 7* P15, K3, P15. *Rows 2, 4, 6 and 8* K15, P3, K15. *Row 9* P14, C2R, K1, C2L, P14. *Row 10* K13, T2L, P3, T2R, K13. *Rows 11 to 14* Continue in this way, shifting the K sts making the branches by 1 st on every row. *Rows 15 and 16* Work the sts as set. *Row 17* Start the leaves on the K sts forming the branches. For each leaf work as follows, working rem sts as set: *Row 1* Make 1 at the edges of the K st (branch). *Row 2 and all even rows* P into made sts of previous row. *Row 3* K1, yo, K1 (central st), yo, K1. *Row 5* K2, yo, K1 (central st), yo, K2. *Row 7* K. *Row 9* Sl1, K1, psso, K3, K2tog, start 2 new branches as row 1. *Row 11* Sl1, K1, psso, K1, K2tog. *Row 13* Sl2, K1, P2sso. Continue 2 new branches, cross the sts as before and spread them to 4 sts from the central st. Work 2 rows without crossing, then work a leaf on each side. These leaves are shorter by 2 rows than the previous ones, so omit rows 5 and 9. As these are finished, start the top leaf: *Row 1* Yo, K1 (central st), yo. *Row 2 and all even rows* P into yo's of previous row. *Row 3* K1, yo, K1 (central st), yo, K1. *Row 5* Sl1, K1, psso, K1, K2tog. *Row 7* Sl2, K1, P2sso. End with 4 rows reverse st st.

Leaves Work over 18 sts. *Rows 1 and 3 (RS)* P18. *Rows 2 and 4* K18. *Row 5* P5, (T2R) twice, (T2L) twice, P5. *Row 6* K5, P1 tbl, K1, P1 tbl, K2, P1 tbl, K1, P1 tbl, K5. *Row 7* P4, T2R, P1, T2L, T2R, P1, T2L, P4. *Row 8* K4, P1 tbl, K3, P2 tbl, K3, P1 tbl, K4. *Row 9* P3, (T2R) 3 times, (T2L) 3 times, P3. *Row 10* K3, (P1 tbl, K1) twice, P1 tbl, K2, (P1 tbl, K1) twice, P1 tbl, K3. *Row 11* P2, (T2R) twice, P1, T2L, T2R, P1, (T2L) twice, P2. *Row 12 and all even rows* Work sts as set. *Row 13* P1, (T2R) 4 times, (T2L) 4 times, P1. *Row 15* As row 11. *Row 17* As row 9. *Row 19* As row 7. *Row 21* As row 5. *Row 23* P7, T2L, T2R, P7. *Row 24* K8, P2 tbl, K8. These 24 rows form the patt.

Decorated lozenge pattern Work on a panel of 22 sts. *Row 1 (WS)* K9, P4, K9. *Row 2* P9, C4B, P9. *Row 3 and all odd rows* Work sts as set. *Row 4* P8, C3B(P), C3F(P), P8. *Row 6* P7, C3B(P), P2, C3F(P), P7. *Row 8* P6, C3B, P4, C3F(P), P6. *Row 10* P5, C3B(P), P1, K4, P1, C3F(P), P5. *Row 12* P4, C3B(P), P1, C3B(P), C3F(P), P1, C3F(P), P4. *Row 14* P3, C3B(P), P1, C3B(P), P2, C3F(P), P1, C3F(P), P3. *Row 16* (P2, C3B(P), P2, C3F(P)) twice, P2. *Row 18* P1, (C3B(P), P4, C3F(P)) twice, P1. *Row 20* P1, K2, P6, C4B, P6, K2, P1. *Row 22* P1, (C3F(P), P4, C3B(P)) twice, P1. *Row 24* (P2, C3F(P), P2, C3B(P)) twice, P2. *Row 26* P3, C3F(P), P1, C3F(P), P2, C3B(P), P1, C3B(P), P3. *Row 28* P4, C3F(P), P1, C3F(P), C3B(P), P1, C3B(P), P4. *Row 30* P5, C3F(P), P6, C3B(P), P5. *Row 32* P6, C3F(P), P4, C3B(P), P6. *Row 34* P7, C3F(P), P2, C3B(P), P7. *Row 36* P8, C3F(P), C3B(P), P8. Rep these 36 rows.

Tree of Life – branches down Work on a panel of 15 sts. *Row 1 (RS)* P2, K1, P4, sl1 P ybk, P4, K1, P2. *Row 2* K2, sl1 P yfwd, K4, P1, K4, sl1 P yfwd, K2. *Row 3* P2, T2L, P3, sl1 P ybk, P3, T2R, P2. *Row 4* K3, sl1 P yfwd, K3, P1, K3, sl1 P yfwd, K3. *Row 5* P3, T2L, P2, sl1 P ybk, P2, T2R, P3. *Row 6* K4, sl1 P yfwd, K2, P1, K2, sl1 P yfwd, K4. *Row 7* P4, T2L, P1, sl1 P ybk, P1, T2R, P4. *Row 8* K5, sl1 P yfwd, K1, P1, K1, sl1 P yfwd, K5. *Row 9* P2, K1, P2, T2L, sl1 P ybk, T2R, P2, K1, P2. *Row 10* K2, sl1 P yfwd, K4, P1, K4, sl1 P yfwd, K2. Rep rows 2 to 10.

Tree of Life – branches up Work on a panel of 9 sts. *Row 1 (RS)* P3, K3, P3. *Row 2* K3, P3, K3. *Row 3* P2, T2R, K1, T2L, P2. *Row 4* K2, (P1, K1) twice, P1, K2. *Row 5* P1, T2R, P1, K1, P1, T2L, P1. *Row 6* K1, (P1, K2) twice, P1, K1. *Row 7* T2R, P1, K3, P1, T2L. *Row 8* P1, K2, P3, K2, P1. Rep these 8 rows.

Interlocked cables Work on a panel of 22 sts. *Rows 1 and 3 (WS)* K2, P2, K3, P2, K4, P2, K3, P2 K2. *Row 2* P2, K2, P3, K2, P4, K2, P3, K2, P2. *Row 4* P2, (C3F(P), P2) twice, (C3B(P), P2) twice. *Row 5 and all odd rows* Work sts as set. *Row 6* P3, C3F(P), P2, C3F(P), C3B(P), P2, C3B(P), P3. *Row 8* P4, C3F(P), P2, C4B, P2, C3B(P), P4. *Row 10* P5, (C3F(P), C3B(P)) twice, P5. *Row 12* P6, C4F, P2, C4F, P6. *Row 14* P5, (C3B(P), C3F(P)) twice, P5. *Row 16* P4, C3B(P), P2, C4B, P2, C3F(P), P4. *Row 18* P3, C3B(P), P2, C3B(P), C3F(P), P2, C3F(P), P3. *Row 20* P2, (C3B(P), P2) twice, (C3F(P), P2) twice. *Rows 22, 24 and 26* As row 2. Rep these 26 rows.

Jacquard knitting
1st method: Twisting yarns
2nd method: Stranding
3rd method: Weaving

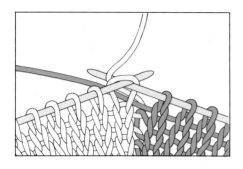

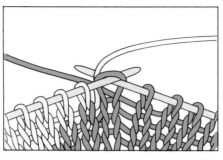

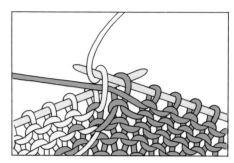

Jacquard knitting: 1st method: Twisting yarns 1. This is the method of changing color for large motifs. Use a ball of yarn for each section and twist them when moving on to the next color, so as not to leave a hole in the work. If the color pattern changes vertically, take the new yarn behind the previous yarn.

2. If the color pattern is diagonal with a slope to the right, pass the right-hand yarn in front of the left, when changing color. On the wrong side of the work, the yarns twist automatically.

3. If the slope is to the left, twist the yarns on the wrong side of the work only. On the right side the yarns twist automatically.

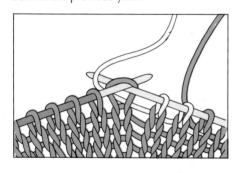

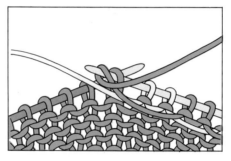

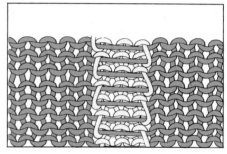

2nd method: Stranding 1. When the design is small (over 3 stitches or fewer), carry the yarn not being used behind the work, crossing the yarns at the point of change so as not to leave a hole. Use both hands to carry the yarn, the first color in the right hand, the second over the left thumb.

2. On the wrong side of the work, purl with the right hand while carrying the second yarn in the left hand. This can also be done with only one hand, dropping the yarns each time, but the resulting work is looser and less regular.

3. This is how the finished work appears on the wrong side. Make sure that an even tension is maintained, so that the work does not become pulled or puckered.

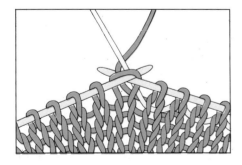

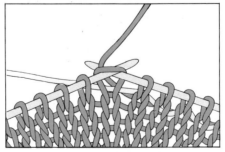

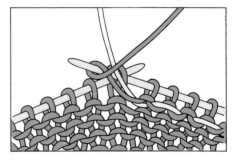

3rd method: Weaving 1. If there are more than 3 stitches in a group, the weaving method is used to avoid loose threads on the wrong side of the work.

2. On the right side of the work, hold the yarn not being used to the left. Put the right-hand needle into the stitch and pass the yarn not in use alternately under and over the working yarn.

3. Work in the same way on the wrong side of the work. Hold the thread not in use at the front of the work, weaving it under and over the working yarn. Take care to use only the working yarn to form the stitches on the needle.

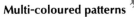

Multi-coloured patterns

Vertical rows	Horizontal rows	Fancy rows
Rectangle stitch	Two-colour Scotch stitch	Star tweed stitch

Vertical rows The stranding or weaving method is used to work 2 to 5 stitches in each color. If the number of stitches in each stripe becomes greater use a separate ball for each color. This makes working with more colors easier too.

Horizontal rows Work 2 rows in each color, keeping the number of rows even. A yarn not in use is carried up the side of the work and caught in the selvedge stitch every couple of rows.

Fancy rows Work over an even number of sts. It is worked in st st in three colors, A, B, and C, spacing them in the following way: 3 rows A, 2 rows C, 1 row B, 1 row C, 1 row B. Then work 1 row as follows: *1 st B, 1 st C, rep from * to end, then 1 row C. Rep these rows.

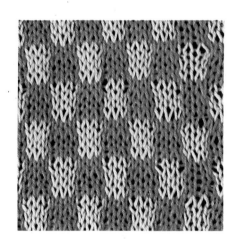

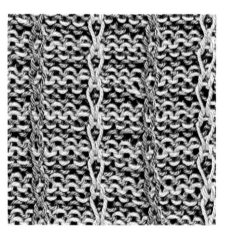

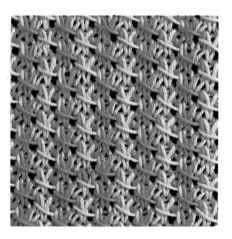

Rectangle stitch Work 3 sts in each color, and change the colors every 4 rows (the number of sts and rows is optional). With a larger number of sts use a ball for each rectangle.

Two-color Scotch stitch Work over a number of sts divisible by 10. Work 2 rows in each color. *Row 1* In A, *P4, K1, P4, sl1 K-wise ybk tbl*. *Row 2* Work the sts as set, sl P-wise ytf the st slipped on previous row. *Row 3* In B, *P4, sl1 K-wise ybk tbl, P4, K1*. *Row 4* As row 2. *Row 5* Rep from row 1.

Star tweed stitch Work over a number of sts divisible by 4 + 1. *Row 1* In B, P. *Row 2* In A, K1, *sl1 P ybk, insert needle under loop before next st and K into it, sl1 P ybk, K1, pass first sl st over 3 sts, K1*. *Row 3* In A, P. *Row 4* In B, K3, *sl1 P ybk, insert needle under loop before next st and K into it, sl1 P ybk, K1, pass first sl st over 3 sts, K1*, end with K2. *Row 5* In B, P. Rep from row 2.

Two-color patterns

Diagonal tweed stitch   Labyrinth stitch
Chevron stitch   Spaced chevron stitch

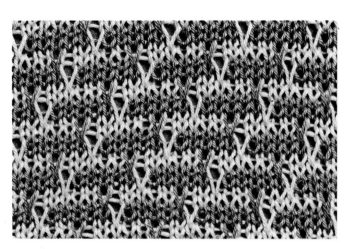

Diagonal tweed stitch Work over a number of sts divisible by 6 + 2 in 2 colors, A and B. Slip all sts P-wise with yarn on WS. *Row 1* In A, P. *Row 2* In B, K1, *sl2, K4*, end with K1. *Row 3* In B, K1, *P4, sl2*, end with K1. *Row 4* In A, K1, *K4, sl2*, end with K1. *Row 5* In A, K1, *sl2, P4*, end with K1. *Row 6* In B, K3, *sl2, K4*, end with sl2, K3. *Row 7* In B, K1, P2, *sl2, P4*, end with sl2, P2, K1. *Rows 8 and 9* In A, as rows 2 and 3. *Rows 10 and 11* In B, as rows 4 and 5. *Rows 12 and 13* In A, as rows 6 and 7. Rep from row 2.

Labyrinth stitch Work over a number of sts divisible by 6 + 1. Slip all sts P-wise with yarn on WS. Work 2 rows for each of the 2 colors, A and B. Cast on with A and work *Row 1* in P. *Row 2* In B, sl 1, *K5, sl1*. *Row 3 and all odd rows* Work the sts as set, sl the slipped sts. *Row 4* In A, K1, *sl1, K5*. *Row 6* In B, K4, *sl1, K5*, end with K2. *Row 8* In A, *K5, sl1 K-wise*, end with K1. *Row 10* In B, K2, *sl1 K-wise, K5*, end with K4. *Row 12* In A, K3, *sl1 K-wise, K5*, end with K3. *Row 14* Rep from row 2.

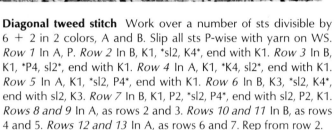

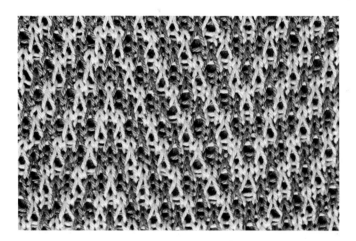

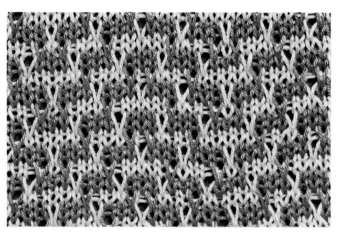

Chevron stitch Work over a number of sts divisible by 24 + 2 in 2 colors, A and B. Slip all sts P-wise with yarn on WS. *Row 1 (RS)* In B, K1, *sl1, K2*, end with K1. *Row 2* In B, K1, *P2, sl1*, end with K1. *Row 3* In A, K1, *K1, sl1, (K2, sl1) 3 times, K3 (sl1, K2) 3 times, sl1*, end with K1. *Row 4* In A, K1, *sl1, (P2, sl1) 3 times, P3, (sl1, P2) 3 times, sl1, P1*, end with K1. *Row 5* In B, K1, *K2, (sl1, K2) 3 times, sl1, K1, sl1, (K2, sl1) 3 times, K1*, end with K1. *Row 6* In B, K1, *P1, (sl1, P2) 3 times, sl1, P1, sl1, (P2, sl1) 3 times, P2*, end with K1. *Rows 7 and 8* In A, as rows 1 and 2. *Rows 9 and 10* In B, as rows 3 and 4. *Rows 11 and 12* In A, as rows 5 and 6. Rep these 12 rows.

Spaced chevron stitch Work over a number of sts divisible by 16 + 3 in 2 colors, A and B. Slip all sts P-wise with yarn on WS. *Row 1* In B, K1, sl1, *K3, sl1*, end with K1. *Row 2* In B, K1, sl1, *P3, sl1*, end with K1. *Row 3* In A, K4, *sl1, K3, sl1, K1, sl1, K3, sl1, K5*, end with K4. *Row 4* In A, K1, P3, *sl1, P3, sl1, P1, sl1, P3, sl1, P5*, end with P3, K1. *Row 5* In B, K3, *sl1, K3*. *Row 6* In B, K1, P2, *sl1, P3*, end with sl1, P2, K1. *Row 7* In A, K2, *sl1, K3, sl1, K5, sl1, K3, sl1, K1*, end with K1. *Row 8* In A, K1, P1, *sl1, P3, sl1, P5, sl1, P3, sl1, P1*, end with K1. Rep these 8 rows.

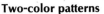
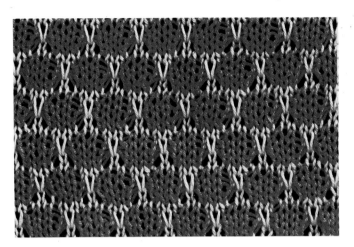

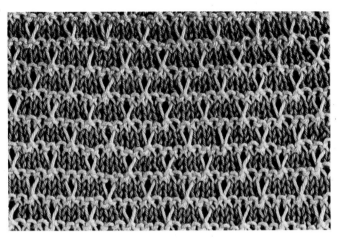

Soap bubbles Work over a number of sts divisible by 4 + 1 in 2 colors, A and B. *Row 1* In A, K. *Row 2* In A, P. *Rows 3 and 5* In B, K. *Rows 4 and 6* In B, P. *Row 7* In A, K2, *drop the next st and let it unravel 4 rows down, picking up A from the 2nd row, insert the needle into this st, under the 4 horizontal threads, in B, and K it keeping the threads behind it, K3*, end with K2. *Row 8* In A, P. *Rows 9 and 11* In B, K. *Rows 10 and 12* In B, P. *Row 13* In A, K4, *let the next st unravel and work it in A 5 rows down, as in row 7, K3*, end with K1. Rep from row 2.

Tile stitch Work over a number of sts divisible by 4 + 3 in 2 colors, A and B. *Rows 1 and 2* In A, K. *Row 3* In B, K1, *sl1 P ybk, K3*, end with sl1 P ybk, K1. *Row 4* In B, P1, *sl1 P yfwd, P3*, end with sl1, P1. *Rows 5 and 6* In A, K. *Row 7* In B, K3, *sl1 P ybk, K3*. *Row 8* In B, P3, *sl1 P yfwd, P3*. Rep these 8 rows.

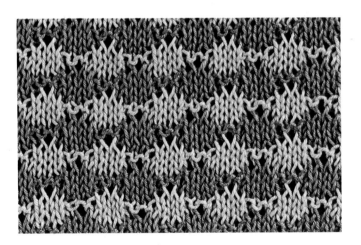

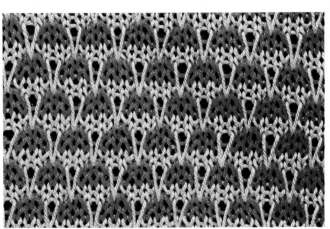

Rows of beads Work over a number of sts divisible by 6 + 5 with 2 colors, A and B. *Row 1 (RS)* In A, K. *Row 2* In A, K1, *P3, K3*, end with P3, K1. *Row 3* In B, K1, *sl3 P ybk, K3*, end with sl3 P ybk, K1. *Row 4* In B, K1, P1, *sl1 P yfwd, P5*, end with sl1 P yfwd, P1, K1. *Row 5* In B, K. *Row 6* In B, K4, *P3, K3*, end with K1. *Row 7* In A, K4, *sl3 P ybk, K3*, end with K1. *Row 8* In A, K1, P4, *sl1 P yfwd, P5*, end with sl1 P yfwd, P4, K1. Rep these 8 rows.

Swallows' flight Work 2 rows for each of the colors, A and B. *Row 1 (WS)* In A, P. *Row 2* *K3, sl1 P ybk*. *Row 3* In B, sl1 P yfwd, *P3, sl1 P yfwd*. *Row 4* *K3, sl1 P ybk*. *Row 5* In A, P. *Row 6* K1, *sl1 P ybk, K3*, end with K2. *Row 7* In B, P2, *sl1 P yfwd, P3*, end with P1. *Row 8* K1, *sl1 P ybk, K3*, end with K2. Rep these 8 rows.

Two-color patterns

Tweedy tapestry stitch   3/1 tweed stitch
Maltese Cross stitch   Knotted tweed stitch

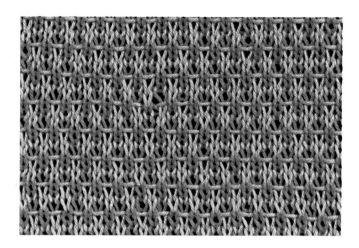

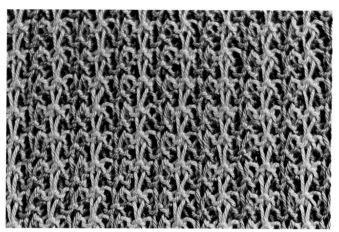

Tweedy tapestry stitch Work over a number of sts divisible by 2 + 1 in 2 colors, A and B. Cast on required number of sts in A and P 1 row. *Row 1 (RS)* In B, K1, *ybk, sl1, K1*. *Row 2* In B, P. *Row 3* In A, K1, *yfwd, sl1, K1*. *Row 4* In A, P. *Row 5* In B, K2, *ybk, sl1, K1*, end with K1. *Row 6* In B, P. *Row 7* In A, K2, *yfwd, sl1, K1*, end with K1. *Row 8* In A, P. Rep these 8 rows.

3/1 tweed stitch Work over a number of sts divisible by 3 + 4 in 2 colors, A and B. Cast on required number of sts in B and K 1 row. *Row 1 (RS)* In A, K3, *ybk, sl1, K3*. *Row 2* In A, K3, *yfwd, sl1, K3*. *Row 3* In B, K1, *ybk, sl1, K3*, end with sl1, K1. *Row 4* In B, K1, *yfwd, sl1, K3*, end with sl1, K1. Rep these 4 rows.

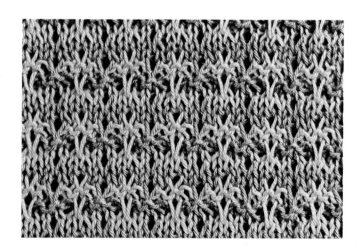

Maltese Cross stitch Work over a number of stitches divisible by 4 + 3 in 2 colors, A and B. *Row 1* In A, P. *Row 2* In B, K3, *sl1 P ybk, K3*. *Row 3* In B, K3, *sl1 P yfwd, K3*. *Row 4* In A, K1, *sl1 P ybk, K3*, end with sl1 P ybk, K3. *Row 5* In A, K1, *sl1 P yfwd, K3*, end with sl1 P yfwd, K1. *Row 6* In B, as row 2. *Row 7* In B, P. *Row 8* In A, as row 4. Rep these 8 rows.

Knotted tweed stitch Work over an odd number of sts in 2 colors, A and B. *Row 1 (WS)* In A, K. *Row 2* In A, K1, *K1D, (work the st below the next st ie. the one worked in the previous row), K1*. *Row 3* In B, K. *Row 4* In B, K2, *K1D, K1*, end with K1. Rep these 4 rows.

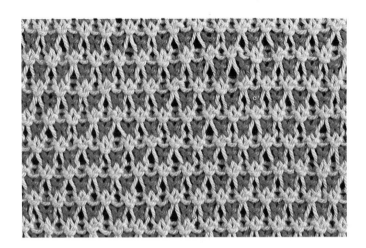

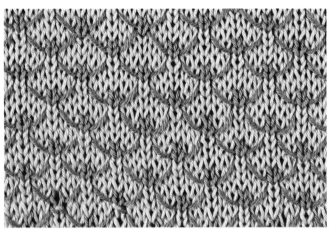

Lacy tweed stitch Work over an odd number of sts in 2 colors, A and B. *Row 1 (WS)* In A, K. *Row 2* In B, K1, *sl1 P ybk, K1*. *Row 3* In B, K1, *sl1 P yfwd, K1*. *Rows 4 and 5* In A, K. *Row 6* In B, K2, *sl1 P ybk, K1*, end with K1. *Row 7* In B, K2, *sl1 P yfwd, K1*, end with K1. *Row 8* In A, K. Rep these 8 rows.

Royal quilt stitch Work over a number of sts divisible by 6 + 3 in 2 colors, A and B. *Row 1 (WS)* In A, K1, P1, *sl5 P ybk, P1*, end with K1. *Row 2* In B, K. *Row 3* In B, K1, P to last st, K1. *Row 4* In A, K1, sl3 P ybk, *insert needle under the loose strand from row 1, K the next st bringing it under the strand to catch it, sl5 P ybk*, rep from * to last 5 sts, end with K the next st under the strand, sl3 P ybk, K1. *Row 5* In A, K1, sl3 P ybk, *P1, sl5 P ybk*, end with P1, sl3 P ybk, K1. *Rows 6 and 7* In B, as rows 2 and 3. *Row 8* In A, K1, *K next st under loose strand from row 5, sl5 P ybk*, end with K st under loose strand, K1. Rep these 8 rows.

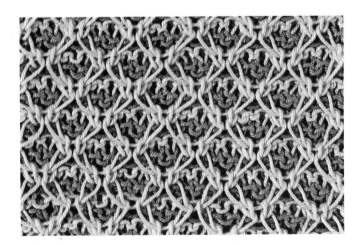

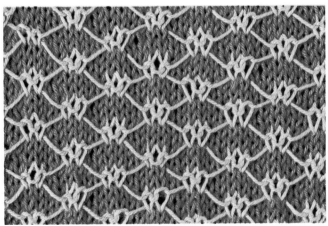

Lacy quilt stitch Work over a number of sts divisible by 6 + 2 in 2 colors, A and B. *Row 1 (WS)* In A, K1, *P1, K4, P1*, end with K1. *Row 2* In B, K1, *sl1 P ybk, K4, sl1 P ybk*, end with K1. *Row 3* In B, K1, *sl1 P yfwd, K4, sl1 P yfwd*, end with K1. *Row 4* In A, K1, *drop sl st in A to front of work, K2, K dropped st, sl2 P ybk, drop sl st in A to front of work, sl same 2 sts back onto left-hand needle, K dropped st, K2*, end with K1. *Row 5* In A, K1, *K2, P2, K2*, end with K1. *Row 6* In B, K1, *K2, sl2 P ybk, K2*, end with K1. *Row 7* In B, K1, *K2, sl2 P yfwd, K2*, end with K1. *Row 8* In A, K1, *sl2 P ybk, drop sl st in A to front of work, sl same 2 sts back onto left-hand needle, K dropped st, K2, drop sl st in A to front of work, K2, K dropped st*, end with K1. Rep these 8 rows.

Crown quilt stitch Work over a number of sts divisible by 8 + 4 in 2 colors, A and B. *Row 1 (RS)* K3A, *K2B, K6A*, end with K1B. *Row 2* K1B, keep ybk, *P6A, K2B, keep ybk*, end with P3A. *Row 3* Take B under left-hand needle ready to work, K1B, *K6A (take right-hand needle under B strand of previous row, K1B) twice*, end with K3A. *Row 4* P3A, *K2B, keep ybk, P6A*, end with K1B. *Row 5* Rep from row 1, taking right-hand needle under B strand when working "K2B".

Pompoms and tassels
Making a pompom
Making a tassel

Making a pompom 1. From a piece of cardboard cut out two circles the size of the finished pompom. Cut out a smaller circle from the center of each of the larger circles. Place the two discs together and begin winding yarn neatly around them with one or more strands as shown.

2. Continue until the small central hole is filled, taking the last strands of yarn through with a blunt needle. Then, with a pair of sharp scissors, cut the yarn all around the outer edge of the discs, pushing the lower blade down between the two discs.

3. Separate the two discs enough to pass a strong strand of yarn between them. Tie a secure knot around the middle of the pompom to hold it together.

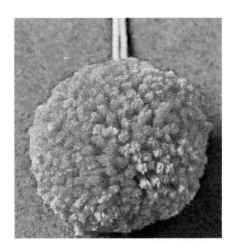

4. Carefully remove the two cardboard discs without pulling out any of the tufts of yarn. Fluff up and trim the tufts to make a thick round pompom. A multicolored pompom can be made by varying the color of the yarn wound around the discs.

Making a tassel 1. From a piece of cardboard, cut a strip of the required depth for the tassel. Wind yarn around it until the tassel is thick enough. Pass a separate strand of yarn through the top of the tassel and tie a knot.

2. Cut through the yarn at the bottom edge of the tassel and remove the cardboard strip. Wind a strand of yarn around the top part of the tassel and knot it. Trim the ends of the tassel with scissors.

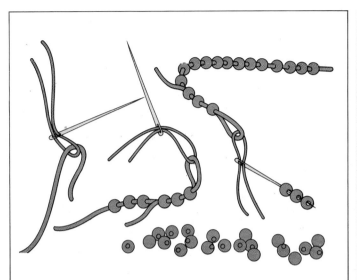

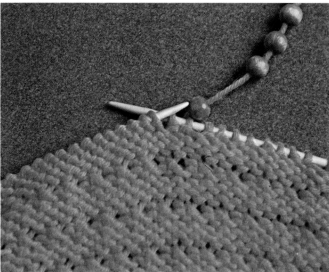

Beads on knitting 1. Before starting to work it will be necessary to thread the beads onto the yarn. Thread a normal sewing needle with a doubled length of strong thread. Pass the end of the yarn through the loop of thread and fold the end back. Thread beads onto the needle and push onto the yarn. Always leave a couple of beads over the yarn end while carrying out the threading to hold the yarn secure.

2. Having threaded the beads, start to work. In these samples the beads are placed with the wrong side of the work facing. Purl to the position of the bead, take the yarn back and slide a bead up the yarn and hold close to the work.

3. To hold the beads firmly, work the next stitch knitwise through the back of the loop. Purl to the position of the next bead and repeat steps 2 and 3.

4. When the work is completed the beads are on the right side of the work. The beads in this sample are spaced two stitches and three rows apart.

INTRODUCTION TO CROCHET

Crochet is a versatile craft with exciting design possibilities. This section contains not only the basic information for beginners in crochet, but also explains the more unusual traditional techniques such as filet crochet, Irish lace, hairpin and Tunisian crochet. In addition, the interesting stitch collection provides a rich source of inspiration.

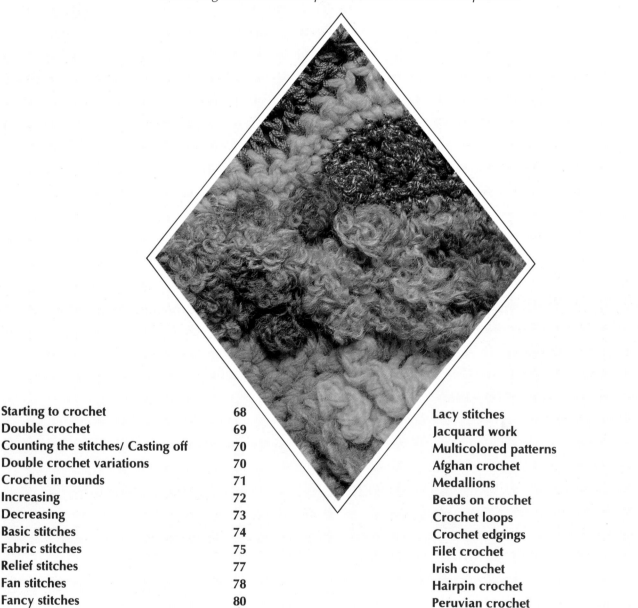

Materials

Hooks A steel hook is used with very fine cotton, linen or silk yarns and sometimes with 3-ply yarn. The length is 5in and the sizes available range from 00 to 5.

An aluminum hook is used for working wool or synthetic yarns, lightweight to heavy. The length is 6in and it is available in sizes B to K. The larger the number, the larger the size.

An afghan needle or hook is used for Tunisian crochet which forms a fabric similar to a knitted fabric. Because stitches are worked onto the hook on one row and off again on the next row, this hook has a knob at one end to prevent the stitches from slipping off. Usually made of aluminum, or sometimes wood, the hook is 12in long and is available in a variety of sizes.

A two-pronged fork is used for hairpin crochet to form a light airy fabric. The size of the forks varies according to width.

A plastic hook is used with rug yarn or fabric strips to make rugs. It is hollow, 5in long and is available in sizes N, P and Q.

Yarns Practically any kind of yarn can be used for crochet, natural or man-made, thin or chunky, ranging from very fine cotton to wool, string, rug wool or even cotton fabric torn into strips. However, some yarns are more suitable than others for certain types of crochet. Filet crochet, which is usually used for edgings or curtains, is best worked in a fine cotton yarn. Bouclé and tweed yarns are generally used for garments which are worked in a simple stitch because complicated patterned stitches would not benefit from a textured or multicolored yarn. Plain yarns, on the other hand, are used to show up textured stitches to best advantage, because the extra work required for these stitches can then be appreciated. Cotton or any suitable washable fabric can be used for crochet by cutting it into bias strips and sewing them together or, for added interest, knotting them together. This can then be used to make bathroom rugs.

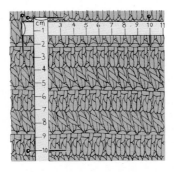

Gauge

Before starting to crochet, whether you are following a pattern or creating an original design, work out an accurate gauge sample using the chosen yarn and stitch for the garment. To begin with, use the hook size recommended on the yarn or thread band. Then if necessary, adjust the hook size to obtain the correct gauge. The gauge can also vary considerably if the yarn is held too tightly or too loosely. An experienced crochet worker will know by the 'feel' of the yarn how to hold it when working. A beginner will only be able to judge how tightly to hold the yarn by practicing.

The number of stitches and rows determines the size of the crochet. If you have more stitches per 4in on your sample than required, try a larger hook. If fewer, you should try a smaller hook.

Measuring the width Lay the sample on a flat surface and place pins vertically 4in apart. For even greater accuracy, leave the work to "rest" for a short while. Then count the number of stitches between the pins.

Measuring the length Lay the sample on a flat surface and place the pins as above but horizontally.

Continue testing until an accurate gauge is obtained.

Abbreviations

beg	beginning	**st**	stitch	
ch	chain	**sT**	simple Tunisian stitch	
cl	cluster	**tr**	treble	
dc	double crochet	**tr tr**	triple treble	
dec	decrease	**Tss**	Tunisian slip stitch	
dtr	double treble	**Ttr**	Tunisian treble	
htr	half treble	**WS**	wrong side	
inc	increase	**yo**	yarn around hook	
lp	loop		yarn over hook	
patt	pattern	**ytf**	yarn to front	
qutr	quadruple treble			
rep	repeat			
RS	right side			
rT	reverse Tunisian stitch			
sc	single crochet			
sp	space			
ss	slip stitch			

An * indicates a repeat. Follow the instructions after the * once, then repeat from the * to the end of the row or as specified. Work the instructions within brackets [ ] the number of times stated. Alternatively, work the instructions within brackets [ ] all into the same place in the pattern. Square brackets [ ] and round brackets ( ) are used together in a pattern where a double set of brackets is required.

Note When working the foundation row of a crochet pattern, the stitches are worked into the chain. On subsequent rows, the stitches are worked by inserting the hook under the two horizontal threads at the top of the stitch in the row below, unless otherwise stated.

Starting to crochet

Making the first chain   Slip stitch
Making a length of chain   Single crochet
Making a length of double chain Reverse single crochet

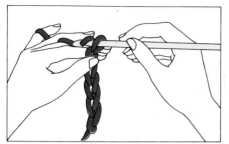

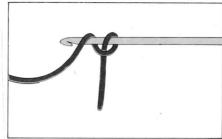

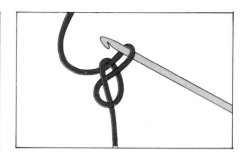

How to hold the crochet hook Hold the crochet hook in the right hand, between the thumb and index finger, placing the thumb on the flat part of the crochet hook. The yarn passes over the index finger and middle finger of the left hand, under the ring finger and around the little finger, folded toward the palm of the hand.

Making the first chain **1.** Hold the end of the yarn between the thumb and index finger of the left hand, closed between the ring and little fingers and the palm of the hand. Insert hook under thread from right to left and twist hook through 360° to make a loop. Insert the crochet hook from front to back under the yarn.

2. Pull hook through the loop to make first chain (ch).

Making a length of chain This is the starting point for all work. Make the first ch, holding the crochet hook horizontally. Then catch the yarn held in the left hand, this step is called yarn over (yo), pulling it through the loop (lp) on the hook and drawing out a new ch.

Making a length of double chain This is used to make a firmer start to work. Make 2 ch. *Insert the crochet hook into the first ch, yo, and pull through a lp, yo and pull through the 2 lps on the crochet hook, closing the st. Repeat the step from * inserting the hook into the side of the st just made.

Slip stitch (ss) Skip first ch. *Insert the hook into the top of next ch, yo, draw a lp through st and lp on hook, rep from *.

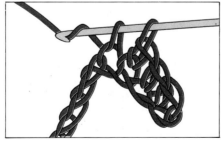

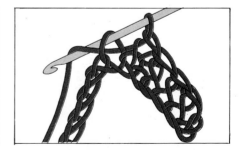

Single crochet (sc) **1.** Insert hook into st, yo and draw it through, so that there are 2 lps on the hook.

2. Yo, draw it through both lps on the hook. Repeat these 2 steps into each st.

Reverse single crochet Work this in the normal way, but making a purl st by catching the yarn over the top instead of the bottom.

Trebles

Half double crochet	Treble	Spaced treble stitches
Double crochet	Double or triple treble	Relief treble stitches
		Turning the work

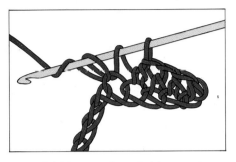

Half double crochet (hdc) Yo, insert hook into top of st, yo and draw through a lp, yo and draw through the 3 lps on the hook.

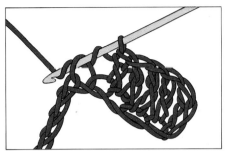

Double crochet(dc) 1. Yo, insert hook into top of st, yo and draw through a lp, yo and draw through the first 2 lps on the hook.

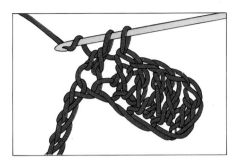

2. Yo again and draw through the last 2 lps on the hook, finishing the st.

Treble (tr) 1. Wind yarn twice around hook then insert hook into top of st.

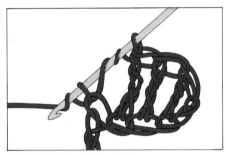

2. [Yo and draw through the first 2 lps on hook] 3 times to complete st.

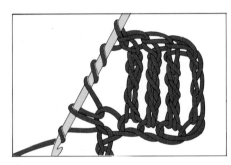

Double treble or triple treble (dtr or trtr) Using the same method as for treble, wind yarn on hook 3 or 4 times, then insert hook into top of st, then work instructions in square brackets 4 or 5 times.

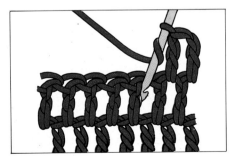

Spaced treble stitches Insert the hook into the space between 2 sts instead of into the top of the st. Work normally, taking care not to pull the yarn too tight.

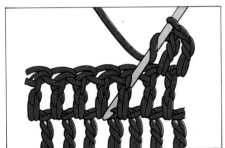

Relief treble stitches Insert the hook horizontally between one st and the next, then bring the hook back to the front of work through foll sp of the row below, then work normally, taking care not to pull the yarn too tight. This way of working results in a textured finish.

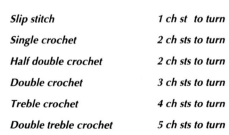

Slip stitch	*1 ch st to turn*
Single crochet	*2 ch sts to turn*
Half double crochet	*2 ch sts to turn*
Double crochet	*3 ch sts to turn*
Treble crochet	*4 ch sts to turn*
Double treble crochet	*5 ch sts to turn*

Turning the work Extra ch are worked at the end of a row before turning to bring the hook to the correct height for the next st being worked.

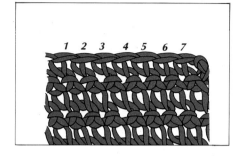

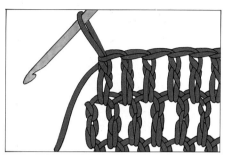

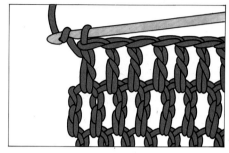

Counting the stitches If working in single crochet, the sts are counted along the top of the work. If working in doubles or trebles, it is easy to count the long sts.

Casting off 1. When the work is the desired length, work the last st in the usual way at the end of the row.

2. Work a chain st, lengthening the lp with the hook, cut the yarn and pull it through the last st.

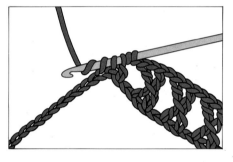

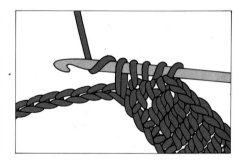

Crossed double crochet stitch 1. *[Yo] twice, insert hook into st, yo and pull through lp, yo and draw through first lp on hook, yo and draw through first 2 lps on hook (3 lps on hook), yo, skip next st, insert hook into next st, yo and pull through lp.

2. [Yo, draw through 2 lps on hook] 4 times, 1ch, 1dc into space where the 2 dcs cross, 1ch, skip next st, rep from *.

Vertical double treble Ch3 to turn, insert hook into first ch, yo, draw through lp [insert hook into next ch, draw through lp] twice, insert hook into next st along row, yo, draw through lp [yo, draw lp through first 2 lps on hook] 4 times to complete first st. Continue in this way, working into 3 lps along side of st.

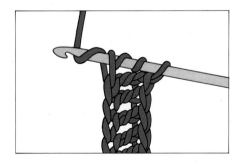

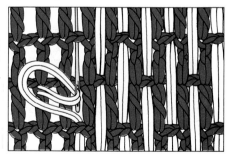

Triple chain This is used as a quick foundation row for a piece of work. Ch4, 1dc in fourth ch from hook, *1dc in base of previous dc, rep from *.

Rolled triple Work on a base of ch. [Yo] 5 times, insert hook in 5th ch from hook, yo, pull through a lp, yo, pull through 7 lps on hook (one at a time), *[yo] 5 times, insert hook in next ch, yo, pull through 7 lps on hook, rep from *.

Woven double crochet Work over a background of dcs separated by ch1 sps. Cut contrasting yarns into lengths long enough to weave vertically through the fabric, allowing extra for weaving and fringing. Use a blunt-ended needle with two lengths of yarn.

Crochet in rounds

Working in rounds   Working a flat circle
Working a square   Working a circle on a ring
                Tubular work

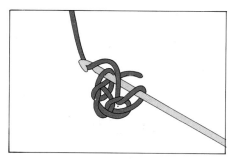

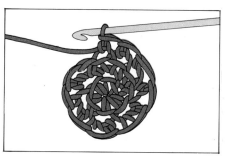

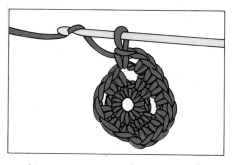

Working in rounds   **1.** Ch4, ss into first ch to form a ring.

2. Continue working, increasing at regular intervals to keep the work flat. *Round 1* Work 2sc in each ch. *Round 2* Work 2sc in every alt sc. *Round 3* Work 2sc in every 3rd sc. *Round 4* Work 2sc in every 4th sc. Continue in this way for size required.

Working a square   Work as in rounds to end of round 1. *Round 2* Work [1sc in each of next 2sc, 1ch] 4 times, ss in first dc. *Round 3* [Work 1sc in each of next 2sc, 1sc/1ch/1sc all in corner ch] 4 times. Continue in this way working 1sc in each sc and 1sc/1ch/1sc in each sc at corner.

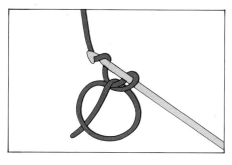

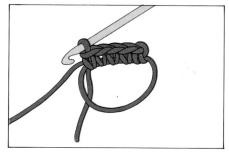

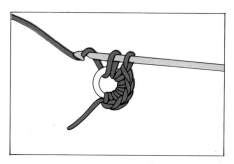

Working a flat circle   **1.** This is an alternative method of working in rounds. Make a lp with the yarn, winding it around the finger a couple of times, and work into the center of it.

2. Work required number of sc around circle, over both strands. Pull loose end firmly to draw circle together and close ring with a ss. Continue work on this base, increasing regularly as explained for working in rounds.

Working a circle on a ring   For decorative motifs it is necessary to work on a plastic ring, covering it completely in sc. When this is done, continue to work normally.

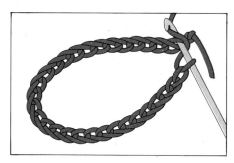

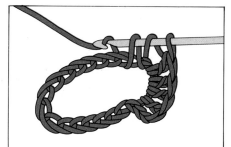

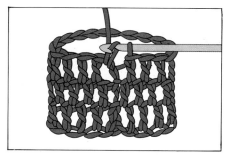

Tubular work   **1.** Make a length of ch (the number of ch required will vary, depending on the circumference of the tube). Ss into first ch to form a ring.

2. Start the rows with 1, 2 or 3 ch according to the st to be used.

3. Each row is completed with a ss worked into the top of the starting ch. This is important to keep changes of color or pattern even.

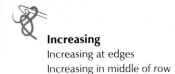

Increasing
Increasing at edges
Increasing in middle of row

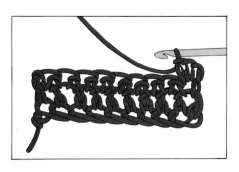

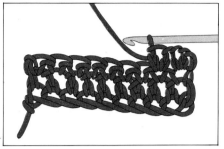

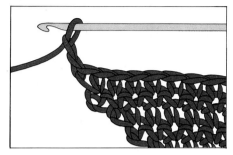

Single increase at each end of a row To increase at the beginning of a row, turn the work with a ch as required, then work 2 sts into the first st. Use the same method at the end of a row, working 2 sts into the penultimate st, then work the last st normally.

Increasing 2 stitches at each end of a row Turn work with ch required. Work 2 sts into each of first 2 sts, work to last 3 sts, 2 sts into each of next 2 sts, 1 st into last st.

Increasing at regular intervals If the sts to be increased are 1 st every row on the same side, work 2 sts into first or last st of every row.

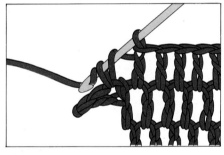

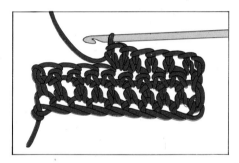

Adding stitches at the beginning of a row Make the same number of ch as sts to be increased, plus the number of ch required for turning. Turn the work and crochet new sts in the ch following the pattern.

Adding stitches at the end of a row To keep increased sts made at both ends of row level, make provision for these sts on previous row. Make same number of extra ch as sts required. Work ss over new ch and continue in pattern. On next row continue to end in pattern, working over ss.

Single increase in middle of row To increase in the middle of a row, work twice into the same st.

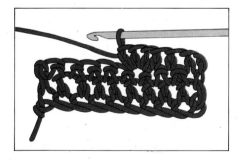

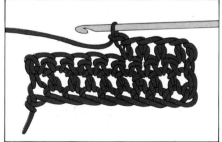

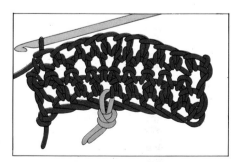

Double increase in the middle of a row To increase 2 sts in the middle of a row, work 3 times into the same st. If this repeat is to be regular and symmetrical, choose a st and work twice into the st on either side of it.

Decorative increasing in the middle of a row Increasing can also be made using ch. On the wrong side of the work, choose the place for increasing. Then work a ch between sts at the chosen place. On the following row, work into the ch.

Increasing evenly in the middle of a row If the increases are to be made at regular intervals, mark the st to be used with a contrasting thread. To work the increase on the right, work twice into the st before the marked st. To increase on the left work twice into the st after the marked st.

Decreasing
Decreasing at edges
Decreasing in middle of row

Decreasing a stitch at the edge of a row 1. To decrease a st at the left-hand edge of a row, work to last 2 sts, skip next st, work into last st, then make turning ch.

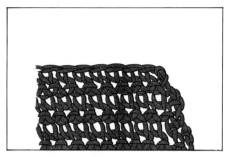

2. To decrease a st on the right of the work, work the first st, skip the second st, and continue normally.

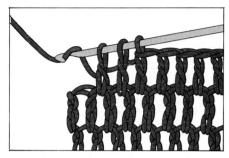

Decreasing double crochet At the beginning of the row [yo, insert hook into next st, yo, draw through a lp, yo, draw through 2 lps on hook] twice, yo, draw through 3 lps on hook (1dc dec). At the end of the row, work the third and second sts from the end in the same way.

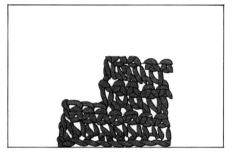

Decreasing any number of stitches at the edge of the work 1. To decrease at the end of the row leave the number of sts to be decreased unworked, then make turning ch.

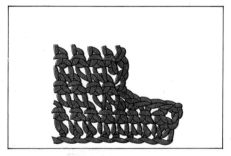

2. To decrease at the beginning of a row work ss over the number of sts to be decreased, then make turning ch.

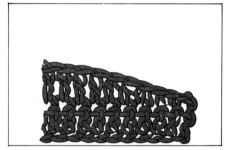

Decreasing at the beginning of row to form a sloping edge At the beginning of the row work the sts to be decreased as follows: 1ss, 1sc, 1hdc, 1dc, then continue with the selected st. More sts can be worked of varying heights to give a longer slope.

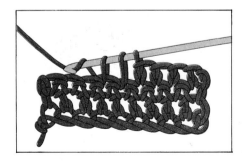

Simple decreasing in the middle of a row To decrease a st in the middle of a row work 2 sts without completing them, leaving 3 lps on the hook, yo and draw through all the lps together.

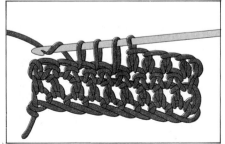

Decreasing more than one stitch in the middle of a row At the required position, work 3 sts without completing them, leaving 4 lps on hook, yo and draw through all the lps together.

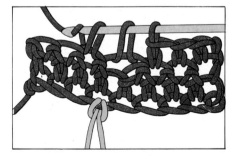

Repeat decreasing in the middle of work If the decreasing is to be repeated on following rows, mark the st to the side of that to be decreased with a contrasting thread, work this st together with the previous and following sts, finishing them all together.

Basic stitches

Single crochet	Albanian single crochet
Ribbed single crochet	Half double crochet
Double crochet	Treble

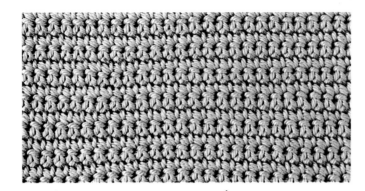

Single crochet Make required no of ch plus 2 for turning. *Foundation row* 1sc in third ch from hook, 1sc in each ch to end, turn. *Row 1* ch2, skip first sc, 1sc in each sc to end. 1sc in 2nd of ch2, turn. Rep this row for a fabric of single crochet.

Albanian single crochet Work the foundation row in sc. The second and following rows are worked in sc by inserting the hook only into the front lp of each sc.

Ribbed single crochet Work the foundation row in sc. The second and the following rows are worked only into the back thread of the sc. This is a softer version of Albanian single crochet, (taking the back instead of the front thread), but the result is different, being ridged and vertically elastic.

Half double crochet Make required no of ch plus 2 for turning. *Foundation row* 1hdc in third ch from hook, 1hdc in each ch to end, turn. *Row 1* ch2, skip first hdc, 1hdc in each hdc to end, 1hdc in second of ch2, turn. Rep this row for a fabric of half double crochet.

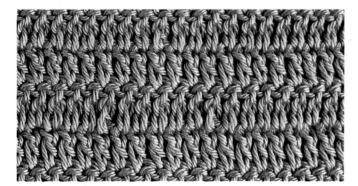

Double crochet Make required no of ch plus 3 for turning. *Foundation row* 1dc in fourth ch from hook, 1dc in each ch to end, turn. *Row 1* ch3, skip first dc, 1dc in each dc to end, 1dc in top of ch3, turn. Rep this row for a fabric of double crochet.

Treble crochet Make required no of ch plus 4 for turning. *Foundation row* 1tr in fourth ch from hook, 1tr in each ch to end, turn. *Row 1* ch4, skip first tr, 1tr in each tr to end, 1tr in top of ch4, turn. Rep this row for a fabric of treble crochet.

Fabric stitches

Alternate stitch   Crossed stitch
Ladder stitch   Leaf stitch
Exchange stitch   Crossed double crochet

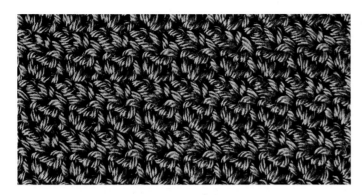

Alternate stitch   Work over a multiple of 2sc. *Row 1* ch1, *skip 1sc, 1sc and 1dc into next st, rep from * to end, turn. *Patt row* ch1, work 1sc and 1dc into each dc, turn. Rep this row to form patt.

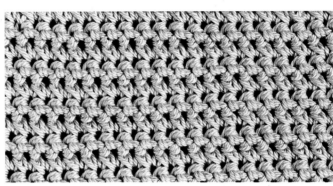

Crossed stitch   Work over an odd no of sc. *Patt row* 1sc in first sc, *insert hook into same place as st just worked, yo and draw loop through, insert hook into next st, yo, and draw loop through, yo and close st. Rep from * to end, turn. Rep this row to form patt.

Ladder stitch   Work over a multiple of 6sc. *Patt row* *1sc in each of next 3sc, 1sc in back lp of next 3sc, rep from * to end, turn. Rep this row to form patt.

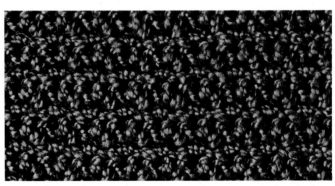

Leaf stitch   Work over a multiple of 2sc. *Patt row* ch1 *skip 1sc, 2sc in next sc, rep from * to end, turn. Rep this row to form patt.

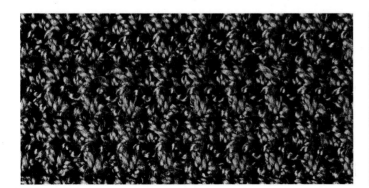

Exchange stitch   Work over an odd no of sc. *Patt row* 1sc in first sc, *skip 1sc, 1sc in next sc, pass hook in front of st just worked and work 1sc into skipped sc, rep from * to end, turn. Rep this row to form patt.

Crossed double crochet   Work over an odd number of double crochet. *Patt row* ch3, *skip next dc, 1dc in next dc, 1dc in skipped dc, rep from * to last 2 sts, 1dc in top of turning ch, 1dc in skipped dc, turn. Rep this row to form patt.

Fabric stitches
Granite stitch   Perforated granite stitch
Diamond stitch   Lacy bricks

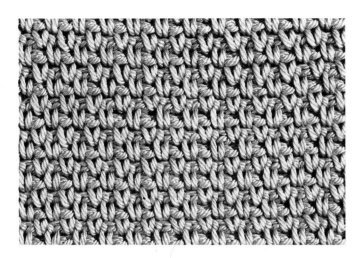

Granite stitch Work over odd no of sc. *Patt row 1* 1sc in first sc, *ch1, skip 1sc, 1sc in next sc, rep from * to end, turn. *Patt row 2* 1sc in first sc, *1sc in 1ch sp, ch1, rep from * to last 2 sts, 1sc in ch1 sp, 1sc in last sc, turn. Rep these 2 rows to form patt.

Perforated granite stitch Work over an odd no of sc. *Patt row 1* ch2, skip first sc, *ch1, skip next sc, work 1 double sc [insert hook into st, yo, draw through 1 lp, yo, draw through 1 lp, yo and close st] into next sc, rep from * to end, turn. *Patt row 2* ch2, 1 double sc in next ch1 sp,*ch1, 1 double sc in next ch1 sp, rep from * to last st, 1 double sc in second of ch2, turn. *Patt row 3* Ch3, *1 double sc in ch1 sp, ch1, rep from *, ending 1sc in second of ch2, turn. Rep rows 2 and 3 to form patt.

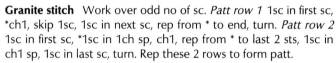

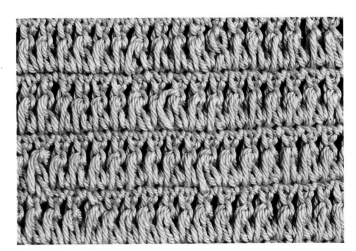

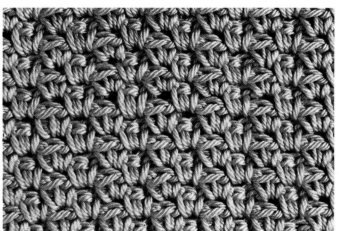

Diamond stitch Work over an even no of sc. *Patt row 1* *Yo, insert hook into first sc and draw 1 lp through, yo, insert hook into next sc and draw 1 lp through, yo and draw through the first 4 lps, yo and close last 2 lps, ch1, rep from * inserting hook into the same place as last part of st just worked, to end of row. 1dc into last sc, turn. *Patt row 2* 1sc into each ch1 sp, 1sc in top of ch3, turn. Rep these 2 rows to form patt.

Lacy bricks Work over an odd no of chain. *Foundation row* 2hdc in third ch from hook, *skip next ch, 2hdc in next ch, rep from * to end, turn. *Patt row* ch2, *skip 2hdc, 2hdc in next sp between hdc, rep from * ending skip 2hdc, 2hdc in top of ch2, turn. Rep this row to form patt.

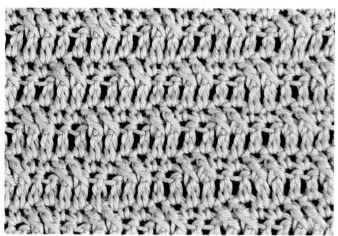

Raised rib stitch Work over a multiple of 3sc + 2sc. *Row 1* 1sc in each sc to end, do not turn. Break off yarn. Return to beg of row. *Row 2* 1sc in each first 2sc, yo, insert hook from right to left around corresponding sc on foundation row, yo then complete as a dc (raised dc), 1sc in each of next 2sc, rep from * to end, turn. *Row 3* 1sc in each st to end, do not turn. Break off yarn. Return to beg of row. *Row 4* 1sc in each of first 2sc, *1 raised dc around stem of previous raised dc, 1sc in each of next 2sc, rep from * to end, turn. Continue in this way working 2 rows on RS then 2 rows on WS, working all raised dcs around stem of previous raised dcs.

Louisa stitch Work over a multiple of 4sc + 2sc. *Row 1* ch3, 1dc in each sc to end, turn. *Row 2 (RS of work)* 1sc in each of next 2dc, *1 raised dc around each of next 2dc, 1sc in each of next 2dc, rep from * to end, turn. Rep these 2 rows to form patt.

Daniella stitch Work over a multiple of 2sc. *Row 1 and all odd rows (WS of work)* Work in dc. *Row 2* *1sc in next dc, 1 raised dc in next dc, rep from * to end. *Row 4* *1 raised dc in next dc, 1sc in next dc, rep from * to end. Rep these 4 rows to form patt.

Wide raised rib Work over a multiple of 6sc + 5sc. *Row 1* 1sc in each of next 5sc, *1 raised dc around next sc, 1sc in each of next 5sc, rep from * to end. *Row 2* 1sc in each of next 5sc, *1 raised dc around next raised dc, 1sc in each of next 5sc, rep from * to end. Rep row 2 to form patt, noting that on alt rows the raised dcs are worked from front and then back of raised dcs.

Fan stitches

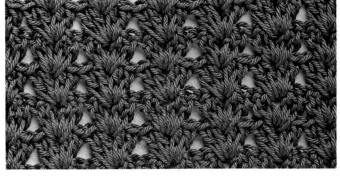

Little fans Work over a multiple of 3sc + 1sc. *Row 1* Ch3 (to count as first dc) *ch1, skip 2sc, 3dc in next sc, rep from* to last 3sc, ch1, skip 2sc, 1dc in last sc, turn. *Row 2* ch3 (to count as first dc), 1dc into center st below ch1 sp, 1dc in ch1 sp, *ch1, 1dc in next ch1 sp, 1dc in center st below ch1 sp, 1dc in same ch1 sp, rep from * working last dc in top of ch3, turn. *Row 3* ch4, * 1dc in next ch1 sp, 1dc in center dc below ch1 sp, 1dc in same ch1 sp, ch1, rep from * to end, 1dc in top of ch3, turn. Rep rows 2 and 3 to form patt.

Columns of fans Work over a multiple of 4sc + 1sc. *Row 1* ch3, skip 2sc, 4dc in next sc, *skip 3sc, 4dc in next sc, rep from * to last 2sc, 1dc in last sc. *Row 2* ch3, work 4dc in center of each 4dc group, 1dc in top of ch3. Rep row 2 to form patt.

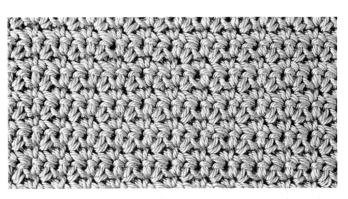

Little leaves stitch Work over a multiple of 2sc. *Row 1* *Skip 1sc, 1sc and 1dc into next sc, rep from * to end, turn. *Row 2* 1sc and 1dc into each sc to end of row, turn. Rep row 2 to form patt.

Little roses stitch Work over a multiple of 2sc. *Row 1* *Skip 1sc, work 2sc into next sc, rep from * to end, turn. *Row 2* *Skip 1sc, 2sc into next sc, rep from * to end, turn. Rep row 2 to form patt.

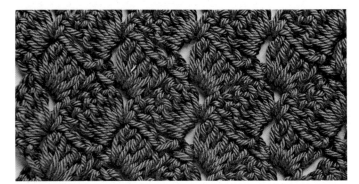

Stepped fans Work over a multiple of 4sc. *Foundation row* *Ss in next sc, ch3, 1dc in next sc, 1hdc in next sc, 1sc in next sc, rep from * to end, turn. *Row 1* Ss into each of first 3 sts, *[1sc, ch3, 4dc] all in next ch3 sp, rep from * to end, turn. Rep row 1 to form patt.

Wickerwork stitch Work over a multiple of 4sc + 1sc. *Row 1* [1sc, 2ch, 2dc] all into the first sc, *skip 3sc, [1sc, 2ch, 2dc] all in next sc, rep from * to end, turn. *Row 2* 2ch, *[1sc, 2ch, 2dc] all into next 2ch sp, rep from * to end, turn. Rep row 2 to form patt.

Fan stitches
Little shell stitch   Shell stitch
Large shell stitch   Double shell stitch

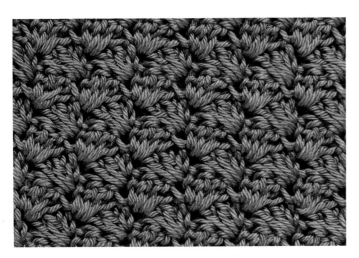

Little shell stitch Work over a multiple of 3sc + 1sc. *Row 1* 1sc and 2dc worked into first sc, *skip 2sc, 1sc and 2dc in next sc, rep from * to last 3sc, 1sc in last sc, turn. *Row 2* Work 1sc and 2dc into each sc to last sc, 1sc in last sc, turn. Rep row 2 to form patt.

Shell stitch Work over a multiple of 6sc + 1sc. *Row 1* 1sc in first st, *skip 2sc, 5dc into next sc, skip 2sc, 1sc in next sc, rep from * to end, turn. *Row 2* ch3, 2dc into first sc, *1sc into third dc of 5dc group, 5dc into next sc, rep from * ending with 3dc in last sc, turn. *Row 3* 1sc in first dc, *5dc in next sc, 1sc in center dc of next 5dc group, rep from * working last sc in top of ch3, turn. Rep rows 2 and 3 to form patt.

Large shell stitch Work over a multiple of 10sc + 1sc. *Row 1* 1sc in first st, *skip 4sc, 9dc into next st, skip 4sc, 1sc in next sc, rep from * to end, turn. *Row 2* ch3, 4dc into first sc, *1sc into 5th dc of 9dc group, rep from * ending with 5dc into last sc, turn. *Row 3* 1sc in first dc, *9dc in next sc, 1sc in center dc of next 9dc group, rep from * ending 1sc in top of ch3, turn. Rep rows 2 and 3 to form patt.

Double shell stitch Work over a multiple of 6sc + 1sc. *Row 1* 1sc in first sc, *skip 2sc, in the next st work [3dc, 1tr, 3dc], skip 2sc, 1sc in next sc, repeat from * to end, turn. *Row 2* 4ch, *leaving last lp of each dc on hook work 1dc in each of next 3dc, yo, draw through all 4 lps on hook, 2ch, 1sc in next tr, 2ch, leaving last lp of each dc on hook. Work 1dc in each of next 3dc, yo and draw through all 4 lps on hook, 1tr in next sc, rep from * to end, turn. *Row 3* 1sc in first tr, *[3dc, 1tr, 3dc] all in next sc, 1sc in next tr, rep from * working last sc in fourth of 4ch, turn. Rep rows 2 and 3 to form patt.

Fancy stitches

Jersey stitch   Slanting alternate stitch
Linked triples   Double slanting stitch

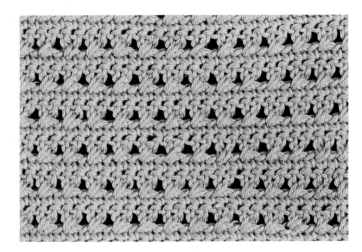

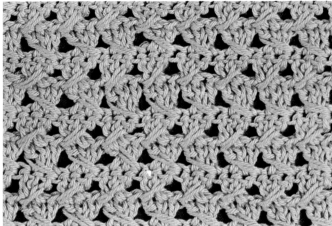

Jersey stitch Work over an even no of sc. *Row 1 (WS of work)* 1sc in each sc to end, turn. *Row 2* 2ch, *skip 1sc, 1dc in next sc, passing in front of the st just worked work 1dc into skipped sc, rep from * to last sc, 1hdc in last sc, turn. Rep rows 1 and 2 to form patt.

Slanting alternate stitch Work over a multiple of 3dc. *Row 1* ch3, skip 1dc, *1dc in each of next 2dc, 1dc in skipped dc, rep from * to last 2 sts, 1dc in each of last 2 sts. Rep this row to form patt.

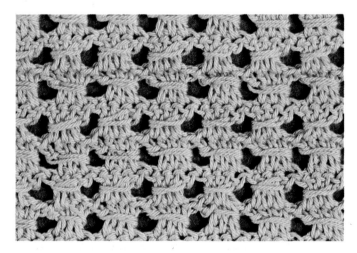

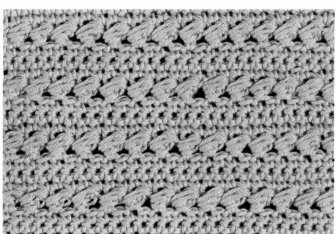

Linked triples Work over a multiple of 4dc + 2dc. *Row 1* ch3, *skip 1dc, 1dc in each of next 3dc, 1dc into sp formed by skipped dc, rep from * to last st, 1dc in top of ch3, turn. Rep this row to form patt.

Double slanting stitch Work over an even no of sc. *Rows 1 and 2* Work in sc. *Row 3* 1sc, *skip 1sc, 1sc in next sc, [yo, insert hook in sp above skipped sc, yo, draw through lp] twice, yo, draw through all 5 lps on hook, rep from * to last st, 1sc in last st, turn. *Row 4* 1sc in each st to end, turn. Rep rows 1 to 4 to form patt.

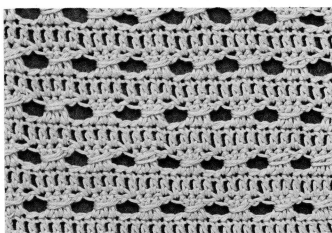

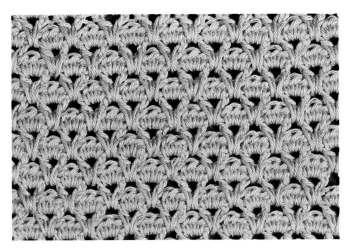

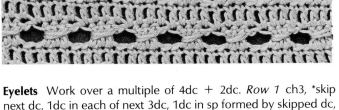

Eyelets Work over a multiple of 4dc + 2dc. *Row 1* ch3, *skip next dc, 1dc in each of next 3dc, 1dc in sp formed by skipped dc, rep from * to last st, 1dc in top of ch3, turn. *Row 2* ch3, 1dc in each st to end, turn. Rep these 2 rows to form patt.

Alternate 'V' stitch Work over a multiple of 4sc. *Row 1* ch3, skip next sc, *[1dc, ch3, 1dc] all in next sc, skip 2sc, rep from * to last 3sc, [1dc, ch3, 1dc] all in next sc, 1dc in last dc, turn. *Row 2* 1hdc in first dc, *3hdc in next ch3 lp, rep from * to end, 1hdc in third of ch3, turn. *Row 3* 4ch, 1dc in first hdc, *skip 3hdc, [1dc, ch3, 1dc] all into sp between 'V' st 2 rows below, rep from * end, [1dc, ch1, 1dc] all in last hdc, turn. *Row 4* 2ch, 1hdc in ch1 lp, *3hdc in next ch3 lp, rep from * ending 1hdc in ch1 lp, 1hdc in 3rd of ch3, turn. *Row 5* ch3, *[1dc, ch3, 1dc] all into sp between 'V' st 2 rows below, rep from * ending 1dc in last sc, turn. Rep rows 2 to 5 to form patt.

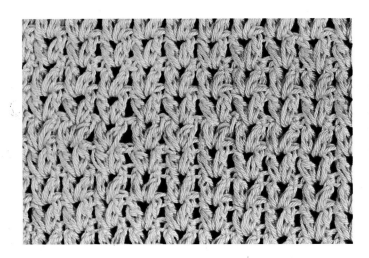

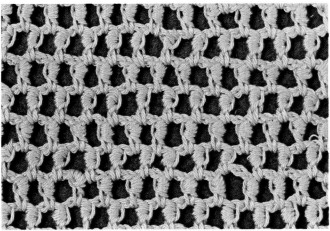

'V' stitch in columns Work over a multiple of 3dc + 1dc. *Row 1* ch3, skip next dc, [1dc, ch1, 1dc] all in next dc, *skip next 2dc, [1dc, ch1, 1dc] all in next dc, rep from * to last 2dc, 1dc in last dc, turn. *Row 2* ch3, work [1dc, ch1, 1dc] all into each ch1 sp along row, 1dc in third of ch3, turn. Rep row 2 to form patt.

Twisted net stitch Work over a multiple of 2sc. *Row 1* ch3, *skip next sc, [yo] 5 times, insert hook in next sc, yo, draw through lp, yo, draw through all 7 lps on hook, ch1*, rep from * to * to end, 1dc in last sc, turn. *Row 2* ch3, work from * to * in row 1 into each ch1 sp, 1dc in third of ch3, turn. Rep row 2 to form patt.

Fancy stitches

Twisted stitch   Lacy blocks
Little crosses   Music sheet

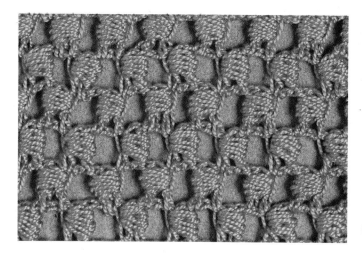

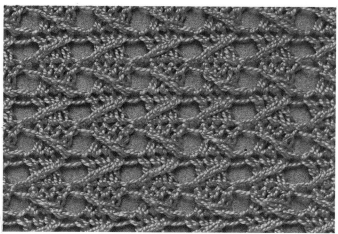

Twisted stitch   Work over a multiple of 4sc. *Row 1* ch3, skip next sc, *1dc in next sc, along side of dc just worked work [yo, insert hook into sp, yo, draw through a lp] 5 times, yo, draw through all lps on hook (a cluster), ch2, skip 3sc, rep from * to last 2sc, 1dc in next sc, make a cluster around dc just made, ch2, 1dc in last sc, turn. *Row 2* ch3, *1dc in next ch1 sp, a cluster around dc, ch2, rep from * ending 1dc in third of ch3, turn. Rep row 2 to form patt.

Lacy blocks   Work over a multiple of 4dc + 2dc. *Patt row* ch3, *skip next dc, 1dc in each of next 3dc, 1dc in skipped dc, rep from * to last st, 1dc in top of ch3, turn. Rep this row to form patt.

Little crosses   Work over a multiple of 2sc. *Row 1* 1sc in first sc, *skip next sc, 1sc in next sc, 1sc in skipped sc, rep from * to last sc, 1sc in last sc, turn. *Row 2* 1sc in each sc to end, turn. Rep these 2 rows to form patt.

Music sheet   Work over any no of dc. *Patt row* ch3, work 1dc in back lp only of each dc, 1dc in third of ch3, turn. Rep this row to form patt.

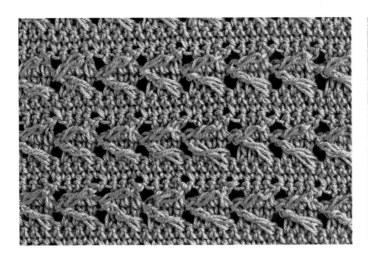

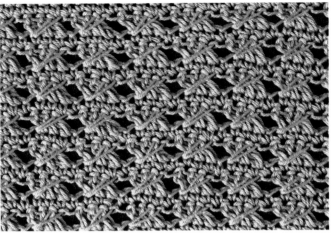

Thorn stitch Work over a multiple of 4sc plus 2sc. *Rows 1 and 2* 1sc into each st, turn. *Rows 3 and 4* ch3, *skip next st, 1dc in each of next 3 sts, 1dc in skipped st, rep from * to last st, 1dc in last st, turn. Rep these 4 rows to form patt.

Andalusian stitch Work over a multiple of 4sc plus 2sc. *Row 1* ch3, *skip next sc, 1dc in each of next 3sc, 1dc in skipped sc, rep from * to last sc, 1dc in last sc, turn. *Row 2* 1sc in each st to end, turn. Rep these 2 rows to form patt.

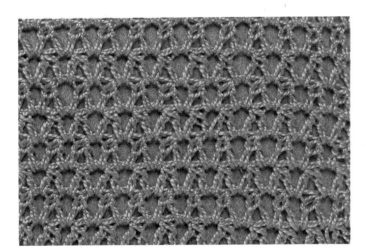

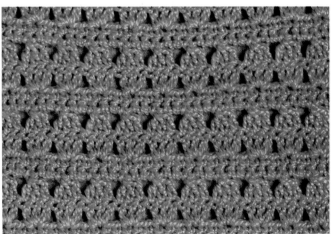

Lacy 'V' Work over a multiple of 2dc. *Row 1* ch4, skip 1dc, 1dc in next dc, ch1, *leaving last lp of each on hook, work 1dc in same place as last dc, skip 1dc, 1dc in next dc, yo, draw through all lps on hook, ch1 to close, ch1, rep from * to end, 1dc in top of ch3, turn. *Row 2* ch4, leaving last lp of each on hook, work 1dc in each of next 2 ch1 sps, yo, draw through all lps on hook, ch1 to close, ch1, *leaving last lp of each on hook, work 1dc in same place as last dc, 1dc in next ch1 sp, yo, draw through all lps on hook, ch1 to close, ch1, rep from * to end 1dc in third of ch4, turn. Rep row 2 to form patt.

Linked oval stitch Work over a multiple of 3sc + 2sc. *Row 1* ch3, skip next sc, 3dc in next sc, *skip 2sc, 3sc in next sc, rep from * to last 2sc, 1dc in last sc, turn. *Row 2* ch4, leaving last lp of each on hook, work 1dc in each of next 3dc, yo, draw through all lps on hook, ch1 to close, ch1, rep from * to end, 1dc in third of ch3, turn. *Row 3* 1sc in first dc, 1sc in next ch1 sp, *1sc in next st, 2sc in ch1 sp, rep from * to end, turn. *Row 4* 1sc in each sc to end, turn. Rep rows 1 to 4 to form the patt.

Cluster stitches

Cluster squares   Open dot stitch
Cluster stitch   Dot stitch

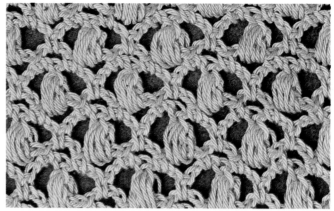

Cluster squares Work over a multiple of 10sc + 3sc. *Row 1* 1sc in first sc, *leaving last lp of each on hook, work 4dc in next sc, yo, draw through all lps, ch1 to close (a cluster made), 1sc in next sc, rep from * to end, turn. *Row 2* 1sc in each st to end, turn. *Row 3* 1sc in first sc, *1 cluster in next sc, 1sc in each of next 9sc, rep from * to last 2sc, 1 cluster in next sc, 1sc in last sc, turn. *Row 4* 1sc in each st to end, turn. *Rows 5 and 6* As rows 3 and 4. *Row 7* 1sc in first sc, *1 cluster in next sc, 1sc in each of next 4sc, rep from * to last 2sc, 1 cluster in next sc, 1sc in last sc, turn. *Row 8* 1sc in each sc to end, turn. *Rows 9 to 12* Rep rows 3 and 4 twice. These 12 rows form the patt.

Open dot stitch Work over a multiple of 6sc + 4sc. *Row 1* 1sc in first sc, *ch3, skip 2sc, 1sc in next sc, rep from * to end. *Row 2* ch4, [yo, insert hook in next ch3 lp, yo, draw through lp] 5 times, yo, draw through all lps on hook, ch1 to close cluster, *ch3, 1sc in next ch3 lp, ch3, 1 cluster in next ch3 lp, rep from * to end, ch1, 1dc in last sc, turn. *Row 3* 1sc in first dc, *ch3, 1sc in next ch3 lp, rep from * to end, working last sc in 3rd of ch4, turn. *Row 4* ch5, 1sc in next ch3 lp, *ch3, 1 cluster in next ch3 lp, ch3, 1sc in next ch3 lp, rep from * to end, ch2, 1dc in last sc, turn. *Row 5* 1sc in first dc, *ch3, 1sc in next ch3 lp, rep from * to end, ch3, 1sc in third of ch5, turn. Rep rows 2 to 5 to form patt.

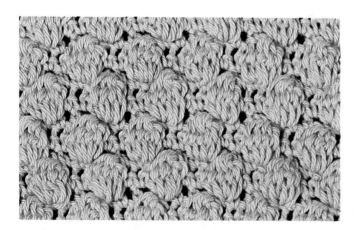

Cluster stitch Work over a multiple of 4sc + 1sc. *Row 1* ch3, leaving last lp of each dc on hook, work 2dc in first sc, yo, draw through 5lps on hook, ch1 to close cluster, *ch1, skip 1sc, 1sc in next sc, ch1, skip next sc, leaving last lp of each dc on hook, work 5dc in next sc, yo, draw through all lps on hook, ch1 to close cluster, rep from * to last 4sc, ch1, skip 1sc, 1sc in next sc, ch1, 3dc cluster in last sc, turn. *Row 2* 1sc in top of first cluster, *ch1, 5dc cluster in next sc, ch1, 1sc in top of next cluster, rep from * to end, turn. *Row 3* ch3, leaving last lp of each dc on hook, work 2dc in first sc, yo, draw through all lps on hook, ch1 to close cluster, *ch1, 1sc in top of next cluster, ch1, 1 5dc cluster in next sc, rep from * ending last rep 3dc cluster in last sc, turn. Rep rows 2 and 3 to form patt.

Dot stitch Work on a multiple of 2sc. *Row 1* ch4, *skip next sc, [yo, insert hook in next sc, draw through a long lp] 5 times, yo, draw through all lps on hook, ch1 to close cluster, rep from * to last sc, 1dc in last sc. *Row 2* ch4, *1 cluster in next sp between clusters, rep from * working last cluster after cluster of previous row, 1dc in third of ch4, turn. Rep row 2 to form patt.

Pineapple stitch This stitch consists of working random clusters on a solid background. *Rows 1 and 2* Work in sc. *Row 3* Work in dc. The clusters are worked on *row 4* as follows: leaving last lp of each st on hook, work 5dc into corresponding sc in row 2, yo, draw through all lps on hook, ch1 to close cluster. The other sts in this row are sc. These 4 rows form the basic st.

Open clusters This stitch consists of working random clusters on a solid background of sc. The clusters are worked into the corresponding st 2 rows below. To work a cluster, leaving last lp of each st on hook, work 5dc into sc, yo, draw through all lps on hook, ch1 to close cluster.

Faggot stitch Work over a multiple of 2sc. *Row 1* ch2, leaving last lp of each dc on hook work 1dc in each of first 3sc, yo, draw through all lps on hook, ch1 to close, ch1, *leaving last lp of each dc on hook work 1dc in same place as last dc, 1dc in each of next 2sc, yo, draw through all lps on hook, ch1 to close, ch1, rep from * to last sc, 1hdc in last sc. *Row 2* 1sc in each st to end. Rep these 2 rows to form patt.

Arches with dots Work over a multiple of ch5 + ch1. *Row 1* 1sc in first ch, *ch5, skip ch4, 1sc in next ch, rep from * to end, turn. *Row 2* *ch5, 1sc [yo, insert hook into ch5 lp, yo, draw through lp] 3 times, yo, draw through all lps on hook (a cluster made), 1sc all in ch5 lp, rep from * ending ch2, 1dc in last sc, turn. *Row 3* *ch5, [1sc, 1 cluster, 1sc] all in next ch5 lp, rep from * to end, ch3, 1dc in third of ch5, turn. Rep rows 2 and 3 to form patt.

Lacy stitches

Net stitch   Lacy fan stitch

Square stitch   Lacy picots

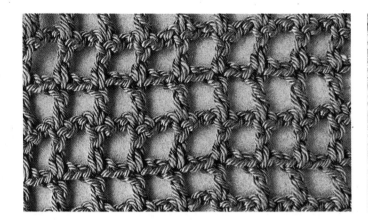

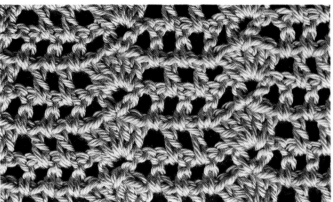

Net stitch Work over a multiple of ch3 + ch8. *Foundation row* 1dc into eighth ch from hook, *ch2, skip ch2, 1dc in next ch, rep from * to end, turn. *Row 1* ch5, 1dc in next dc, *ch2, 1dc in next dc, rep from * to end, turn. Rep row 1 to form patt.

Lacy fan stitch Work over a multiple of 6dc + 9dc. *Row 1* ch4, skip 1dc, 1dc in next dc, ch1, skip 1dc, 5dc in next dc, *[ch1, skip 1dc, 1dc in next dc] twice, ch1, skip 1dc, 5dc in next dc, rep from * to last 4dc, [ch1, skip 1dc, 1dc in next dc] twice, turn. *Row 2* ch3, 1dc in next ch1 sp, ch1, 1dc in next ch1 sp, skip 2dc, [1dc, ch1, 1dc] all in next dc, *[1dc in next ch1 sp, ch1] twice, 1dc in next ch1 sp, skip 2dc, [1dc, ch1, 1dc] all in next dc, 1dc in next ch1 sp, ch1, 1dc in next ch1 sp, 1dc in third of ch4, turn. *Row 3* ch4, 1dc in next ch1 sp, ch1, 5dc in next ch1 sp, *[ch1, 1dc in next ch1 sp] twice, ch1, 5dc in next ch1 sp, rep from * ending ch1, 1dc in next dc, ch1, 1dc in third of ch3, turn. Rep rows 2 and 3 to form patt.

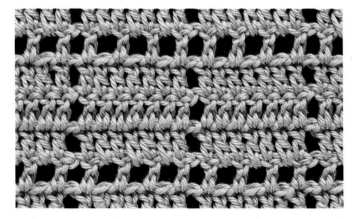

Square stitch Work over a multiple of 8dc + 7dc. *Row 1* ch3, 1dc in each of next 6dc, *ch1, skip 1dc, 1dc in each of next 7dc, rep from * to end, turn. *Rows 2 and 3* ch3, 1dc in each of next 6dc, *ch1, 1dc in each of next 7dc, rep from * to end, turn. *Row 4* ch4, skip next dc, 1dc in next dc, [ch1, skip 1dc, 1dc in next dc] twice, *ch1, 1dc in next dc, [ch1, skip 1dc, 1dc in next dc] 3 times, rep from * to end, turn. *Row 5* ch3, [1dc in next ch1 sp, 1dc in next dc] 3 times, *ch1, 1dc in next dc, [1dc in next ch1 sp, 1dc in next dc] 3 times, rep from * to end, turn. Rep rows 2 to 5 to form patt.

Lacy picots Work over a multiple of 5sc + 1sc. *Row 1* 1sc in first sc, *ch6, 1ss in fourth ch from hook (picot formed), 6ch, skip 4sc, 1sc in next sc*, rep from * to * to end. *Row 2* ch9, *skip ch4, 1sc in next ch, ch6, 1ss in fourth ch from hook, ch6, skip 1sc and ch4, 1sc in next ch, rep from * ending ch6, 1ss in 4th ch from hook, ch2, 1tr in last sc, turn. *Row 3* 1sc in first tr, rep from * to * in row 1 working last sc in fifth of ch9, turn. Rep rows 2 and 3 to form patt.

86

Lacy stitches
Cluster net   Lacy dot stitch
Fancy clusters   Mazzetti stitch

Cluster net Work over a multiple of 8dc + 7dc. *Row 1* ch3, 1dc in each of next 6dc, *ch1, skip next dc, 1dc in each of next 7dc, rep from * to end, turn. *Row 2* ch3, 1dc in next dc, ch1, skip 1dc, leaving last lp of each on hook, work 5dc in next dc, yo, draw through all lps on hook, ch1 to close cluster (a 5dc cluster made), ch1, skip next dc, 1dc in each of next 2dc, *ch1, 1dc in each of next 2dc, ch1, skip 1dc, 1 5dc cluster in next dc, ch1, skip 1dc, 1dc in each of next 2dc, rep from * to end, turn. *Row 3* ch3, 1dc in next dc, 1dc in next ch sp, 1dc in top of cluster, 1dc in next ch sp, 1dc in each of next 2dc, *ch1, 1dc in each of next 2dc, 1dc in next ch1 sp, 1dc in top of cluster, 1dc in next ch1 sp, 1dc in each of next 2dc, rep from * to end, turn. *Row 4* ch4, skip next dc, 1dc in next dc, [ch1, skip 1dc, 1dc in next dc] twice, *ch1, 1dc in next dc, [ch1, skip 1dc, 1dc in next dc] 3 times, rep from * to end, turn. *Row 5* ch3, [1dc in next ch1 sp, 1dc in next dc] 3 times, *ch1, 1dc in next dc, [1dc in next ch1 sp, 1dc in next dc] 3 times, rep from * to end, turn. Rep rows 2 to 5 to form patt.

Lacy dot stitch Work over a multiple of ch6 + ch1. *Foundation row* 1dc in eighth ch from hook, ch2, *skip ch2, 1dc in next ch, rep from * to end, turn. *Row 1* ch5, leaving last lp of each on hook, work 7dc in next dc, yo, draw through all lps on hook, ch1 to close cluster, *ch2, 1dc in next dc, ch2, 1 cluster in next dc, rep from * ending ch2, 1dc in 3rd of 7ch, turn. *Row 2* ch5, 1dc in top of next cluster, *ch2, 1dc in next dc, ch2, 1dc in top of next cluster, rep from * ending ch2, 1dc in third of 5ch, turn. Rep rows 1 and 2 to form patt.

Fancy clusters Work over a multiple of 6dc + 1dc. *Row 1* ch5, skip next 2dc, 4dc in next dc, remove hook from lp, insert hook into top of first dc, draw lp from 4dc through, ch1 to close cluster, *ch2, skip next 2dc, 1dc in next dc, ch2, skip 2dc, 1 cluster in next dc, rep from * to last 3 sts, ch2, 1dc in last st, turn. *Row 2* ch3, *2dc in next ch2 sp, 1dc in top of next cluster, 2dc in next ch2 sp, 1dc in next dc, rep from * working last dc in third of ch5, turn. Rep rows 1 and 2 to form patt.

Mazzetti stitch Work over a multiple of 2sc + 1sc. *Row 1* ch3 [yo, insert hook in next sc, draw through lp] 3 times all in same sc, yo, draw through all sts on hook, ch1, to close cluster, *ch1, skip next sc, 1 cluster in next sc, rep from * to last sc, 1dc in last sc, turn. *Row 2* 1sc in first dc, 1sc in next cluster, *1sc in next ch1 sp, 1sc in next cluster, rep from * ending 1sc in third of ch3, turn. Rep rows 1 and 2 to form patt.

Lacy stitches

Mesh stitch   Columns

Chequerboard stitch   Eyelet bands

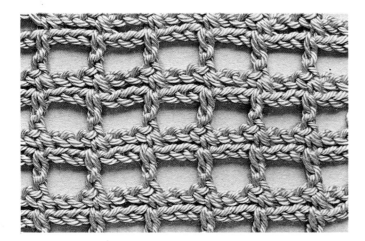

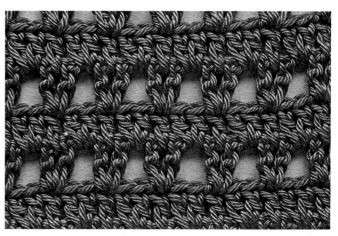

Mesh stitch Work over a multiple of ch4 + ch1. *Foundation row* 1sc in first ch, ch3, skip ch3, 1sc in next ch, rep from * to end, turn. *Row 1* ch6, 1dc in next sc, *ch3, 1dc in next sc, rep from * to end, turn. *Row 2* 1sc in first dc, ch3, 1sc in next dc, rep from * working last sc in fourth of 6ch, turn. Rep rows 1 and 2 to form patt.

Columns Work over a multiple of 3dc. *Row 1* ch5, *skip next 2dc, 2tr in next dc, ch1, rep from * to end, 1tr in top of ch3, turn. *Row 2* ch3, 1dc in first sp, *1dc in each of next 2tr, 1dc in next ch1 sp, rep from * to end, 1dc in fourth of ch5, turn. Rep these 2 rows to form patt.

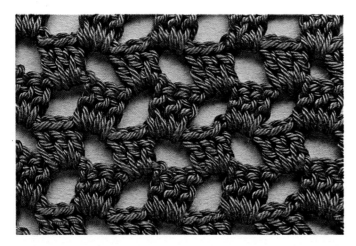

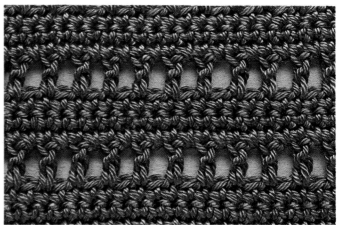

Chequerboard stitch Work over a multiple of 6dc + 3dc. *Row 1* ch3, 1dc in each of next 2dc, *ch3, skip 3dc, 1dc in each of next 3dc, rep from * working last dc in third of ch3, turn. *Row 2* ch5, *3dc in next ch3 sp, ch3, rep from * ending ch2, 1dc in 3rd of ch3, turn. *Row 3* ch3, 2dc in ch2 sp, *ch3, 3dc in ch3 sp, rep from * ending 2dc in turning ch, 1dc in third of ch5, turn. Rep rows 2 and 3 to form patt.

Eyelet bands Work on a multiple of 2sc + 1sc. *Rows 1 and 2* Work 1sc in each sc, turn. *Row 3* ch4, skip next sc, 1dc in next sc, *ch1, skip 1sc, 1dc in next sc, rep from * to end, turn. *Row 4* 1sc in first dc, *1sc in next ch1 sp, 1sc in next dc, rep from * ending 1sc in turning ch, 1sc in third of ch4, turn. Rep rows 1 to 4 to form patt.

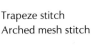
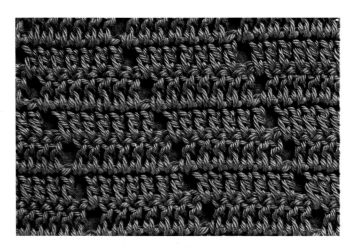

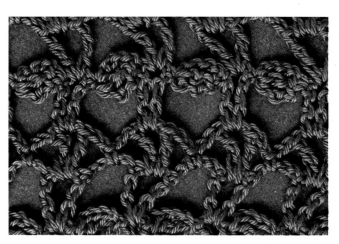

Trapeze stitch Work over a multiple of 8dc + 7dc. *Row 1* ch3, 1dc in each of next 6dc, *ch1, skip 1dc, 1dc in each of next 7dc, rep from * to end, working last dc in top of ch3, turn. *Row 2* ch3, 1dc in each of next 5dc, *ch1, skip 1dc, 1dc in next ch1 sp, 1dc in each of next 6dc, rep from * ending 1dc in top of ch3, turn. *Row 3* ch4, skip next dc, *1dc in each of next 6dc, 1dc in next ch1 sp, ch1, skip 1dc, rep from * ending 1dc in each of next 4dc, 1dc in top of ch3, turn. Continue in this way moving the ch1 sp 1 st on every row.

Mesh stitch with clusters Work over a multiple of ch5 + ch1. *Foundation row* 1dtr in fifth ch from hook, *ch4 skip ch4, [1dtr, ch2, 1dtr] all in next ch, rep from * to last 6ch, ch4, skip ch4, 1dtr in each of last ch2, turn. *Row 1* ch4, 1dtr in next dtr, *ch2, 1sc in next ch4 lp, ch2, [1dtr, ch2, 1dtr] all in next ch2 sp, rep from * ending ch2, 1sc in last ch4 lp, ch2, 1dtr in next dtr and top of ch4, turn. *Row 2* ch4, 1dtr in next dtr, *ch4, leaving last lp of each on hook, work 2dtr in top of last dtr, yo, draw through all lps on hook (a 2dtr cluster made), rep from * ending ch4, 1dtr in next dtr and top of ch4, turn. *Row 3* ch4, 1dtr in next dtr, *ch4, 1dtr in next dtr, ch2, 1dtr in next dtr, rep from * ending ch4, 1dtr in next dtr and top of ch4, turn. Rep rows 1 to 3 to form patt.

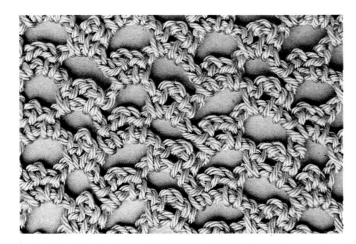

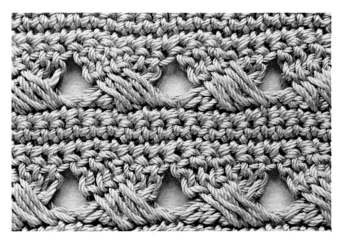

Arched mesh stitch Work over a multiple of 4sc + 1sc. *Row 1* 1sc in first sc, *ch5, skip 3sc, 1sc in next sc, rep from * to end, turn. *Row 2* *ch5, [1sc, ch3, 1sc] all in next ch5 lp, rep from * to end, ch2, 1dc in last sc, turn. *Row 3* 1sc in first dc, *ch5, 1sc in next ch5 lp, rep from * working last sc in third of ch5, turn. Rep rows 2 and 3 to form patt.

Crossed treble stitch Work over a multiple of 6sc + 2sc. *Row 1* 1sc in each sc to end, turn. *Row 2* As row 1. *Row 3* ch3, skip 3sc, 1dtr in each of next 3sc, 1dtr in each of 3 skipped sc, rep from * to last sc, 1dc in last sc, turn. *Row 4* 1sc in first dc, 1sc in each dtr to end, 1sc in top of ch3, turn. Rep rows 1 to 4 to form patt.

Lacy stitches

Simple diadem stitch   Lace stitch
Beehive stitch   Sunrise stitch

Simple diadem stitch Work over a multiple of 8sc + 1sc. *Row 1* ch6, *skip 3sc, [1dc, ch1, 1dc] all in next sc, ch3, skip 3sc, 1dc in next sc, ch3, rep from * omitting ch3 at end of last rep, turn. *Row 2* 1sc in first dc, *3sc in next ch3 lp, 5sc in next ch1 lp, 3sc in next ch3 lp, ch1, rep from * omitting ch1 at end of last rep and working 1sc in third of 6ch, turn. *Row 3* ch4, *skip 3sc, [into next sc work 2dtr leaving last lp of each on hook, yo, draw through all lps on hook, ch1 to close cluster, ch1] 5 times, 1dc in next ch1 sp, ch1, rep from * omitting ch1 at end of last rep and working 1dc into last sc, turn. *Row 4* 1sc in first dc, *1sc in each of next 3 ch1 sp, ch1, rep from * omitting ch1 at end of last rep and working 1sc into third of ch4, turn. *Row 5* ch6, *[1dc, ch1, 1dc] all in next ch1 sp, ch3, 1dc in next ch1 sp, ch3, rep from * omitting ch3 at end of last rep and working last dc in last sc, turn. Rep rows 2 to 5 to form patt.

Lace stitch Work over a multiple of 8sc + 1sc. *Row 1* 1sc in first sc, *ch3, skip 3sc, 1sc in next sc, rep from * to end, turn. *Row 2* 1sc in first sc, 1sc in next ch3 lp, ch3, *1sc in same ch3 lp, 1sc in next sc, 1sc in next ch3 lp, ch3, rep from * ending 1sc in same ch3 lp, 1sc in last sc, turn. *Row 3* 1sc in first sc, *ch2, 1sc in next ch3 lp, ch2, skip 1sc, 1sc in next sc, rep from * to end, turn. *Row 4* 1sc in first sc, ch1, 1sc in first ch2 lp, 1sc in next sc, *1sc in next ch2 lp, ch3, 1sc in next ch2 lp, 1sc in next sc, rep from * ending 1sc in next ch2 lp, ch1, 1sc in last sc, turn. *Row 5* 1sc in first sc, *ch3, 1sc in next ch3 lp, rep from * ending last rep 1sc in last sc, turn. Rep rows 2 to 5 to form patt.

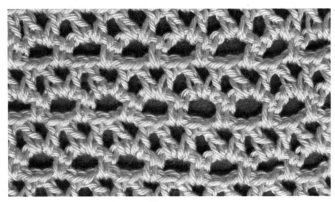

Beehive stitch Work over a multiple of 4sc + 1sc. *Row 1* ch6, skip 3sc, 1dc in next sc, *ch3, skip 3sc, 1dc in next dc, rep from * to end, turn. *Row 2* ch5, *1sc in next ch3 sp, ch2, 1dc in next dc, ch2, rep from * ending 1sc in next ch3 sp, ch2, 1dc in third of 6ch, turn. *Row 3* ch6, 1dc in next dc, *ch3, 1dc in next dc, rep from * ending ch3, 1dc in third of 5ch, turn. Rep rows 2 and 3 to form patt.

Sunrise stitch Work over a multiple of 3sc + 1sc. *Row 1* 1sc in first sc, *ch4, skip 2sc, 1sc in next sc, rep from * to end, turn. *Row 2* ch3 [1dc, ch2, 1dc] all in each ch4 lp to end, 1dc in last sc, turn. *Row 3* 1sc in first dc, ch2, 1sc in next ch2 lp, *ch4, 1sc in next ch2 lp, rep from * to end, ch2, 1sc in top of ch3, turn. *Row 4* ch4, 1dc in first sc, [1dc, ch2, 1dc] all in each ch4 lp, [1dc, ch1, 1dc] in last sc, turn. *Row 5* 1sc in first dc, *ch4, 1sc in next ch2 lp, rep from * to end, ch4, 1sc in third of ch4, turn. Rep rows 2 to 5 to form patt.

90

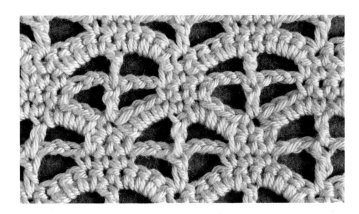

Half arch stitch Work over a multiple of 10sc + 5sc. *Row 1* 1sc in each of next 3sc, *ch3, skip 3sc, 1dc in next sc, ch3, skip 3sc, 1sc in each of next 3sc, rep from * ending last rep 1sc in each of last 2sc, turn. *Row 2* 1sc in first 1sc, ch1, skip next sc, 1sc in next sc, * 3sc in next ch3 lp, 1sc in next dc, 3sc in next ch3 lp, 1sc in next sc, ch1, skip 1sc, 1sc in next sc, rep from * to end, turn. *Row 3* ch3, 1dc in next ch1 sp, *ch3, skip 3sc, 1sc in each of next 3sc, ch3, 1dc in next ch1 sp, rep from * to end, 1dc in last sc, turn. *Row 4* ch3, 1dc in next dc, *ch3, 1sc in each of next 3sc, ch3, 1dc in next dc, rep from * to end, 1dc in top of ch3, turn. *Row 5* 1sc in each of first 2dc, *4sc in next ch3 lp, 1sc in next sc, ch1, skip next sc, 1sc in next sc, 4sc in next ch3 lp, 1sc in next dc, rep from * to end, 1sc in top of ch3, turn. *Row 6* 1sc in first sc, ch1, skip next sc, 1sc in next sc, *ch3, 1dc in next ch1 sp, ch3, skip 4sc, 1sc in next sc, ch1, skip 1sc, 1sc in next sc, rep from * to end, turn. Rep rows 2 to 6 to form patt.

Row of 'V's Work over a multiple of 4sc + 2sc. *Row 1* ch3, skip next sc, *[1dc, ch2, 1dc] all in next sc, skip 3sc, rep from * ending 1dc in last sc, turn. *Row 2* 1sc in first dc, *1sc in next sp between dc, 3sc in next ch2 sp, rep from * to end, 1sc in top of ch3, turn. *Rows 3 and 4* Work 1sc in each sc to end, turn. Rep rows 1 to 4 to form patt.

Single tulip stitch Work over a multiple of 4dtr + 2dtr. *Row 1* ch4, *4dtr in next dtr, skip 3dtr, rep from * to end, 1dtr in top of ch4, turn. Rep this row to form patt.

Double tulip stitch Work over a multiple of 5dtr + 2dtr. *Row 1* ch4, skip 2dtr, *leaving last lp of each on hook, work 3dtr in next dtr, yo, draw through all lps to close cluster (a 3dtr cluster formed), ch2, 1 3dtr cluster into same place as last cluster, skip 4dtr, rep from * ending last repeat skip 2dtr, 1dtr in top of ch4, turn. *Row 2* ch4, *[1 3dtr cluster, ch2, 1 3dtr cluster] into next ch2 sp, rep from * to end, 1dtr in top of ch4, turn. Rep row 2 to form patt.

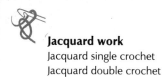

Jacquard work
Jacquard single crochet
Jacquard double crochet

Simple vertical stripes, squares, zigzag patterns and many other designs can be worked using this method of crochet. It is a useful way of using up remnants of the same type of yarn to produce an interesting decorative effect. The method used is the same as in knitting, the difference being that in crocheted jacquard work, the stitches are longer than in knitting and so less detailed designs are possible. For this reason, single crochet is most often used in this work.

The number of balls of yarn required depends on the number of colors being used. When changing color, close the last stitch with the next color, holding the yarn at the back of the work. When the color changes are close together, the result is a firm, even fabric suitable for bags, mats etc. When using two colors, hold the working yarn over the left index finger and the second-color yarn below this finger, working with the two yarns together so that each can be picked up in turn without tangling them. Always work with the right side of the work facing, or in the round, cutting the yarns at the end of each row.

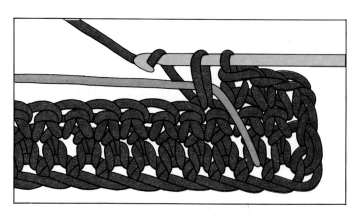

Jacquard single crochet 1. Join in the second color several stitches before it is needed, laying the yarn above the previous row and including it in the work.

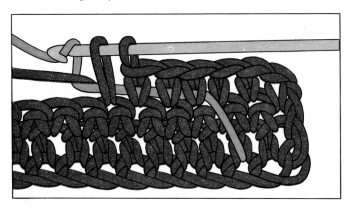

2. Where the color change is required, yo with the second color to close the last stitch. Lay the first-color yarn along the previous row, including it in the work.

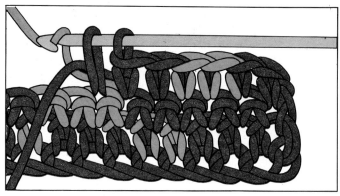

3. Whenever the color being carried along the WS of the work is to be used again, pick it up during the closing stitch of the previous color.

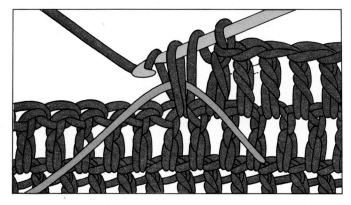

Jacquard double crochet 1. Bring the second color along the previous row, including it in the work as described for single crochet.

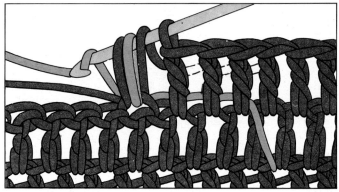

2. When changing the color, yo with the first color, insert the hook and yo with both colors, drawing both through, yo with the new yarn, draw through both the single and the double stitch, yo again and close the stitch.

A great variety of attractive motifs and all-over geometric patterns can be achieved with jacquard crochet. Remember that the colors not in use are carried along on the wrong side of the work. If a color is to be carried more than three stitches, it is better to pick it up once every two stitches. If, however, all the stitches are worked over the yarn not in use, ie. the yarn is 'woven in', a reversible effect can be achieved, but it is not always possible to conceal the carried thread completely. For really neat jacquard work, it is best to work with small balls of yarn for each area of color, especially where large and small areas of color are combined.

When the color changes are frequent, and more than two colors are being used, as in the Fancy rhombus pattern, it is advisable to use the weaving method of working.

In the following examples of jacquard motifs, one square corresponds to one stitch and one row. The motifs are worked in two colors, except for the Fancy rhombus, which is worked in three.

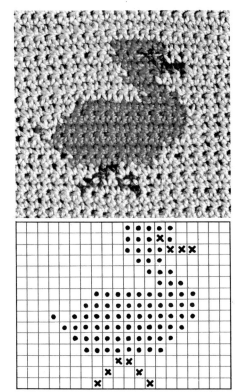

Bird This is worked over a base of 14 sts and a height of 15 rows.

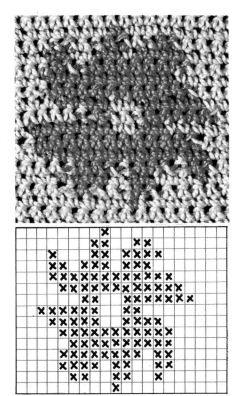

Star This is worked over a base of 15 sts and a height of 15 rows.

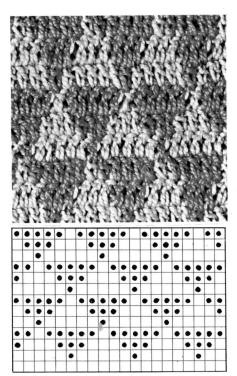

Triangles This is worked over a base of 20 sts and a height of 12 rows.

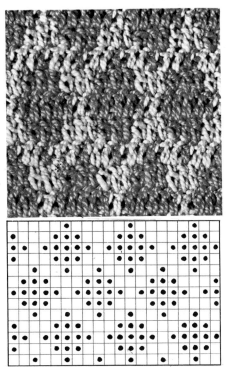

Diamonds This is worked over a base of 20 sts and a height of 13 rows.

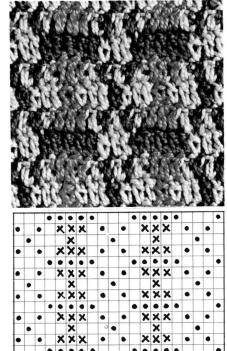

Fancy rhombus This is worked over a base of 20 sts and a height of 13 rows.

Multi-colored patterns

Rows of single crochet   Random single crochet
Rows of double crochet   Irregular rows

Rows of single crochet This is the simplest way of changing color as it is done at the end of the row. The yarn is either cut or held aside to be picked up later. There is no RS or WS of the work, both sides being the same. When changing color at the beginning of a row, make sure that the last stitch of the previous row is closed with the new color.

Random single crochet This is useful for using up remnants of yarn. The color change can be made in any position, perhaps several times in the same row. Take care to close the last stitch of one color with the next color to be used.

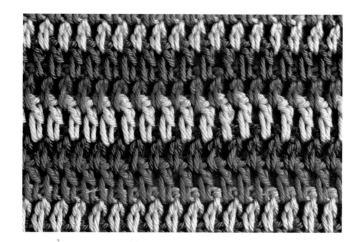

Rows of double crochet As in single crochet the color change takes place at the end of a row, the yarn being cut or kept aside to be picked up later. *Row 1* Work in dc. *Row 2 and following rows* Work in dc, inserting the hook between one stitch and the next. Again as for single crochet, there is no RS or WS to this work.

Irregular rows This stitch is shown using 3 colors, but it is possible to use more. The color changes every row; cut the yarn at the end of the row, working the cut end into the first stitch of the next row, or keep it aside to be picked up a few rows later. *Row 1* Work in dtr. *Row 2* Work in sc. *Row 3* Work in dc. Rep rows 1 to 3 to form patt.

Horizontal rib stitch Work on a base of ch. *Row 1* In A, work in sc. Cut the yarn leaving at least 2in. *Row 2* In B, return to the beg and work in sc, inserting the hook into the back of the sc sts of previous row. Cut the yarn. *Row 3 and following rows* Rep row 2, changing colors each row. This stitch lends itself to pillow covers with fringe, as the threads at each end of the rows can be trimmed to the same length and knotted in two's to make a two-toned fringe.

Cock's foot stitch Work over a multiple of 2sc + 1sc using 2 colors. *Row 1* In A, 1sc in first sc, *ch1, skip next sc, 1sc in next sc, rep from * to end, turn. *Row 2* In A, 1sc in first sc, 1sc in next ch sp, *ch1, 1sc in next ch sp, rep from * ending 1sc in last sc, turn. Working 2 rows B and 2 rows A, rep to form patt.

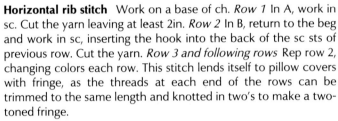

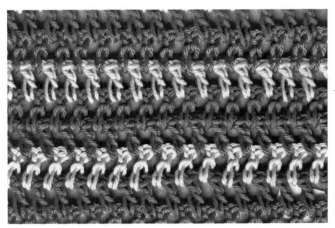

Threaded chain stitch Work on a multiple of ch2 + ch8 in A. *Row 1* 1dtr into eighth ch from hook, *ch1, skip ch1, 1dtr into next ch, rep from * to end, turn. *Row 2* ch6, *1dtr into next dtr, ch1, rep from * working last dtr in 6th of ch7, turn. Repeating row 2 forms an even mesh through which can be threaded a chain in color B.

Multi-colored mesh stitch Work over a multiple of 2dc + 1dc using 3 colors. *Row 1* In A, ch4, skip 2dc, 1dc in next dc, *ch1, skip 1dc, 1dc in next dc, rep from * to end, turn. *Row 2* In B, ch4, 1dc in next ch sp, *ch1, 1dc in next ch sp, rep from * to end, 1dc in third of ch4, turn. *Row 3* In C, ch4, *1dc in next ch sp, ch1, rep from * ending 1dc in third of ch3, turn. Rows 2 and 3 form the patt, working 1 row each of A, B, C.

Multi-colored patterns

Three color zigzag
Chequered wtitch
Half loop stitch

Three color zigzag Work over a multiple of ch22 + ch1 + 3 turning ch using 3 colors. *Row 1* In A, 1dc in fourth ch from hook, 2dc in same place as last dc, 1dc in each of next ch8, leaving last dc of each on hook work [1dc in next ch, skip next ch] twice, 1dc in next ch, yo, draw through all lps on hook, ch1 to close (a 5dc dec made), 1dc in each of next ch8, 5dc in next ch, rep from * ending last rep 3dc in last ch, turn. *Patt row* In A, ch3, 2dc in first dc, *1dc in each of next 8dc, 5dc ˙dec, 1dc in each of next 8dc, 5dc in next dc, rep from * ending last rep 3dc in top of ch3, turn. Working in stripes of 2 rows B, 2 rows C, 2 rows A, rep patt row to form patt.

Checkered stitch Work over a multiple of 6dc + 3dc using 2 colors. *Row 1* In B, ch3, 1dc in each of next 2dc; in A, *1dc into each of the next 3dc; in B, work 1dc into each of the next 3dc, rep from * to end. *Row 2* As row 1, reading A for B and B for A. Rep these 2 rows, twisting the colors together at the end of each row, to form patt.

Half loop stitch Work over a multiple of 10dc + 8dc using 2 colors. *Row 1* In A, ch4, skip next dc, *1dc in each of next 4dc, ch1, skip 1dc, rep from * to end, 1dc in top of ch3, turn. *Row 2* In A, ch3, 1dc in first ch1 sp, *ch1, 4dc in next ch1 sp, rep from * to last ch1 sp, 1dc in last ch1 sp, 1dc in third of ch4, turn. *Row 3* In B, ch4, *[2dc, ch1, 2dc] in next ch1 sp, ch1, rep from * to end, 1dc in third of ch3, turn. *Row 4* In A, ch4, 1dc in next ch1 sp, ch1, leaving last lp of each on hook, work 4dc around stem of dc just made, yo, draw through all lps on hook, ch1 to close (a cluster made), ch1, *4dc in next 1 ch sp, ch1, 1dc in next ch1 sp, ch1, a cluster around previous dc, ch1, rep from * to end, 1dc in third of ch4, turn. *Row 5* In A, ch3, 1dc in first ch1 sp, ch1, *4dc in next ch1 sp, ch1, rep from * to last ch1 sp, 1dc in last 1 ch sp, 1dc in third of ch4, turn. Rep rows 3 to 5 to form patt.

Multi-colored patterns
Shell stitch
Two color squares
Alternating square stitch

Shell stitch Work over a multiple of 8sc + 1sc using 2 colors. *Row 1* In A, 1sc in first sc, *skip 3sc, 7dc in next sc, skip 3sc, 1sc in next sc, rep from * to end, turn. *Row 2* In B, ch3, 3dc in first dc, *1sc in center dc of 7dc group, 7dc in next sc, rep from * ending 4dc in last sc, turn. *Row 3* In A, 1sc in first dc, *7dc in next sc, 1sc in center dc of 7dc group, rep from * ending 1sc in top of ch3, turn. Rep rows 2 and 3 to form patt.

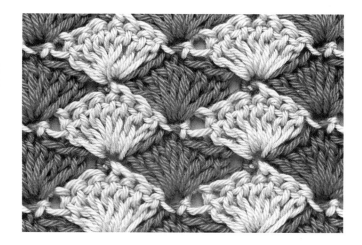

Two color squares Work over a multiple of 6dc + 3dc using 2 colors. *Row 1* In A, ch3, 1dc in each of next 2dc, * ch3, skip 3dc, 1dc in each of next 3dc, rep from * to end, turn. *Row 2* In A, ss in first dc, ch2, *1dc in each of 3 skipped dc on previous row working over the ch, ch3, rep from * ending ch2, ss in top of ch3, turn. *Rows 3 and 4* In B, as rows 1 and 2. Rep rows 1 to 4 to form patt.

Alternating square stitch Work over a multiple of 6dc + 3dc using 2 colors. *Row 1* In A, ch3, 1dc in each of next 2dc, *ch3, skip 3dc, 1dc in each of next 3dc, rep from * to end, do not turn. *Row 2* In B, ss into top of ch3, ch2, *1dc in each of 3 skipped dc on previous row working over the ch, ch3, rep from * ending ch2, ss in last dc, turn. Working 1 more row B, 2 rows A, 2 rows B, rep rows 1 and 2 to form patt.

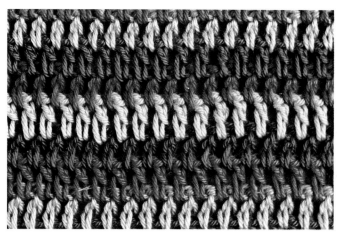

Rows and squares Work over a multiple of 6dc + 3dc. Using 3 colors, change color every row. The pattern is made up of 3 rows of dcs (one for each color) and 3 rows in Alternating square stitch (see page 97).

Rows of double crochet Work over any no of dc using 3 colors. *Patt row and following rows* Work in dcs, inserting the hook between one st and the next of the previous row. Change colors at the end of each row.

Three color squares Work over a multiple of 6dc + 3dc using 3 colors. Work as given for Alternating square stitch (see page 97), changing color every row.

Tile stitch Using 3 colors and changing color every row, work as for Stepped fans stitch (see page 78).

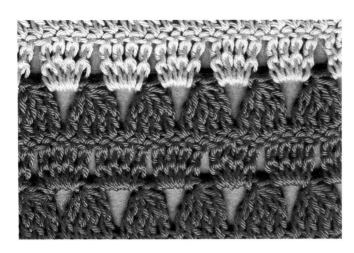

Serpentine stitch Work over a multiple of 4dtr + 1dtr using 3 colors. *Row 1* In A, ch4, skip next dtr, 4dtr in next dtr, *skip 3dtr, 4dtr in next dtr, rep from * to last 2dtr, 1dtr in last dtr, turn. *Row 2* In A, ch3, leaving last lp of each on hook, work 1dtr in each of next 4dtr, yo, draw through all lps on hook, *ch3, leaving last lp of each on hook work 1dtr in each of next 4dtr, yo, draw through all lps on hook, rep from * to last 3dtr, ch3, leaving last lp of each on hook work 1dtr into each of last 2dtr and 3rd of ch3, yo, draw through all lps on hook, turn. *Row 3* In B, ch4, *4dtr in next ch3 lp, rep from * to end, 1dtr in last st, turn. Working 1 more row B, then 2 rows C, 2 rows A, 2 rows B, rep rows 2 and 3 to form patt.

Three color dot stitch Work as given for Dot stitch (see page 84), using 3 colors.

Three color fans Work over a multiple of 5sc + 2sc using 3 colors. *Row 1* In A, ch3, 2dc in first sc, *skip 2sc, [3dc, ch1, 3dc] all in next sc, rep from * to last 3sc, 3dc in last sc, turn. *Row 2* In B, ch3, 2dc in first dc, *[3dc, ch1, 3dc] all in next ch1 sp, rep from * to end, 3dc in third of ch3, turn. Working 1 row C, 1 row A, 1 row B, rep row 2 to form patt.

Three color shell stitch Work over a multiple of 4sc + 1sc using 3 colors. *Row 1* In A, 1sc in first sc, *skip next sc, 3dc in next sc, skip next sc, 1sc in next sc, rep from * to end, turn. *Row 2* In B, ch3, 1dc in first sc, skip 1dc, 1sc in next dc, *3dc in next sc, skip 1dc, 1sc in next dc, rep from * ending 2dc in last sc, turn. *Row 3* In C, 1sc in first dc, 3dc in next sc, skip 1dc, 1sc in next dc, rep from * working last sc in third of ch3, turn. Working 1 row each of A, B, C, rep rows 2 and 3 to form patt.

Square 1. In A, ch6, ss into first ch to form a ring. *Round 1* ch3, into the circle work 2dc, (ch1, 3dc) 3 times, ch1, ss into top of ch3. Fasten off. *Round 2* Join B at any one of the ch1 spaces and work ch3; into the same space work (2dc, ch1 and 3dc), *ch1, in the next ch space work (3dc, ch1 and 3dc)*; rep from * to * twice, ch1, ss into top of ch3. Fasten off.

2. *Round 3* Join C at any one of the spaces at a corner and work the first corner as in round 2; (ch1, 3dc into next space, ch1, 1 corner into the next corner space) 3 times; ch1, 3dc into next space, ch1, ss in top of ch3. Fasten off. *Round 4* Join D at any one of the corner spaces and work the first corner, [(ch1, 3dc into next space) twice, ch1, 1 corner into next corner space] 3 times; (ch1, 3dc into next sp) twice, ch1, ss into top of ch3. Fasten off. *Round 5* Join E at any one of the corner spaces and work 1 corner [(ch1, 3dc into next space) 3 times, ch1, 1 corner into next corner] 3 times, (ch1, 3dc in next sp) 3 times, ch1, ss into top of ch3. Fasten off.

Triangle (equal to ½ the square) In A, ch5. *Row 1* Into each of the ch5 work (3dc, ch1, 3dc, ch1 and 1dc). Fasten off. *Row 2* Join B to the third of ch4, ch4, 3dc into first ch sp, ch1, into the next space work (3dc, ch1 and 3dc) (a corner), ch1; into the last space work 3dc, ch1 and 1dc. Fasten off. *Row 3* Join C to the third of ch4, ch4, 3dc into first ch sp, ch1, 3dc into next ch sp, ch1, 1 corner into next ch sp, ch1, 3dc into next sp, ch1, into the last sp work (3dc, ch1, 1dc). Fasten off. *Row 4* Join D to the third of ch4, ch4, 3dc into first ch sp (ch1, 3dc in next ch sp) twice, ch1, 1 corner into next ch sp, (ch1, 3dc in next ch sp) twice, ch1, into last sp work (3dc, ch1, 1dc). Fasten off. *Row 5* Join E to the third of ch4, ch4, 3dc into first ch sp, (ch1, 3dc in next ch sp) 3 times, ch1, 1 corner into next ch sp, (ch1, 3dc in next ch sp) 3 times, ch1, into last sp work (3dc, ch1, 1dc). Fasten off.

Pentagon In A, ch4, ss into first ch to form a ring. *Round 1* ch3, into circle work 1dc, (ch1, 2dc) 4 times, ch1, end with ss into third of ch3. Fasten off. *Round 2* Join B with a ss in the space of ch1, ch3, into same space work (1dc, ch2, 2dc) (first corner), *ch1, into next space work (2dc, ch1, 2dc)*; rep from * to * 3 times more (5 corners), ch1, ss into third of ch3. Fasten off. *Round 3* Join C with a ss in a corner sp, work first corner in this same space, *(ch1, 2dc) into next space, ch1, 1 corner at the next corner*; rep from * to * 3 times more; ch1, 2dc in next ch sp. Fasten off. Continue in this way, keeping the corners one above the other, and working 2dc into the ch sps between corners separated by ch1.

Hexagon Using A, ch6, ss into first ch to form a ring. *Round 1* ch3, into circle work 1dc, (ch1, 2dc) 5 times, ch1, ss into third of ch3, Fasten off. *Round 2* Join B with a ss, in a space of ch1 work ch3, in the same space work (1dc, ch2, 2dc) (first corner), *ch1, into next sp work (2dc, ch1, 2dc)*, rep from * to * 4 times more, ch1, ss in third of ch3. Fasten off. *Round 3* Join C with a ss in a corner sp, work first corner in this same sp, *(ch1, 2dc) into next sp, ch1, 1 corner in the next corner space*, rep from * to * 4 times more (6 corners); ch1, 2dc in next ch sp, ch1, ss into third of ch3. Fasten off. Continue in this way keeping the corners one above the other, working 2dc into the ch sps between corners, separated by ch1.

Octagon Using A, ch6, ss into first ch to form a ring. *Round 1* ch3, into the circle work 2dc, (ch1, 3dc) 3 times, ch1, ss into third of ch3. Fasten off. *Round 2* Join B with a ss into ch1 sp, work ch3, into same sp work 2dc, ch1, 3dc (first corner), *ch1, into next space work (2dc, ch1, 2dc)*, rep from * to * twice more (4 corners), ch1, ss into third of ch3. Fasten off. *Round 3* Join C with a ss into next ch sp, ch3, into same sp work (1dc, ch1, 2dc) (first corner), *ch1, into next sp work (2dc, ch1, 2dc)*, rep from * to * 6 times (8 corners), ch1, ss in top of ch3. Fasten off. *Round 4* Join D with a ss into ch1 sp, work a corner as in round 3, ch1, 2dc into next sp, *ch1, (2dc, ch1, 2dc) in next ch sp*, ch1, 2dc in next ch sp, ch1, rep from * to * 6 times more, ss in third of ch3. Fasten off. Continue in this way, keeping the corners one above the other, and working 2dc into the ch sp between corners, separated by ch1.

Medallions
Star in a wheel
Hexagonal star
Six-pointed star

NOTE On the following instructions work ch3 at beg of round in place of the first dc, when required.

Star in a wheel Ch8, ss into first ch to form a ring. *Round 1* Into the circle work ch6, (1dc, ch3) 7 times, ss in third of ch6. *Round 2* Into first sp work (ss, ch3, 1dc, ch3, 2dc, ch1); into each of next 7 ch3 sp work (2dc, ch3, 2dc, ch1), ss in third of ch3. *Round 3* Ss in next dc and ch3 lp, *into next ch3 lp work (2dc, ch3 2dc, ch1), 1sc in next ch1 sp, ch1, rep from * to end, ss in third of ch3. *Round 4* Ss in next 2dc and ch3 lp, *into next ch3 lp work (3dc, ch3, 3dc, ch2), 1sc in next sc, ch2, rep from * to end, ss in third of ch3. *Round 5* Ss in next 2dc and ch3 lp, *into next ch3 lp work (4dc, ch3, 4dc, ch3), 1dc in next sc, ch3, rep from * to end, ss in third of ch3. *Round 6* Ss in next 3dc, *1sc in next ch sp, 1sc in each of next 4dc, ch3, 1dc in next dc, ch3, 1sc in each of next 4dc, rep from * working last 4sc in first 4ss. *Round 7* *1sc in next sc, 7ch, 1dc in next dc, skip 4sc, rep from * to end, ss in first sc. Fasten off.

Hexagonal star Ch8, ss into first ch to form a ring. *Round 1* Work (3dc, ch2) 6 times in the circle, ss in top of ch3. *Round 2* Work (1dc in each of next 3dc, ch2, 1dc in ch2 sp, ch2) 6 times, ss in top of ch3. *Round 3* *ch3 to count as first dc, 1dc in each of next 2dc (ch2, 1dc in next ch sp) twice, ch2, rep from * to end, ss in top of ch3. *Round 4* *ch3 to count as first dc, 1dc in each of next 2dc, (ch2, 1dc in next ch sp) 3 times, ch2, rep from * to end, ss in top of ch3. *Round 5* *ch3 to count as first dc, 1dc in each of next 2dc, 3dc into next space, (ch2, 1dc in next ch sp) twice, ch2, 3dc into next sp, rep from * to end, ss in top of ch3. *Round 6* *ch3 to count as first dc, 1dc in each of next 8dc, 3dc in next ch sp, ch2, 1dc in next sp, ch2, 3dc in next ch sp, rep from * to end, ss in top of ch3. *Round 7* *ch3 to count as first dc, 1dc in each of next 11dc, 2dc into next sp, ch3, 2dc into next sp, rep from * to end, ss in top of ch3. Fasten off.

Six-pointed star Ch6, ss in first ch to form a ring. *Round 1* ch3, 1dc, (ch3, 2dc) 5 times, ch3 into the ring, ss in top of ch3. *Round 2* *1dc in next dc, 2dc in next dc, ch4, rep from * to end, ss in top of ch3. *Round 3* *2dc in next dc, 1dc in next dc, 2dc in next dc, ch5, rep from * to end, ss in top of ch3. *Round 4* *1dc in each of next 2dc, (1dc, ch2, 1dc) worked in next dc, 1dc in each of next 2dc, ch5, rep from * to end, ss in top of ch3. *Round 5* *1dc in each of next 3dc, ch3, 1dc in the ch2 sp, ch3, 1dc in each of next 3dc, ch4, rep from * to end, ss in top of ch3. *Round 6* *1dc in each of next 3dc, ch3, (3dc cluster, ch3, 3dc cluster) in next dc, ch3, 1dc in each of next 3dc, ch3, rep from * to end, ss in top of ch3. *Round 7* *1dc in each of next 3dc, ch3, skip ch3, (3dc cluster, ch3) 3 times in next ch3 lp, 1dc in each of next 3dc, ch3, rep from * to end, ss in top of ch3. *Round 8* *1dc in each of next 3dc, ch3, skip ch3 (3dc cluster, ch3) twice in next ch3 lp, 3dc cluster in top of next cluster, (3dc cluster, ch3) twice in next ch3 lp, 1dc in each of next 3dc, rep from * to end, ss in top of ch3. *Round 9* *1dc in each of next 2dc, (ch3, 1sc in next ch3 lp) 3 times, ch4, (1sc in next ch3 lp, ch3) 3 times, rep from * to end, ss in top of ch3. Fasten off.

NOTE On the following instructions work ch3 at beg of round in place of the first dc, when required.

Lacy star Ch6, ss in first ch to form a ring. *Round 1* ch5, *(1dc, ch2 into ring) 7 times, ss in third of ch5; *Round 2* *4dc cluster in ch2 lp, ch5, rep from * to end, ss in top of first cluster. *Round 3* *ch3, skip ch2, (1dc, ch5, 1dc) in next ch, ch3 1sc in top of next cluster, rep from * to end. *Round 4* *3sc in next ch3 lp, 5sc in next ch5 lp, 3sc in next ch3 lp, rep from * to end, ss in first sc. Fasten off.

Festooned star Ch6, ss in first ch to form a ring. *Round 1* Work 14sc in ring. *Round 2* *1sc in next sc, 2sc in next sc, rep from * to end. *Round 3* *1sc in each of next 2sc, 2sc in next sc, rep from * to end. *Round 4* *1sc in each of next 6sc, 2sc in next sc, rep from * to end (32 sts). *Round 5* On the 32 sts work *ch5, skip 1sc, 1sc in next sc, rep from * to end (16 arches). *Round 6* Ss in each of next ch2, 1sc in ch5 lp, *ch5, 1sc in next lp, rep from * ending with ss in first sc. *Round 7* Ss in each of next ch2, 1sc in ch5 lp, *9ch, skip one ch5 lp, 1sc in center of the next ch5 lp, rep from * ending with ss in first sc. *Round 8* Into each ch9 lp work (6sc, ch2, ss in first ch, 6sc), ss in first sc. Fasten off.

Star with picots Ch6, ss in first ch to form a ring. *Round 1* Work 24sc into ring. *Round 2* ch5, 1dc in first sc, ch1, skip 2sc, *(1dc, ch2, 1dc) in next sc, ch1, rep from * to end, ss in third of ch5. *Round 3* *(ch3 to count as first dc, 1dc, ch2, 2dc) in next ch2 sp, 1sc in next ch sp, rep from * to end, ss in top of ch3. *Round 4* *(ch3 to count as first dc, 2dc, ch1, 3dc) in next ch2 sp, 2sc in next sc, rep from * to end, ss in top of ch3. *Round 5* *1sc in each st to ch1 sp, (1sc, ch2, 1sc) in ch1 sp, rep from * to end, ss in first sc. Fasten off.

Beads on crochet
Single crochet with beads
Double crochet with beads

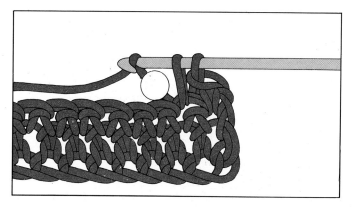

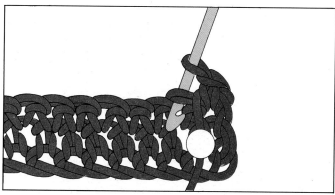

Before starting work, thread the beads along the yarn, ready for use.

Single crochet: adding beads on WS row Insert hook and draw a lp through, slide a bead close to the 2 sts on the hook, yo and close the st.

Single crochet: adding beads on RS row **1.** Slide a bead up to the st on the hook, insert hook into back of st.

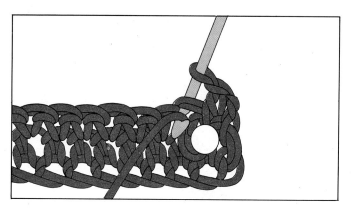

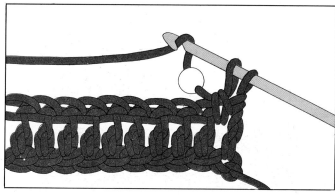

2. Yo and draw a lp through to back of work, yo and close the st. Slide another bead close to the st on the hook, and rep the process.

Double crochet: adding beads on WS row Before closing the dc, slide a bead up to the 2 lps on hook, yo and close the st.

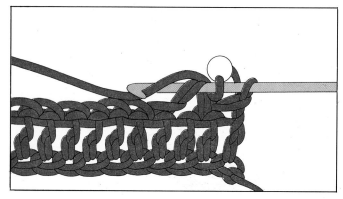

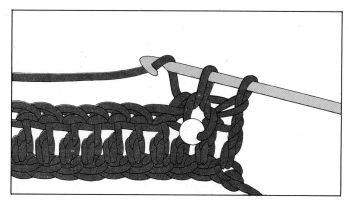

Double crochet: adding beads on RS row **1.** Yo and slide a bead onto the hook, insert hook into st, yo.

2. Draw through 2 lps on hook, passing the hook behind the bead. Yo and close the st. Yo, slide a bead onto the hook and rep the process.

Crochet loops
Using a ruler
Using the index finger

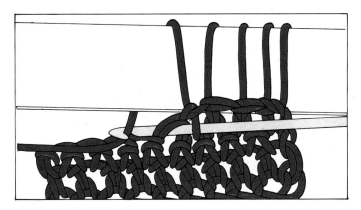

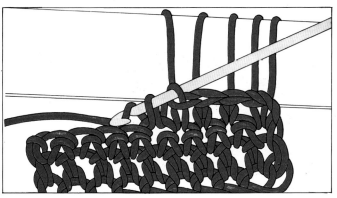

Loop stitch using a ruler 1. Use a ruler, or any suitable straight-edged flat object of the required height for the fringe. Work an initial row of sc, starting the loop stitch on the next row, *insert hook into first base st, yarn around the ruler (held in left hand) from front to back, yo.

2. Draw the yarn through the st into which the hook was inserted, yo again.

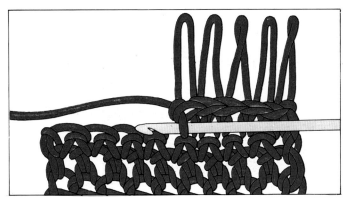

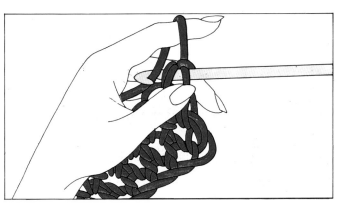

3. Close the st to make a sc*, rep from * to * in each st. Work the return row in sc. Rep these 2 rows. This method is used for extra long fringes.

Loop stitch using the index finger 1. Work an initial row of sc. *Insert hook into st (or into back of st), and pass the yarn up and over the index finger of the left hand, yo.

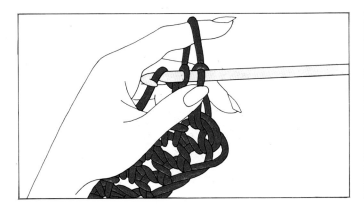

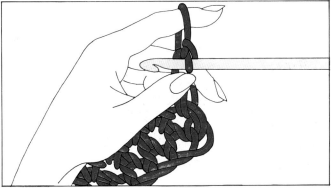

2. Draw the yarn through the st, yo and close the st to make a sc*, rep from * to * into each st.

3. The st making the loop lies behind the work. Work the return row in sc. Rep these 2 rows.

Crochet edgings

Fan edging
Fan outline edging
Suspended fan edging
Open cluster edging
Three color ribbon edging

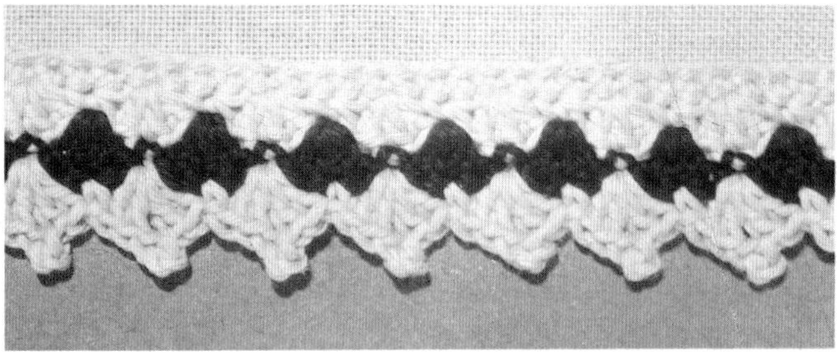

Fan edging Work on a base of a multiple of 4sc + 1sc, using 3 colors. *Row 1* In A, 1sc in first sc, skip 1sc, *3dc into next sc, skip 1sc, 1sc in next sc, rep from * to end. Fasten off. *Row 2* In B, ch3, 2dc into first sc, 1sc into center of group of 3dc, 3dc in next sc, rep from * to end. Fasten off. *Row 3* In C, 1sc in center of group of 3dc, *[2dc, ch2, 2dc] into next sc, 1sc at center of group of 3dc, rep from * to end. Fasten off.

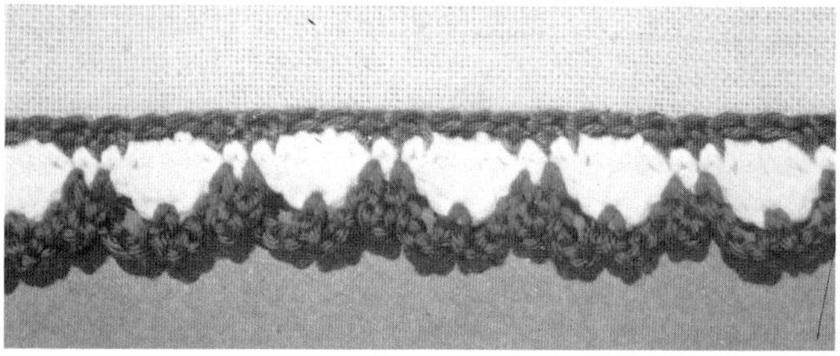

Fan outline edging Work on a base of ch4 + ch2, using 3 colors. *Row 1* In A, 1sc in each of first ch2, *ch3, skip ch2, 1sc in each of next ch2, rep from * to end. *Row 2* In B, 1sc into each of first 2sc, *[1sc, 3dc and 1sc] into next ch3 lp, 1sc in each of next 2sc, rep from * to end. Fasten off. *Row 3* In C, 1sc in first sc, ch2, 1sc in next sc, *ch2, skip 1dc, 1sc in next dc, ch2, skip next sc, 1sc in next sc, ch2, 1sc in next sc, rep from * to end. Fasten off.

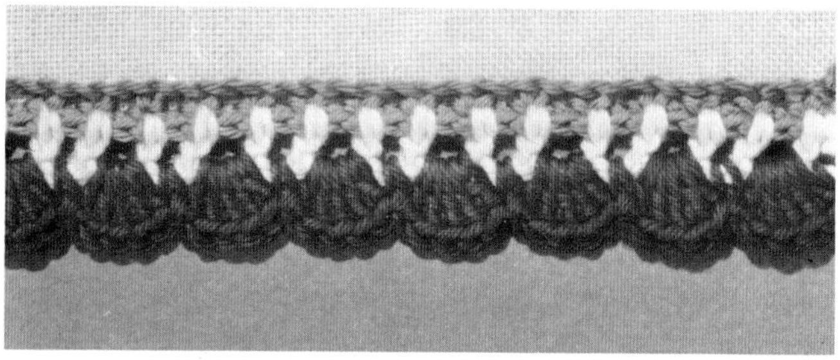

Suspended fan edging Work on a base of a multiple of ch4 + ch3, using 3 colors. *Row 1* In A, 1sc in first ch, *ch1, skip ch1, 1sc in next ch, rep from * to end. Fasten off. *Row 2* In B, ch4, 1dc into next sc, *ch1, 1dc in next sc, rep from * to end. Fasten off. *Row 3* In C, 1sc in first ch sp, 1dc in next sc, *5dc into next ch sp, 1sc in next ch sp, rep from * to end. Fasten off.

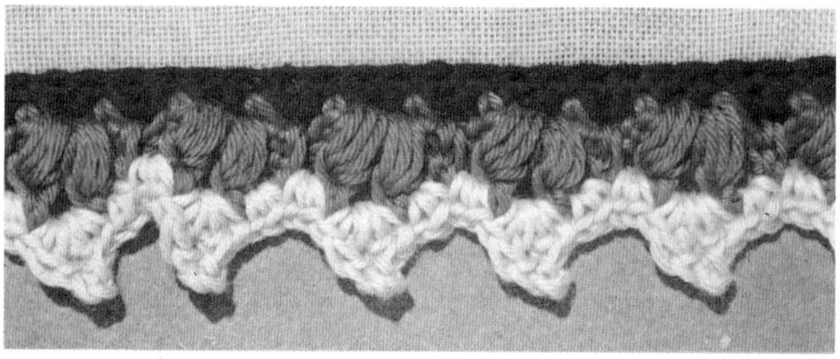

Open cluster edging Work on a base of ch4 + ch3, using 4 colors. *Row 1* In A, 1sc in first ch, *ch1, skip ch1, 1sc in next ch, rep from * to end. Fasten off. *Row 2* Attach B to first sc, ch5, *1dc in each of next 2sc, ch2, rep from * to last sc, 1dc in last sc. Fasten off. *Row 3* Attach C to third of ch5, ch2, [one 3dc cluster, ch3, one 3dc cluster] in next ch2 lp, *ch2, 1sc into sp between 2dc, ch2, work [1 cluster, ch3, 1 cluster] into next ch2 lp, rep from * to end, ch2, ss in top of last dc. Fasten off. *Row 4* Attach D to first ch3 sp, work [2sc, ch2, 2sc] in first ch3 sp, *2sc in each of next ch2 sps, [2sc, ch2, 2sc] in next ch3 sp, rep from * to end. Fasten off.

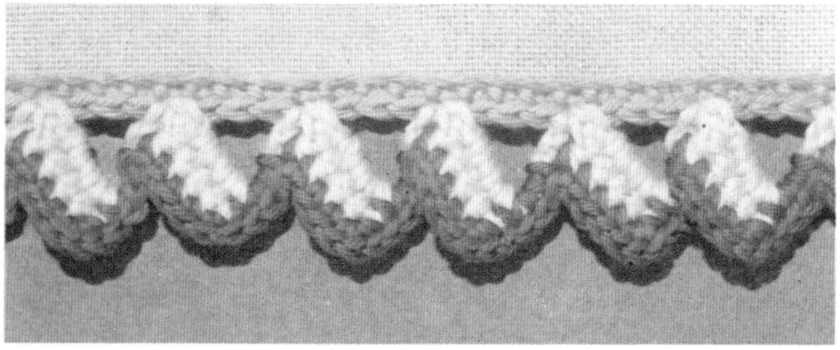

Three color ribbon edging Work on a base of ch4 + ch1, using 3 colors. *Row 1* In A, work 1sc in each ch to end. Fasten off. *Row 2* In B, 1sc in first sc, *ch7, skip 3sc, 1sc in next sc, ch1, turn the work and into the arch work 4sc, turn the work, 1sc in each of next 4sc, 1sc into same place as sc worked at beg of arch, rep from * to end, turn and fasten off. *Row 3* Attach C to last sc worked, *1sc in each of next 5sc, 1sc in side of next sc, 3sc in ch3 lp, rep from * to end, 1sc in last sc. Fasten off.

Crochet edgings
Festoon edging   Serpentine edging
Curved edging   Looped edging
Trefoil edging

Festoon edging Work on a base of a multiple of ch5 + ch1. *Row 1* 1sc in first ch, *ch1, skip ch1, 1sc in next sc, rep from * to end, turn. *Row 2* 1sc in first sc, *ch6, skip next sc, 1sc in next sc, rep from * to end, turn. *Row 3* 1sc in first sc, *into ch6 lp work [3sc, ch3, ss into first ch, 3sc], 1sc in next sc, rep from * to end. Fasten off.

Curved edging Work on a base of a multiple of ch10 + ch1. *Row 1* 1sc in first ch, *ch1, skip ch1, 1sc in next sc, rep from * to end, turn. *Row 2* 2sc in first sc, *ch5, skip 4 sts, 1sc in next st, ch7, 1sc into same st as last sc, ch5, skip 4 sts, 2sc in next st, rep from * to end, turn. *Row 3* 1sc in each of first 2sc, 5sc into the ch5 lp, into the arches of the ch7 work [1ss, 1sc, 1hdc, 2dc, 1hdc, 1sc, 1ss], 5sc into the ch5, 1sc in each of next 2sc, rep from * to end. Fasten off.

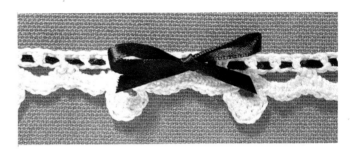

Serpentine edging Ch7. *Row 1* 1sc in fourth ch from hook, 1sc in each of next ch3, turn. *Row 2* ch7, 1sc in each of next 4sc, turn. *Row 3* ch3, 1sc in each of next 4sc, turn. Rep rows 2 and 3 for length required ending with row 1. *Ending row* *ch1, 1sc in next ch3 lp, rep from * to end. Fasten off.

Looped edging Work on a base of a multiple of ch8 + ch3. *Row 1* 1sc in first sc, *ch1, skip ch1, rep from * to end, turn. *Row 2* 1sc in each of first 3 sts, *ch10, 1sc in each of next 5 sts, ch2, turn, 1sc into seventh and eighth ch just worked, turn, ch6, 1sc in each of next 3 sts, rep from * to end. Fasten off.

Trefoil edging Work over a multiple of ch8 + ch1. *Row 1* 1sc in first ch, *ch1, skip ch1, 1sc in next ch, rep from * to end, turn. *Row 2* 1sc in first sc, *ch3, skip 3 sts, into next 1sc work [ch5, ss into first ch – picot – 1dtr, 1 picot, 1dtr, 1 picot, 1sc], ch3, skip 3 sts, 1sc into next sc, rep from * to end. Fasten off.

Filet crochet
Working a simple mesh
Working filled squares
Working open squares

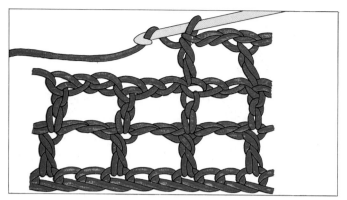

Working a simple mesh Make required number of ch in a multiple of 3 + 5. For the foundation row work: 1dc into eighth ch from hook, *skip ch2, 1dc into next ch, rep from * to end. On following rows work: ch5 (to count as first dc and ch2 sp), 1dc into next dc*, ch2, 1dc into next dc, rep from * to end.

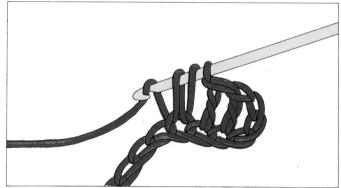

Working filled squares on foundation row To start the foundation row with a filled square, work 1dc into fourth ch from hook, then 1dc into each of next ch2. For every subsequent filled square work 1dc into each of next ch3. A filled square is made up of 2dc instead of a ch2 space with 1dc each side of it, making 4dc altogether.

Working open squares on foundation row Work 1dc into eighth ch from hook. For every subsequent open square work ch2, skip ch2, 1dc into next ch. An open square is made up of a ch2 sp with 1dc each side of it.

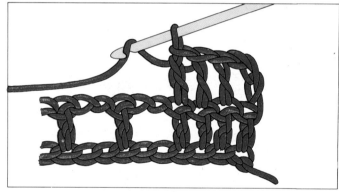

Working filled squares at beginning of rows At the beginning of the row, ch3 to count as first dc. Now work 2dc over either the next 2dc or ch2 sp, then work 1dc into next dc.

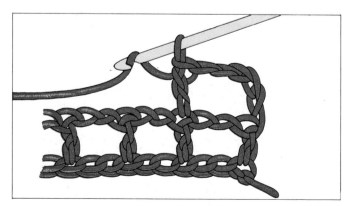

Working open squares at beginning of rows At the beginning of the row, ch5 to count as first dc and ch2 sp. Now skip either the next 2dc or ch2 sp, then work 1dc into next dc.

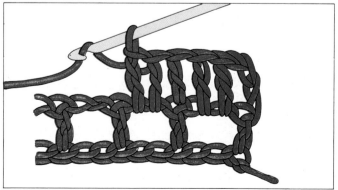

Working more than 1 filled square together After working a filled square at the beginning of a row, only 3dc are required for each subsequent filled square – 2dc over the central ch2 sp, then 1dc to complete the square.

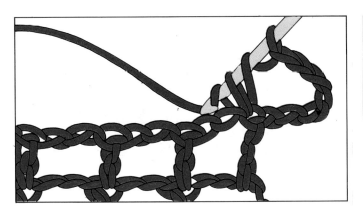

Increasing an open square at the beginning of a row At the end of the previous row, ch7, then turn. Work 1dc into first dc (last dc of previous row), then continue in pattern to end.

Increasing an open square at the end of a row Work in pattern to end of row, ch2, then work 1dtr (yarn 2 times around hook) into base of last dc of row.

Increasing more than 1 square at the end of a row Increase first square at end of the row as already given above, then make subsequent squares as follows: ch2, 1dtr (yarn 2 times around hook) into corner formed by previous increased square.

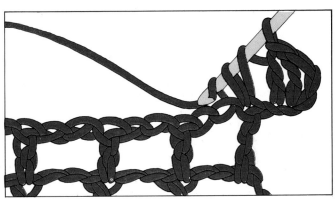

Increasing a filled square at the beginning of a row At the end of the previous row, ch5, then turn. Work 1dc into fourth ch from hook, 1dc into next ch, then 1dc into next dc (last dc of previous row), then continue in pattern to end.

Increasing a filled square at the end of a row Work in pattern to end of row, then work a dtr into base of last dc of row, [work 1dtr into base of previous dtr] twice.

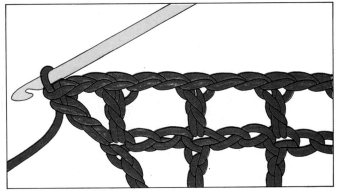

Graduated increasing At the beginning of the row, ch5 (to count as 1dc and ch2), then 1dc into first dc. At the end of the row work: 1dc as the last st of the row, then work ch2 and 1dc into same place as last dc.

Decreasing an open or filled square at the beginning of a row
Ss into the top of each of the first 4 sts of first square, make either ch3 for a filled square or ch5 for an open square, then work in pattern to end of row.

Decreasing an open or filled square at the end of a row Work in pattern to the last square of the row, then turn leaving the last 3 sts unworked. Make either ch3 for a filled square or ch5 for an open square, then work in pattern to end of row.

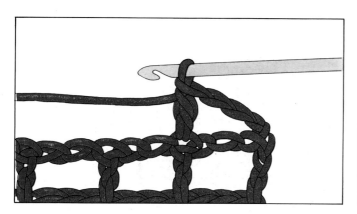

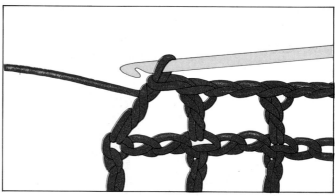

Graduated decrease of an open square at the beginning of a row Make ch3 instead of ch5 at beginning of row (omitting ch2 sp), then work 1dc into second dc of row.

Graduated decrease of an open square at the end of a row Work to first dc of last square of row, work 1dc but do not work ch2 sp, then work 1dc into third of turning ch.

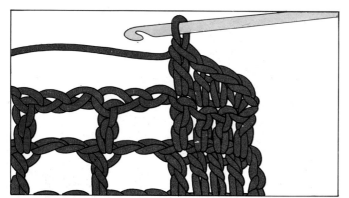

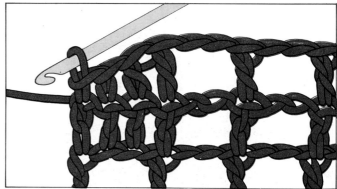

Graduated decrease of a filled square at the beginning of a row Begin the row by working 1ss into first dc, 1sc into next st, 1hdc into next st, then 1dc into next dc, work in pattern to end of row.

Graduated decrease of a filled square at the end of a row Work to first dc of last square of row, work 1dc into dc, 1hdc into next st, 1sc into next st, 1ss into last st, turn and ss to first dc ready to begin next row.

Working corners 1. When working crochet borders in rounds the corners are worked by increasing stitches at regular intervals each side of the point. In filet crochet, which is generally worked backwards and forwards in rows across the width of the edging, a different method is used. If you have never worked a corner in filet crochet before, you will notice that the pattern changes at the corner enabling a symmetrical pattern to be worked without spoiling the allover design. In the example you will notice that the last 8 rows are shown in the chart, and that there is a heavier line, forming a step pattern, running diagonally to the corner. The heavier line shows where you must turn the work to form the corner, ie. on the first row work 1 filled square, 5 open squares, then 1 filled square, turn and leave any remaining squares unworked. On the next row work 3 filled squares, 3 open squares, then 1 filled square. Turn again and work 1 filled, 2 open and 2 filled squares – you have again reached the heavier line so turn and work back by working 2 open, 1 filled, 1 open and 1 filled square.

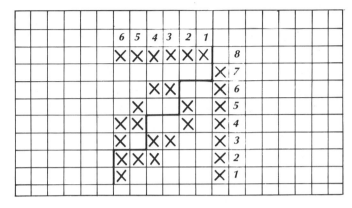

2. Continue in this way, working 2 fewer squares on every 2 rows until the last single square (1 open square) has been worked.

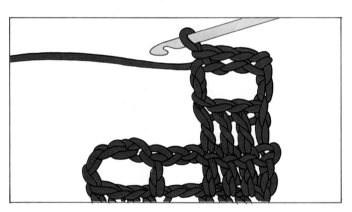

3. At the end of the last row, turn the work so that the right side is facing, then ss along to the left-hand side of the top square.

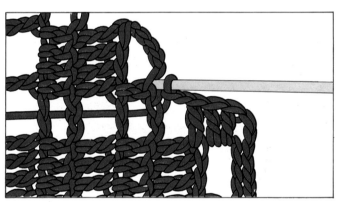

4. Turn work 90° so that stitch still on hook is at the right-hand edge. Working along side edges of previous corner rows, work the first row of the second side by making 1 filled and 1 open square, ss to corner to secure end of row.

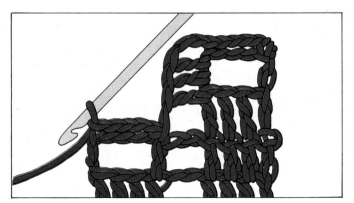

5. Ss along the top of the next stitch to bring the yarn to the appropriate point to start the next row.

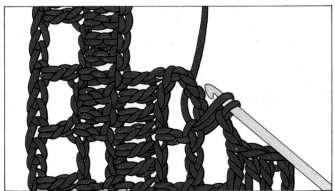

6. Turn and work the second row by working 1 open and 1 filled square. Then continue in this way, working extra squares every 2 rows until the corner is complete.

Irish crochet

Picot and arch stitch
Scattered picot stitch
Gothic stitch

Picot grill stitch
Diamond picot stitch
Single mesh stitch

Picot and arch stitch Make required number of ch, a multiple of 4 + 2. *Row 1* 1sc into second ch from hook, *ch5, skip ch3, 1sc into next ch, rep from * to end. *Row 2* ch4, 1sc into first ch5 arch, *ch5, 1sc into next arch, rep from * to last arch, ch2, 1dc into last sc. *Row 3* 3sc into ch2 sp, *into ch5 arch work [3sc, ch4, 1ss into first of ch4, 2sc, ch4, 1ss into first of ch4, 2sc], rep from * to end, ch4, 3sc into ch4 sp. *Row 4* 1sc into first sc, *ch5, 1sc between central 2sc of arch, rep from * to end, working last sc into end sc. Rep rows 2 to 4 to form patt.

Picot grill stitch Make required number of ch, a multiple of 5 + 2. *Row 1* 1sc into second ch from hook, *ch5, 1ss into third ch from hook to form picot, ch4, 1ss into third ch from hook to form picot, ch2, skip ch4, 1sc into next ch, rep from * to end. *Row 2* ch4, *into ch1 sp between picots work [1sc, 1dc, 1sc], ch5, 1ss into third ch from hook, ch4, 1ss into third ch from hook, ch2, rep from * to last arch, into ch1 sp between picots work [1sc, 1dc, 1sc], ch2, 1dc into last sc. *Row 3* 1sc into top of dc of previous row, *ch5, 1ss into third ch from hook, ch4, 1ss into third ch from hook, ch2, 1sc into ch1 sp between picots, rep from * to end, working last sc into second of 4 turning ch. Rep rows 2 and 3 to form patt.

Scattered picot stitch Make required number of ch, a multiple of 4 + 1. *Row 1* 1dtr into fourth ch from hook, 1 picot (ch3, 1ss into first of ch3), into same ch as dtr work [1dtr, ch1, 1dtr], *skip next ch3, into next ch work [1dtr, 1 picot, 1dtr, ch1, 1dtr], rep from * to end. *Row 2* ch3, *into ch1 sp between dtr work [1dtr, 1 picot, 1dtr, ch1, 1dtr], rep from * to end, 1dtr into top of turning ch. Rep row 2 to form patt.

Diamond picot stitch Make required number of ch, a multiple of 5 + 2. *Row 1* 1sc into second ch from hook, ch7, 1ss into fifth ch from hook, ch8, 1ss into fifth ch from hook, ch2, skip ch4, 1sc into next ch, rep from * to end. *Row 2* ch7, 1ss into fifth ch from hook, [ch8, 1ss into fifth ch from hook] twice, ch2, 1sc into central ch3 of first arch, *ch7, 1ss into fifth ch from hook, ch8, 1ss into fifth ch from hook, ch2, 1sc into central ch3 of next arch, rep from * to end. Rep row 2 to form patt.

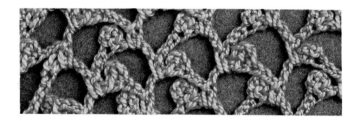

Gothic stitch Make required number of ch, a multiple of 4 + 2. *Row 1* 1sc into second ch from hook, *ch8, 1ss into fifth ch from hook, ch3, skip ch3, 1sc into next ch, rep from * to end. *Row 2* *ch8, 1ss into fifth ch from hook, ch3, 1sc into third ch of arch (st before next picot), rep from * to end. Rep row 2 to form patt.

Single mesh stitch Make required number of ch, a multiple of 4 + 10. *Row 1* 1dc into tenth ch from hook, *ch4, skip ch3, 1dc into next ch, rep from * to end. *Row 2* ch8, 1dc into first sp, *ch4, 1dc into next sp, rep from * to end. Rep row 2 to form patt.

Irish crochet edgings

Crown edging   Crested edging
Convoluted edging   Stepped picot edging
Fancy loop edging   Simple loop edging

Crown edging Make required number of ch, a multiple of 6 + 1.
Row 1 1sc into second ch from hook, 1sc into each ch to end.
Row 2 1sc into first sc, *ch3, skip 2sc, [1dc, ch5, 1dc] into next sc, ch3, skip 2sc, 1sc into next sc, rep from * to end. Row 3 Ss to ch5 arch, into each ch5 arch work 4dc, [ch4, 1ss into first of ch4] 3 times, then 4dc. Fasten off.

Crested edging Make required number of ch, a multiple of 18 + 5. Row 1 1dc into eighth ch from hook, *ch2, skip ch2, 1dc into next ch, rep from * to end. Row 2 1sc into first ch2 sp, *ch5, 1sc into next ch2 sp, 1hdc into next dc, [1dc and 1tr] into next ch2 sp, 1dtr into next dc, [ch4, 1ss into first ch4] 5 times, 1hdc into top of dtr, 1dtr into same dc as previous dtr, [1tr and 1dc] into next ch2 sp, 1hdc into next dc, 1sc into next ch2 sp, rep from * to last ch2 sp, ch5, 1sc into last sp. Fasten off.

Convoluted edging Make required number of ch, a multiple of 5 + 2. Row 1 (WS) 1sc into second ch from hook, 1sc into each ch to end. Row 2 1sc into first sc, *[ch4, 1ss into first of ch4] 3 times, skip 1sc, 3dtr into next sc, skip 2sc, 1sc into next sc, rep from * to end. Fasten off.

Stepped picot edging Make required number of ch, a multiple of 12 + 4. Row 1 (WS) 1dc into sixth ch from hook, *ch1, skip ch1, 1dc into next ch, rep from * to end. Row 2 1sc into first dc, *[1sc into next ch1 sp, 1sc into next dc] twice, ch1, 1dc into next dc, 1 picot (ch4, 1ss into first of ch4), 1tr into next dc, 1 picot, 1dtr into next dc, 4 picots, 1sc into next dc, rep from * to end. Fasten off.

Fancy loop edging Make required number of ch, a multiple of 6 + 2. Row 1 (RS) 1dc into eighth ch from hook, *ch2, skip ch2, 1dc into next ch, rep from * to end. Break off yarn. Row 2 With right side still facing, rejoin yarn to third of ch8, 3sc into first ch2 sp, *into next ch2 sp work [2sc, ch3, 2sc], ch8, working backwards 1sc into first of 4sc just worked so making an arch, into arch work [3sc, ch3, 2sc, ch3, 2sc, ch3, 3sc], 3sc into next ch2 sp, rep from * to end. Fasten off.

Simple loop edging Make required number of ch, a multiple of 3 + 8. Row 1 (RS) 1dc into eighth ch from hook, *ch2, skip ch2, 1dc into next ch, rep from * to end. Break off yarn. Row 2 With RS still facing, rejoin yarn to third of ch8, *[work 3sc into next ch2 sp] 3 times, ch8, working backwards skip 5 of sc just worked, ss into sixth sc to make an arch, into arch work [3sc, ch3, 2sc, ch3, 2sc, ch3, 3sc], rep from * to last ch2 sp, 3sc into last ch2 sp. Fasten off.

Irish crochet motifs
Working over a cord
Flower motif

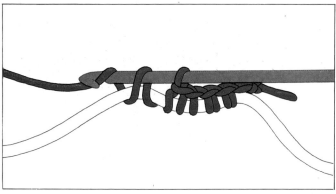

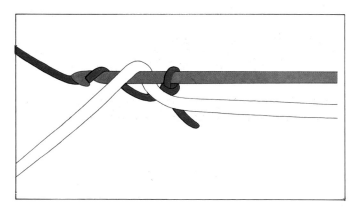

Working over a cord 1. This method gives a firm, slightly ridged, base to the stitches, giving more control to the shape for motifs. Make a slip knot and place on hook. Holding the cord in the left hand, pass hook under the cord, then wind yarn around hook.

2. Bring loop up in front of cord, then passing hook over the cord, wind yarn around hook and draw through both loops on hook. Continue in this way for required number of single crochet stitches, then gently push all the stitches close together along the cord.

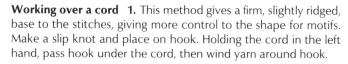

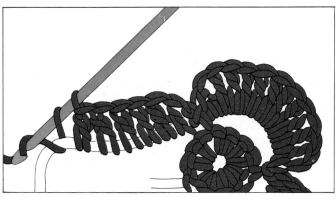

Flower motif 1. *Center* Make a circle with the cord and work 12sc into it. Pull the 2 ends of the cord to tighten the stitches together. Join the circle with a ss into first sc.

2. *Petals* *Over the cord work 1sc, 12dc, 1sc, tighten the cord, skip 3sc of center circle, 1ss into next sc, rep from * twice more.

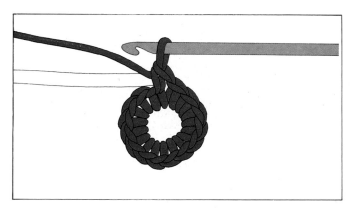

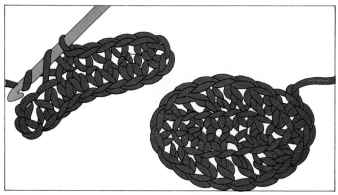

3. *Stalk* Work in sc over cord until the stalk is required length. Pull the cord to tighten. Still working over the cord, turn the work and work 1sc into back loop of each sc of stalk, ending with 1ss to edge of petal.

4. *Leaf* Without using the cord, make several chain. Work 1sc into each ch, 3sc into end ch, then 1sc into each ch down second side of chain. Work a second round by working 1hdc into each sc, and 3hdc at each end.

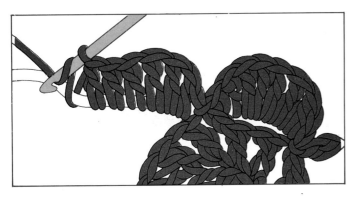

Simple rose Work the center as for the flower motif on page 114. Now work ch4, 1dc into next sc, *ch1, 1dc into next sc, rep from * to end, finishing with 1ss into third of ch4. Ss into ch1 sp. Working over cord, work 1sc, 5dc, 1sc, skip 2dc, then ss into next ch1 sp of center. Continue working petals in this way, ending with ss to sc of first petal.

Rose in relief 1. Make center as for the flower motif on page 114. Now work ch6, skip next sc, 1dc into next sc, *ch3, skip next sc, 1dc into next sc, rep from * to end, finishing with 1ss into third of ch6. Into each ch3 sp work [1sc, 3dc, 1sc].

2. *Round 2* Make ch2, then working behind first round of petals work 1sc at base of second dc of petal, *ch4, 1sc at base of second dc of next petal, rep from * to end. Into each ch4 loop work [1sc, 3dc, 1sc].

3. Continue in this way, working 2 more rounds of petals and working extra chains and double crochet to make petals larger as necessary.

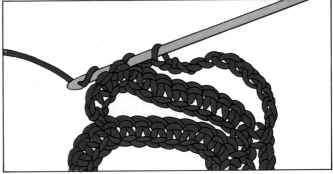

Trefoil *Stalk* Work sc tightly over cord to required length. *Leaf* Work in sc over cord for required length of leaf, then still working over cord, work 1sc into base of each sc to end. Do not cut off cord, but work 1 or 2 rounds of sc without cord, ending with ss into last st. Work 2 more leaves in same way, then fasten off.

Bars Worked without cord. Make a loop of chain, then work back in sc. Make a bar of several chain and fix to other side of loop with a ss, turn and work back over it in sc. Continue in this way until required number of bars have been worked. Fasten off.

Hairpin crochet
Single crochet strip
Finishing with single crochet edging
Finishing with crossed loops

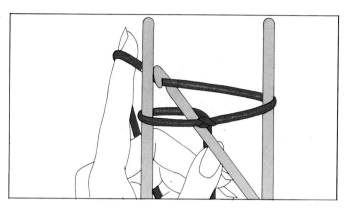

Single crochet strip 1. Make a slip knot and place the loop on the left prong of the hairpin, so that the knot lies in the center. Wind the yarn around the right prong from front to back. Insert the hook through the loop and catch the yarn.

2. Holding the hairpin in the left hand and the hook in the right hand, draw through a loop, yo and draw through loop on hook.

3. *Turn the hairpin to the left, allowing the yarn to wind around the prong of the hairpin as you turn it. Insert the hook under the top loop of the left prong, yo and draw a loop through.

4. Yo and draw a loop through both loops on hook*. Rep from * to * until the required number of loops have been worked. If there are too many loops on the hairpin, pull the hairpin out and re-insert it through the last 2 or 3 on each side.

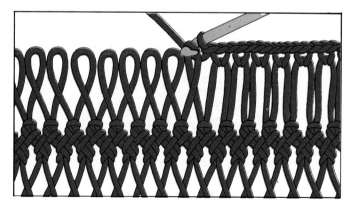

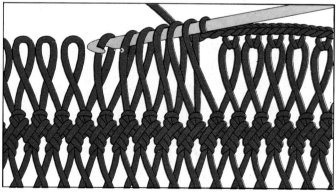

Finishing with single crochet edging The simplest way to finish a strip of hairpin crochet, whether it is to be used as a border or an insertion is as follows: join yarn to first loop at one edge, insert hook into loop and ch1. Taking care that the loops are not twisted, work 1sc into each loop to end. Fasten off.

Finishing with crossed loops Join yarn to first loop and ch1. *Inserting hook from front to back of twisted loop, work 1sc into each of first 6 loops. Insert hook through center of next 6 loops, then work [ch2, 1sc, ch2]. Rep from * to end.

Hairpin crochet
Alternative ways of forming strips
Working a circular piece

Some alternative ways of forming the hairpin crochet strips

Strips made with 2 single crochet Work as given for single crochet strips on page 116, working 2sc into front of each loop (see diagram right).

Strips made with 3 single crochet Work as given for single crochet strips, working 3sc into front of each loop.

Strips made with 1sc and 2dc Work as given for single crochet strips, working 1sc and 2dc into front of each loop.

Strips made with groups of stitches Work as given for single crochet strips, working around each loop as follows: yo 3 times, insert hook under loop on left prong of hairpin, yo and draw loop through, yo and draw through all 5 loops on hook.

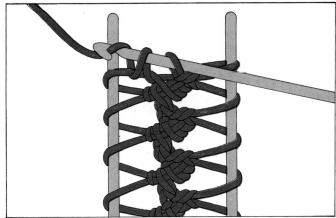

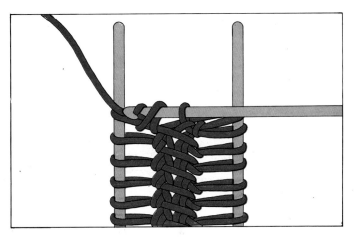

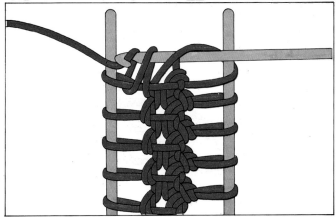

Strips made with single crochet and closed loops Work as given for single crochet strips, inserting hook below each loop on left prong instead of through it.

Strips made with double crochet and closed loops Work as given for single crochet strips, working 1dc around each loop and inserting hook below each loop on left prong instead of through it.

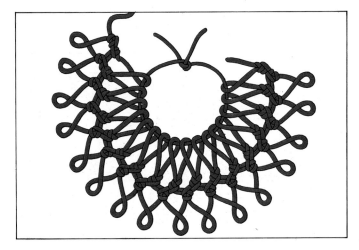

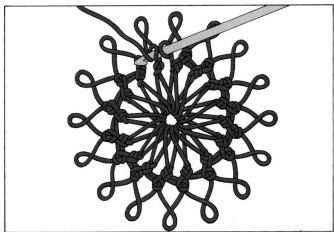

Working a circular piece of hairpin crochet 1. Make a strip of hairpin crochet and remove hairpin, but do not cut off yarn. Thread a spare length of matching yarn through all the loops on one edge, taking care that the loops are all twisted the same way, then draw up tightly and secure.

2. Insert hook back into last stitch from last loop and join to first stitch with a slipstitch. Finish the outer edge by working 1sc into each loop, working 1 or 2 chain between each loop as required.

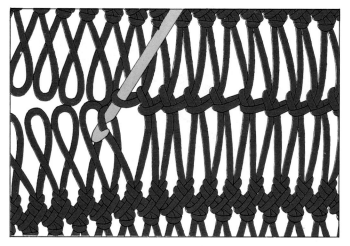

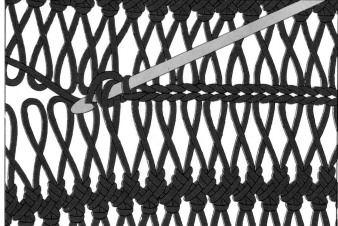

Joining 2 strips by weaving Lay the 2 strips edge to edge, with the right sides facing upward. Insert hook through first loop in top strip, then through first loop in bottom strip, draw second loop through first loop. *Insert hook through next loop in top strip and draw through loop on hook, insert hook through next loop in bottom strip and draw through loop on hook, rep from * to end. Fasten off.

Joining 2 strips with chain stitch Lay the 2 strips edge to edge, with the right sides facing upward. Join yarn to first loop in top strip, insert hook through first loop in top strip, then through first loop in bottom strip, yo and draw through a loop, yo and draw through loop on hook, *insert hook through next loop in top strip, then through next loop in bottom strip, yo and draw through a loop, yo and draw through loop on hook, rep from * to end. Fasten off.

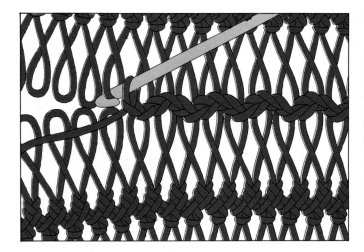

Joining 2 strips with zigzag chain stitch Lay the 2 strips edge to edge, with the right sides facing upward. Join yarn to first loop in top strip, insert hook through first loop in top strip, yo and draw through a loop, yo and draw through loop on hook, insert hook through first loop in bottom strip, yo and draw through a loop, yo and draw through loop on hook, *insert hook through next loop in top strip, yo and draw through a loop, yo and draw through loop on hook, insert hook through next loop in bottom strip, yo and draw through a loop, yo and draw through loop on hook, rep from * to end. Fasten off.

Joining 2 strips by weaving groups of stitches Lay the 2 strips edge to edge, with the right sides facing upward. Insert hook through first 2 or 3 loops in top strip, then through same number of loops in bottom strip, draw second group of loops through first group. *Insert hook through next group of loops in top strip and draw through loops on hook, insert hook through next group of loops in bottom strip and draw through loops on hook, rep from * to end. Fasten off.

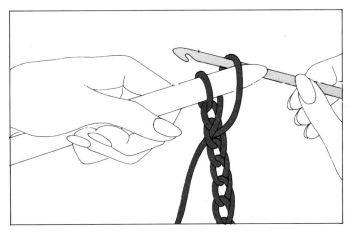

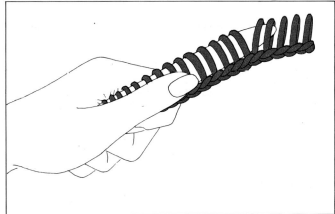

Peruvian crochet 1. This stitch is worked by using one large knitting needle and a hook. Each row is made up of two parts – a forward and a return row, each worked with the right side facing. Make the required number of chain, which in this example is divisible by 5. On the forward row begin by placing the first chain loop on to the needle. *Insert the hook through the next ch, yo, draw a loop through and place on to the needle.

2. Holding the needle in the left hand, rep from * to end of chain, taking care to keep all loops the same length. Note that this row forms the foundation row for the work.

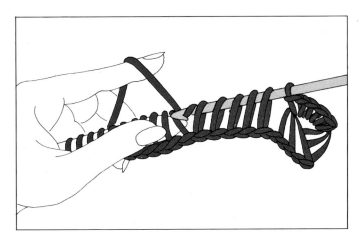

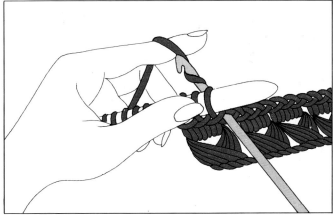

3. Working from right to left and holding the needle in the left hand and the hook in the right hand, insert the hook through the first 5 loops, yo and draw through a loop, yo and draw through loop on hook. Now working through all 5 loops again, work 5sc, *inserting hook through the center of the next 5 loops, work 5sc, rep from * to end.

4. Working from left to right and holding the needle in the left hand and the hook in the right hand, insert the hook into the first sc, yo, draw a loop through and place on the needle. *Insert the hook into the next sc, yo, draw a loop through and place on the needle, rep from * to end. Repeat steps 3 and 4 to form pattern, ending with row 3.

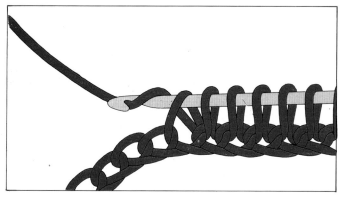

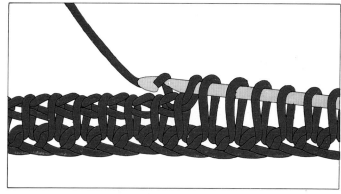

Simple Tunisian stitch 1. This stitch is worked with a special Tunisian crochet hook on a base of ch stitch. *Row 1 (forward)* Insert hook into second ch from hook, yo, draw loop through and leave on hook, *insert hook through next ch, yo, draw through loop and leave on hook, rep from * to end. Do not turn the work.

2. *Row 1 (return)* Still with right side of work facing, work yo, draw through first loop on hook, *yo, draw through 2 loops on hook, rep from * to end. This completes the 2 sections of the first row.

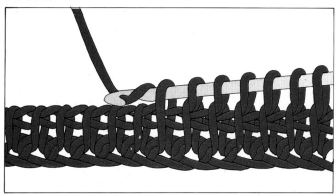

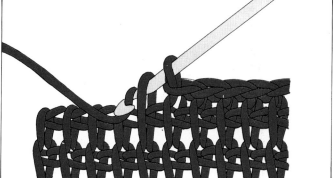

3. *Row 2 (forward)* Insert hook from right to left under second vertical loop of last row, yo, draw loop through, *insert hook under next vertical loop, yo, draw loop through, rep from * to end.

4. Work the *return row* as given for row 1, then repeat row 2 (forward and return) to form pattern. This stitch forms the basic technique for simple Tunisian stitch patterns.

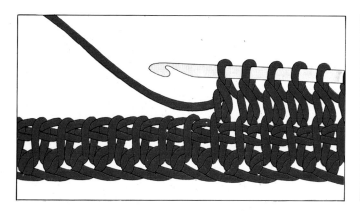

Double Tunisian stitch Make req no of ch and work *row 1* as simple Tunisian st. *Row 2 (forward)* Yo, draw through lp on hook, *insert hook through next vertical lp of prev row, yo, draw lp through, yo, draw through lp on hook, rep from * to end. Work return row as simple Tunisian st; rep row 2 to form patt.

Finishing the work Although the work seems finished at the end of a return row, the edge can be a bit ragged and tends to 'curl'. To give a neat edge, work 1 row of sc, inserting hook under vertical loop of each stitch and completing each stitch as it is worked.

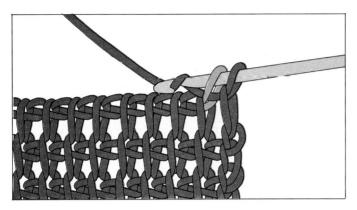

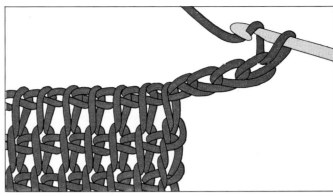

Increasing a stitch at the edge of a row A stitch can be increased at either end of the row, but it must be worked on the forward row. At the beginning of the row, work the first stitch, then insert hook through horizontal stitch between first and second stitches and draw a loop through. Work in same way at end of row.

Increasing more than 1 stitch at the beginning of a row Make the same number of chain as the required number of increased stitches, then work these stitches in the normal way.

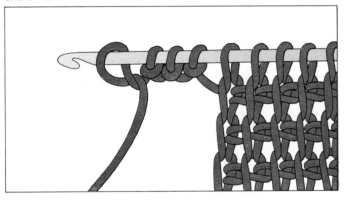

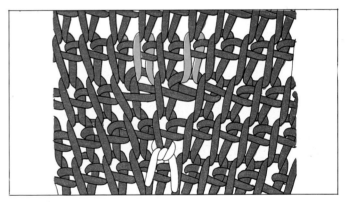

Increasing more than 1 stitch at the end of a row Work to end of a forward row, then make extra stitches by forming a loop in the yarn, twisting it to place it on hook. Tighten the stitch, then form the next one until the required number of stitches has been increased. Work these stitches off the hook in the normal way.

Increasing in the middle of a row Mark the position for the increased stitches. Work to the position of the increase, then make an extra stitch by inserting the hook under the horizontal thread between the stitches and drawing a loop through.

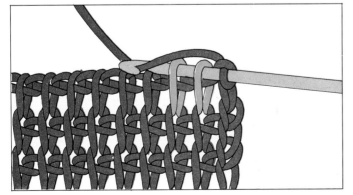

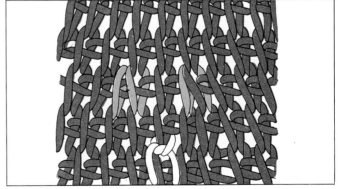

Decreasing at the edge of a row If decrease is at beginning work the first stitch normally, then insert hook through next 2 vertical loops together and draw through only 1 loop. If it is at the end work to last 3 stitches, work 2 together, then work last stitch.

Decreasing in the middle of a row Mark the position for the decreased stitches. Work to the position for the decrease, then work the next 2 stitches together as for the decrease at the edge of a row.

Tunisian crochet

Simple Tunisian stitch   Textured rib
Crossed Tunisian stitch   Triple rib
Reverse Tunisian stitch

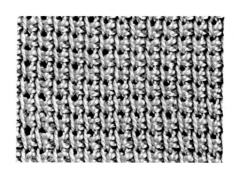

Simple Tunisian stitch Make required number of ch. *Row 1 (forward)* Insert hook into second ch from hook, yo, draw loop through and leave on hook, *insert hook through next ch, yo, draw through loop and leave on hook, rep from * to end. *Row 1 (return)* Yo, draw through first loop on hook, *yo, draw through 2 loops on hook, rep from * to end. *Row 2 (forward)* Insert hook through second vertical loop of last row, yo, draw loop through, *insert hook through next vertical loop, yo, draw loop through, rep from * to end. *Row 2 (return)* Yo, draw through first loop on hook, *yo, draw through 2 loops on hook, rep from * to end. Rep row 2 (forward and return) to form patt.

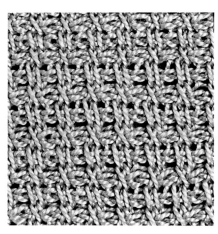

Crossed Tunisian stitch Make required number of ch, a multiple of 2 + 1. Work *Row 1 (forward and return rows)* as given for simple Tunisian stitch. *Row 2 (forward)* Insert hook under vertical loop of third st, yo, draw loop through, passing hook back across front of work, insert through vertical loop of second st, yo, draw loop through, *skip next loop, insert hook under next loop, yo, draw loop through, passing hook back across in front of work, insert under skipped loop, yo and draw loop through, rep from * to end. *Row 2 (return)* Yo, draw through first loop on hook, *yo, draw through 2 loops on hook, rep from * to end. *Row 3 (forward)* Insert hook through second vertical loop of last row, yo, draw loop through, *insert hook through next vertical loop, yo, draw loop through, rep from * to end. *Row 3 (return)* Yo, draw through first loop on hook, *yo, draw through 2 loops on hook, rep from * to end. Rep rows 2 and 3 (forward and return) to form patt.

Textured rib Make required number of ch, a multiple of 2 + 1. Work *Row 1 (forward and return rows)* as given for simple Tunisian stitch. *Row 2 (forward)* Skip the first st, insert hook under second vertical loop, yo and draw loop through, *yo twice, insert hook through next 2 vertical loops tog, yo and draw loop through, yo and draw through 2 loops on hook, rep from * to last st, insert hook under last st, yo and draw loop through. *Row 2 (return)* Yo, draw through first loop on hook, *yo, draw through 2 loops on hook, rep from * to end. Rep row 2 (forward and return) to form patt.

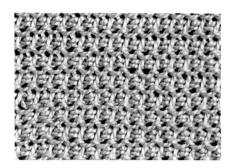

Reverse Tunisian stitch Make required number of ch. Work *Row 1 (forward and return rows)* as given for simple Tunisian stitch. *Row 2 (forward)* With yarn at front of work, insert hook through second vertical loop of last row, yo from back to front, draw through a loop and leave on hook, *ytf, insert hook through next vertical loop, yo from back to front, draw through loop, rep from * to end. *Row 2 (return)* Yo, draw through first loop on hook, *yo, draw through 2 loops on hook, rep from * to end. Rep row 2 (forward and return) to form patt.

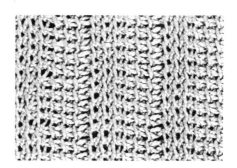

Triple rib Make required number of ch, a multiple of 6 + 1. Work *Row 1 (forward and return rows)* as given for simple Tunisian stitch. *Row 2 (forward)* Work alternately 3 simple Tunisian stitches, then 3 reverse Tunisian stitches to end of row. *Row 2 (return)* Yo, draw through first loop on hook, *yo, draw through 2 loops on hook, rep from * to end. Rep row 2 (forward and return) to form patt.

Butterfly stitch Make required number of ch, a multiple of 10 + 6. Work *Row 1 (forward and return rows)* as given for simple Tunisian stitch. *Rows 2 to 5* Work as simple Tunisian stitch. *Row 6 (forward)* *Work 5sT, (insert hook through center of st 4 rows below third st to left, draw a long loop through, insert hook back into next vertical loop of row 5, yo and draw through a long loop on hook – called Loop 1), [work 1sT, then Loop 1 through same st as before] twice, rep from * to last 5 sts, work 5sT. *Row 6 (return)* Yo, draw through first loop on hook, *yo, draw through 2 loops on hook, rep from * to end. *Rows 7 to 10* Work 5 rows simple Tunisian st. *Row 11 (forward)* Work 3sT, *[Loop 1, 1sT] twice, loop 1, work 5sT, rep from * to last 2 sts, work 2sT. *Row 11 (return)* Yo, draw through first loop on hook, *yo, draw through 2 loops on hook, rep from * to end. Rep rows 2 to 11 (forward and return) to form patt.

Scattered eyelet stitch Make required number of ch, a multiple of 6 + 4. Work *Row 1 (forward and return rows)* as given for simple Tunisian stitch. *Row 2 (forward)* Skip first st, [insert hook under vertical loop of next st, yo and draw loop through] 3 times, *yo twice, skip next 2 sts, [insert hook under vertical loop of next st, yo and draw loop through] 4 times, rep from * to end. *Row 2 and all return rows (return)* Yo, draw through first loop on hook, *yo, draw through 2 loops on hook, rep from * to end. *Row 3 (forward)* Work in simple Tunisian st. *Row 4 (forward)* Skip first st, insert hook under vertical loop of next st, yo and draw loop through, *yo twice, skip next 2 sts, [insert hook under vertical loop of next st, yo and draw loop through] 4 times, rep from * to last 6 sts, yo twice, skip next 2 sts, [insert hook under vertical loop of next st, yo and draw loop through] twice. *Row 5 (forward)* Work in simple Tunisian st. Rep rows 2 to 5 (forward) and return) to form patt.

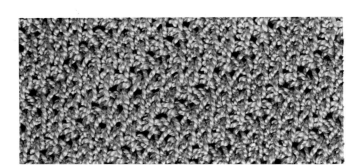

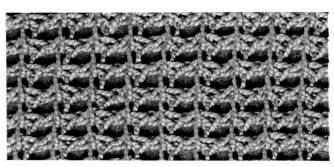

Diagonal stitch Make required number of ch, a multiple of 5. Work *Row 1 (forward and return rows)* as given for simple Tunisian stitch. *Row 2 (forward)* *Work 4sT (simple Tunisian), 1rT (reverse Tunisian), rep from * to end. *Row 2 and all return rows (return):* Yo, draw through first loop on hook, *yo, draw through 2 loops on hook, rep from * to end. *Row 3* 3sT, *1rT, 4sT, rep from * to last 2 sts, 1rT, 1sT. *Row 4* 2sT, *1rT, 4sT, rep from * to last 3 sts, 1rT, 2sT. *Row 5* 1sT, *1rT, 4sT, rep from * to last 4 sts, 1rT, 3sT. *Row 6* *1rT, 4sT, rep from * to end. Rep rows 2 to 6 (forward and return) to form patt.

Mesh stitch Make required number of ch, a multiple of 2 + 1. *Row 1 (forward)* *Yo, skip next ch, draw loop through next ch, rep from * to end. *Row 1 and all return rows (return)* Yo, draw through first loop on hook, *yo, draw through 2 loops on hook, rep from * to end. *Row 2 (forward)* *Yo, insert hook through vertical loop of next st, yo and draw loop through, rep from * to end. Rep row 2 (forward and return) to form patt.

Tunisian crochet

Simple grain of rice stitch   Double grain of rice stitch
Horizontal ridge stitch   Full Tunisian stitch
Tunisian stocking stitch

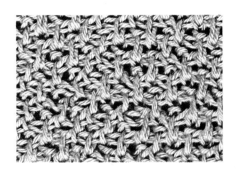

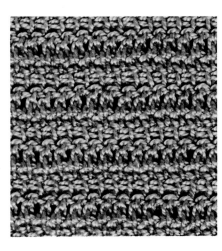

Simple grain of rice stitch Make required number of ch, a multiple of 2 + 1. Work *Row 1 (forward and return rows)* as given for simple Tunisian stitch. *Row 2 (forward)* *Work 1sT, 1rT, rep from * to end. *Row 2 (return)* Yo, draw through first loop on hook, *yo, draw through 2 loops on hook, rep from * to end. *Row 3 (forward)* *Work 1rT, 1sT, rep from * to end. *Row 3 (return)* Yo, draw through first loop on hook, *yo, draw through 2 loops on hook, rep from * to end. Rep rows 2 and 3 to form patt.

Horizontal ridge stitch Make required number of ch. Work *Row 1 (forward and return rows)* as given for simple Tunisian stitch. *Row 2 (forward)* Ch1, *yo, insert hook under vertical loop of next st, yo and draw through loop, yo and draw through first 2 loops on hook, rep from * to end. *Row 2 (return)* Yo, draw through first loop on hook, *yo, draw through 2 loops on hook, rep from * to end. *Row 3 (forward)* Work 1 row simple Tunisian st. *Row 3 (return)* Yo, draw through first loop on hook, *yo, draw through 2 loops on hook, rep from * to end. *Row 4 (forward)* *Insert hook below vertical loop of next st, yo and draw through a loop, rep from * to end. *Row 4 (return)* Yo, draw through first loop on hook, *yo, draw through 2 loops on hook, rep from * to end. Rep rows 2 to 4 (forward and return) to form patt.

NOTE **A Tunisian treble (Ttr) is worked as given for *Row 2 (forward)* in Horizontal ridge stitch (above), beginning at the asterisk.**

Double grain of rice stitch Make required number of ch, a multiple of 4 + 1. Work *Row 1 (forward and return rows)* as given for simple Tunisian stitch. *Row 2 (forward)* *Work 2sT, 2rT, rep from * to end. *Row 2 (return)* Yo, draw through first loop on hook, *yo, draw through 2 loops on hook, rep from * to end. *Row 3 (forward)* *Work 2rT, 2sT, rep from * to end. *Row 3 (return)* Yo, draw through first loop on hook, *yo, draw through 2 loops on hook, rep from * to end. Rep row 2 (forward and return) to form patt.

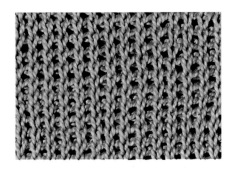

Tunisian stocking stitch Make required number of ch. Work *Row 1 (forward and return rows)* as given for simple Tunisian stitch. *Row 2 (forward)* *Insert hook from front to back through center of next st (between the 2 vertical loops), yo and draw loop through, rep from * to end. *Row 2 (return)* Yo, draw through first loop on hook, *yo, draw through 2 loops on hook, rep from * to end. Rep row 2 (forward and return) to form patt.

Full Tunisian stitch Make required number of ch. Work *Row 1 (forward and return rows)* as given for simple Tunisian stitch. *Row 2 (forward)* *Insert hook under horizontal thread between next 2 vertical loops, yo and draw loop through, rep from * to end, work last st into end vertical loop. *Row 2 (return)* Yo, draw through first loop on hook, *yo, draw through 2 loops on hook, rep from * to end. Rep row 2 (forward and return) to form patt.

Tunisian crochet

Slanting rib   English rib
Open fan stitch   Granite stitch
                 Cable pattern

Slanting rib Make required number of ch, a multiple of 6 + 1. Work *Row 1 (forward and return rows)* as given for simple Tunisian stitch. *Row 2 (forward)* *Work 3sT, 3rT, rep from * to end. *Row 2 (return)* Yo, draw through first loop on hook, *yo, draw through 2 loops on hook, rep from * to end. *Row 3 (forward)* Work 1rT, *3sT, 2rT, rep from * to last 5 sts, work 3sT, 2rT. *Row 3 (return)* Yo, draw through first loop on hook, *yo, draw through 2 loops on hook, rep from * to end. Continue working in this way, moving the patt over 1 st on every row to form diagonal patt.

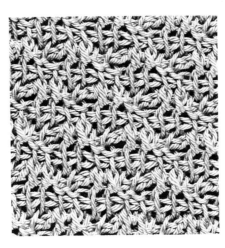

Granite stitch Make required number of ch, a multiple of 4 + 1. Work *Row 1 (forward and return rows)* as given for simple Tunisian stitch. *Row 2 (forward)* *Work 2sT, 2rT, rep from * to end. *Row 2 (return)* Yo, draw through first loop on hook, *yo, draw through 2 loops on hook, rep from * to end. *Row 3 (forward)* Work in simple Tunisian st. *Row 3 (return)* Yo, draw through first loop on hook, *yo, draw through 2 loops on hook, rep from * to end. *Row 4 (forward)* *Work 2rT, 2Ttr, rep from * to end. *Row 4 (return)* Yo, draw through first loop on hook, *yo, draw through 2 loops on hook, rep from * to end. *Row 5 (forward)* Work in simple Tunisian st. *Row 5 (return)* Yo, draw through first loop on hook, *yo, draw through 2 loops on hook, rep from * to end. *Row 6 (forward)* *Work 2Ttr, 2rT, rep from * to end. *Row 6 (return)* Yo, draw through first loop on hook, * yo, draw through 2 loops on hook, rep from * to end. Rep rows 3 to 6 (forward and return) to form patt.

English rib Make required number of ch, a multiple of 4 + 1. Work *Row 1 (forward and return rows)* as given for simple Tunisian stitch. *Row 2 (forward)* *Work 2sT, 2rT, rep from * to end. *Row 2 (return)* Yo, draw through first loop on hook, *yo, draw through 2 loops on hook, rep from * to end. Rep row 2 (forward and return) to form patt.

Open fan stitch Make required number of ch, a multiple of 4 + 1. Work *Row 1 (forward)* as given for simple Tunisian stitch. *Row 1 (return)* ch3, *yo and draw loop through first st on hook, yo, draw through 4 loops on hook, rep from * to end. *Row 2 (forward)* *Insert hook into top of 4 st group, yo and draw loop through [yo draw loop through next ch] 3 times, rep from * to end. *Row 2 (return)* Yo, draw through first loop on hook, *yo, draw through 2 loops on hook, rep from * to end. Rep row 2 (forward and return) to form patt.

Cable pattern Make required number of ch, a multiple of 6 + 1. *Row 1 (forward)* *Work 4sT, 2rT, rep from * to end. *Row 1 (return)* Yo, draw through first loop on hook, *yo, draw through 2 loops on hook, rep from * to end. *Rows 2 to 4 (forward and return)* As row 1. *Row 5 (forward)* *Skip next 2sT sts, work 1sT into each of next 2sT sts, crossing in front of last 2sts work 1sT into each of the 2 skipped sT sts, work 2rT, rep from * to end. *Row 5 (return)* Yo, draw through first loop on hook, *yo, draw through 2 loops on hook, rep from * to end. *Row 6 (forward and return)* As row 1. Rep rows 1 to 6 (forward and return) to form patt.

Tunisian crochet

Natalie stitch   Laura stitch
Julia stitch   Erica stitch

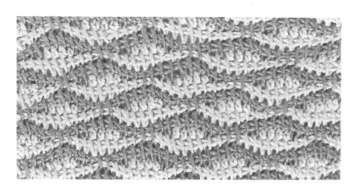

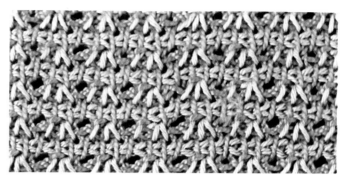

Natalie stitch In A make required number of ch, a multiple of 10 + 2. Work *Row 1 (forward and return rows)* in A, as given for simple Tunisian stitch. *Row 2 (forward)* In B, work 1Tss (insert hook through next loop but do not draw loop through), *work 2sT, 4Ttr, 2sT, 2Tss, rep from * to end. *Row 2 (return)* In B, yo, draw through first loop on hook, *yo, draw through 2 loops on hook, rep from * to end. *Row 3 (forward)* In A, work in simple Tunisian st. *Row 3 (return)* In A, yo, draw through first loop on hook, *yo, draw through 2 loops on hook, rep from * to end. *Row 4 (forward)* In B, work 2Ttr, *work 2sT, 2Tss, 2sT, 4Ttr, rep from * to end. *Row 4 (return)* In B, yo, draw through first loop on hook, *yo, draw through 2 loops on hook, rep from * to end. *Row 5 (forward)* In A, work in simple Tunisian st. *Row 5 (return)* In A, yo, draw through first loop on hook, *yo, draw through 2 loops on hook, rep from * to end. Rep rows 1 to 5 (forward and return) to form patt.

Laura stitch In A make required number of ch, a multiple of 4 + 1. Work *Row 1 (forward and return rows)* in A, as given for simple Tunisian stitch. *Row 2 (forward and return)* In A, work in simple Tunisian st. *Row 3 (forward)* In B, *insert hook through vertical loops of next 3 sts, yo and draw through a loop, then working into the third of the 3 loops only work 1sT and 1rT, 1sT into next loop, rep from * to end. *Row 3 (return)* In B, yo, draw through first loop on hook, *yo, draw through 2 loops on hook, rep from * to end. Rep rows 2 and 3 (forward and return) to form patt.

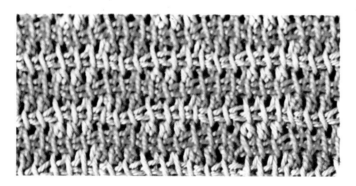

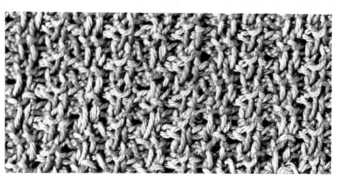

Julia stitch In A make required number of ch, a multiple of 6 + 1. Work *Row 1 (forward and return rows)* in A, as given for simple Tunisian stitch. *Row 2 (forward)* In B, *work 3Ttr, 3sT, rep from * to end. *Row 2 (return)* In B, yo, draw through first loop on hook, *yo, draw through 2 loops on hook, rep from * to end. *Row 3 (forward)* In A, *work 3sT, 3Ttr, rep from * to end. *Row 3 (return)* In A, yo, draw through first loop on hook, *yo, draw through 2 loops on hook, rep from * to end. Rep rows 2 and 3 (forward and return) to form patt.

Erica stitch In A make required number of ch, a multiple of 4 + 1. *Row 1 (forward)* In A, *work 2sT, 2rT, rep from * to end. *Row 1 (return)* In A, yo, draw through first loop on hook, *yo, draw through 2 loops on hook, rep from * to end. *Row 2 (forward)* In B, *work 2rT, 2sT, rep from * to end. *Row 2 (return)* In B, yo, draw through first loop on hook, *yo, draw through 2 loops on hook, rep from * to end. Rep rows 2 and 3 (forward and return) to form patt.

126

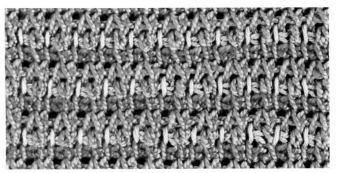

Nicola stitch In A make required number of ch, a multiple of 2 + 1. Work *Row 1 (forward and return rows)* in A, as given for simple Tunisian stitch. *Row 2 (forward)* In A, *insert hook through next 2 vertical loops, yo and draw loop through, insert hook into horizontal bar before next vertical loop, yo and draw loop through, rep from * to end. *Row 2 (return)* In B, yo, draw through first loop on hook, *yo, draw through 2 loops on hook, rep from * to end. *Row 3 (forward)* In B, work as given for row 2. *Row 3 (return)* In C, yo, draw through first loop on hook, *yo, draw through 2 loops on hook, rep from * to end. *Row 4 (forward)* In C, work as given for row 2. *Row 4 (return)* In A, yo, draw through first loop on hook, *yo, draw through 2 loops on hook, rep from * to end. Rep rows 2 to 4 (forward and return) to form patt.

Anna stitch In A make required number of ch, a multiple of 2 + 1. Work *Row 1 (forward and return rows)* in A, as given for simple Tunisian stitch. *Row 2 (forward)* In B, *skip next loop, work 1sT into next loop, rep from * to end. *Row 2 (return)* In B, yo, draw through 1 loop, *ch1, yo, draw through next 2 loops on hook, rep from * to last st, yo and draw through last 2 loops. *Row 3 (forward)* In C, *1sT into next loop, 1Ttr into ch1 sp, rep from * to last st, 1sT into last st. *Row 3 (return)* In C, yo, draw through first loop on hook, *yo, draw through 2 loops on hook, rep from * to end. *Row 4 (forward)* In A, 1sT into next loop, *insert hook through vertical loops of sT and Ttr, yo and draw through loop, rep from * to end. *Row 4 (return)* In A, yo and draw loop through 1 loop, *ch1, yo and draw through 2 loops, rep from * to last st, yo and draw through last 2 loops. Rep rows 2 to 4 (forward and return) to form patt.

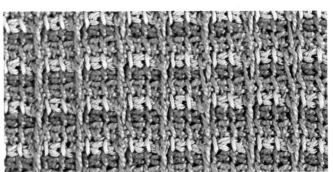

Gwendoline stitch In A make required number of ch, a multiple of 2 + 3. Work *Row 1 (forward and return rows)* in A, as given for simple Tunisian stitch. *Row 2 (forward)* In B, *yo, insert hook through next 2 vertical loops, yo and draw through loop, rep from * to last 2 sts, 1sT into each of last 2 loops. *Row 2 (return)* In C, yo, draw through first loop on hook, *yo, draw through 2 loops on hook, rep from * to end. *Row 3 (forward)* In C, work as given for row 2. *Row 3 (return)* In A, yo, draw through first loop on hook, *yo, draw through 2 loops on hook, rep from * to end. *Row 4 (forward)* In A, work as given for row 2. *Row 4 (return)* In B, yo, draw through first loop on hook, *yo, draw through 2 loops on hook, rep from * to end. Rep rows 2 to 4 (forward and return) to form patt.

Victoria stitch In A make required number of ch, a multiple of 3. Work *Row 1 (forward and return rows)* in A, as given for simple Tunisian stitch. *Row 2 (forward)* In B, *work 2sT, skip next loop, rep from * to last 2 loops, work 2sT. *Row 2 (return)* In B, yo and draw through 1 loop, yo and draw through 2 loops, ch1, *[yo and draw through 2 loops] twice, ch1, rep from * to last 3 sts, [yo and draw through 2 loops] 3 times. *Row 3 (forward and return)* In C, work as given for row 2. *Row 4 (forward)* In A, *work 2sT, 1Ttr into ch loop, rep from * to last 2 sts, 2sT. *Row 4 (return)* In A, yo, draw through first loop on hook, *yo, draw through 2 loops on hook, rep from * to end. Rep rows 2 to 4 (forward and return) to form patt.

INTRODUCTION TO EMBROIDERY & NEEDLEPOINT

This section introduces the fascinating craft of embroidery with a wide selection of beautiful stitches and techniques for decorative or practical purposes. It explains the basics of drawn thread work, smocking, appliqué and needlepoint to name just a few, and provides an invaluable stitch reference for those working their own designs.

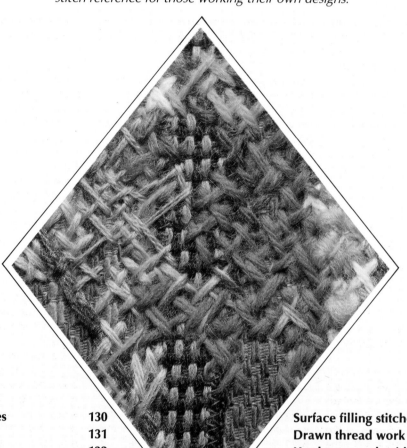

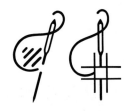

Embroidery is an exciting field to explore because of its sheer versatility. Depending on the technique and on the fabric and thread chosen, the result can be as delicate as a lacy tablecloth or as bold as a colorful wall hanging. It can be put to a practical purpose such as a hard-wearing needlepoint chair seat cover or it can be purely decorative, to enhance a collar or a child's dress for example.

The range of fabrics, threads and needles is extensive and it is important to use the correct combination for the results you want to achieve.

Fabrics Some embroidery stitches can be worked on practically any fabric from fine linen and cotton to silk, tulle, velvet and even felt. Certain techniques, however, have more specific requirements. Counted thread and drawn thread work must be done on an evenweave fabric, which has an equal number of warp and weft threads over a square inch.

Needlepoint is worked on canvas which is a firm material woven with either single or double threads. The number of threads (or double threads) to the inch varies from coarse rug canvas with $3\frac{1}{3}$ threads to the inch to fine canvas with 26 threads to the inch. Most needlepoint, however, is worked on canvas in the range of 12 to 20 threads to the inch. Plastic canvas is also available and, being more rigid, is useful for bags or boxes which do not then need to be backed.

Threads Some embroidery techniques require certain types of thread, whereas with others you can experiment to achieve different effects. Stranded cotton, pearl cotton and coton à broder are all shiny threads which can be used for free embroidery and for counted thread work. Stranded cotton is useful as it can be separated into six strands which can then be combined to achieve different thicknesses. Soft embroidery cotton is a matt cotton thread also suitable for free embroidery.

Woollen threads include crewel wool, tapestry wool and rug wool. Although needlepoint traditionally uses woollen threads, any embroidery thread can be used for special effects, including knitting yarns and even fine ribbon.

For sumptuous work such as gold work, there is a variety of metallic and silk threads available, including pure gold.

Needles It is important to use the correct needle for the type of embroidery you are working. The needle should be large enough to carry the thread through the fabric easily without distorting the woven threads.

All types of needles come in a range of sizes. Crewel and chenille needles have a sharp point and a large eye suitable for holding a variety of embroidery threads. For counted thread work and needlepoint, tapestry needles with blunt ends are necessary in order not to split the fabric threads. For sewing on beads, a special fine beading needle is required.

Frames Although some embroidery can be worked in the hand, the finished result is more satisfactory, with neater stitches, if the fabric is stretched in a frame. Ring frames are versatile and easy to use for embroidery. Different types are available – some can be hand-held, others clamped to a table or fixed to a floor stand. They consist of an inner ring and an adjustable outer ring which is tightened by means of a screw. Before using a ring frame, bind the inner ring with bias binding to protect the fabric.

Canvas may be mounted on a rectangular slate frame which has two cross bars and two side bars and is available in different sizes. It is tightened either by a screw method or by positioning pegs in peg holes, and can be held in the hand or mounted on a stand. Alternatively the fabric or canvas can simply be stretched over a plain wooden frame and tacked or stapled down.

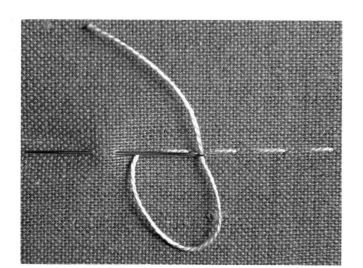

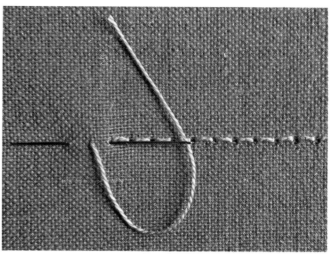

Running stitch Some embroidery stitches are used to outline motifs in a design. They can also be used in a decorative border. The easiest of these stitches, also used in plain sewing, is running stitch. Work from right to left in a straight line. The needle passes in and out of the fabric making a row of evenly spaced, even-sized stitches.

Backstitch *1* This stitch is also frequently used in plain sewing. In embroidery, it is mainly used to make an outline, or as a base line for other decorative stitches. One variation is to weave a thread of a different color through the stitches. Working from right to left, bring the needle through to the right side of the fabric and make a small backward stitch. Bring the needle out the same number of threads to the left. Continue in this way, always returning to the end of the previous stitch.

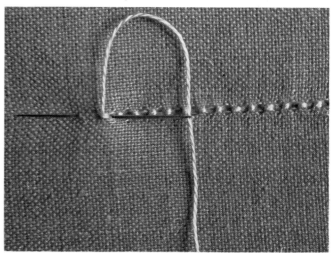

Backstitch *2* and Seeding Use a stepped backstitch to create geometric shapes with even-sized stitches. Small separate back-stitches can be used to fill spaces, giving the effect of scattered small dots. To make them more obvious go over each stitch twice, doubling them. This technique is called seeding.

Double backstitch Working from right to left, make a backstitch over three threads, bringing the needle out at the starting point. Work a second stitch over the first, bringing the needle out three threads to the left. Pull all stitches firmly. Continue in this way, forming a type of reinforced back stitch and pulled threads. This resembles a stitch used in drawn fabric work. It is the main variation of backstitch and is most often used for finishing off household linen such as tablecloths.

Stem stitches

Stem stitch	Threaded stem stitch
Alternating stem stitch	Darned stem stitch
Cable stem stitch	Whipped stem stitch

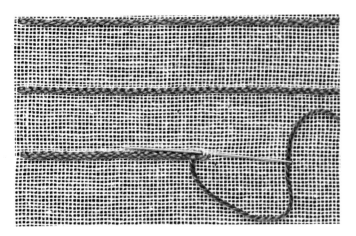

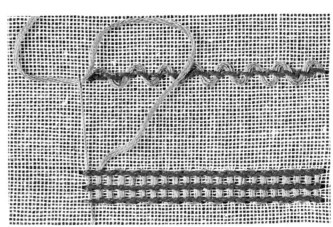

Stem stitch This is a widely used stitch as it is complementary to satin stitch and other filling stitches and is good for outlining and making curving lines. Working from left to right, pass the needle to the left under two or three threads of the fabric. Move along the line of the design to the right and make a second stitch to the left, picking up the same number of threads. The needle always emerges just above the previous stitch, giving the effect of a fine twisted cord.

Threaded stem stitch Work a row of ordinary stem stitch, then with a thread of a contrasting color, weave in and out of the stitches. Start by passing the thread under the first stitch from the top, and then under the second stitch from the bottom. Use a fine thread for the stem stitch and a thicker one for the undulating threading.

Darned stem stitch Sew three or more rows of ordinary stem stitch, one under the other. Then pass another thread up and down under alternate stitches. To achieve a relief effect, use threads of both different color and thickness.

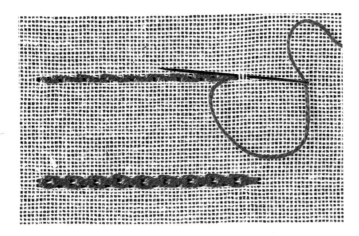

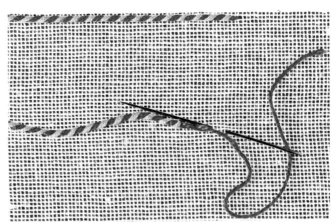

Alternating stem stitch Make a row of stem stitch with the needle emerging alternately above and below the previous stitch, giving a different effect from the twisted cord. Use a long stitch and a thick thread for a relief effect.

Cable stem stitch Make two rows of alternating stem stitch, so that the stitches lie together or apart alternately, giving a chain effect. This makes a pleasing border, and can also be worked in curves.

Whipped stem stitch Work a row of stem stitch using fairly long stitches. Then using a thread of a contrasting color, pass the needle through each stitch without going through the fabric. Work from left to right.

Curving whipped stem stitch Work a row of curving stem stitch, keeping the stitches diagonal by inserting the needle slightly lower with each stitch on a downward curve and the reverse on an upward curve. Working from left to right, whip these stitches with a contrasting color.

Chain stitches

Chain stitch   Zigzag chain stitch
Sloping chain stitch   Open chain stitch
Russian chain stitch   Lazy daisy or Detached chain stitch

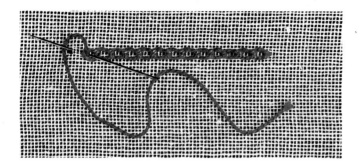

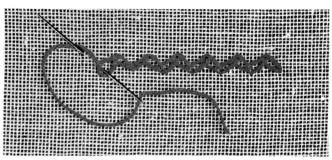

Chain stitch   Work from right to left. Bring the needle through to the right side of the fabric. Stitch into the same point, picking up several threads of the fabric, and loop the embroidery thread around the emerging point of the needle. Pull the needle through and make a second stitch, again catching the loop. Keep the stitches fairly loose.

Zigzag chain stitch   Work from right to left. Work simple chain stitches diagonally, one upward and one downward alternately. Make them of regular size and spacing.

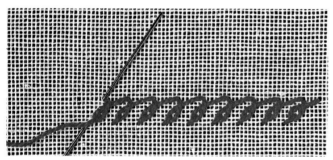

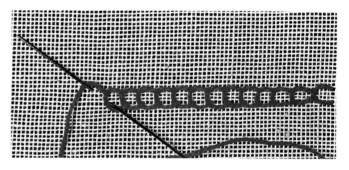

Sloping chain stitch   Working in a straight line, bring the thread through to the right side of the fabric. Stitch not into the same point, but several threads of the fabric to the left, leaving a loop. Bring the needle out diagonally downward, and wind the loop around the tip of the needle before pulling the thread through. Catch the loop with a small oblique stitch.

Open chain stitch   Work from right to left. This is similar to ordinary chain stitch, but instead of making the next stitch by stitching back into the same hole, stitch several threads of the fabric lower, inside the loop, slanting the needle up and forward. Loop the thread around the point of the needle.

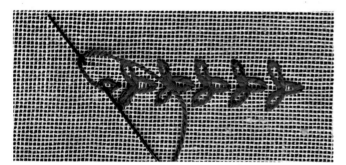

Russian chain stitch   This is a variation of simple chain stitch. Make an ordinary single chain stitch. Start the second stitch inside the loop, and catch it down with a tiny stitch to one side of the first stitch. Make a third stitch in the same way on the other side. Start a second group of three stitches to the left of the first, and continue to form a row.

Lazy daisy or Detached chain stitch   This is similar to Russian chain stitch and is used to make flowers and leaves. First decide how many petals a flower needs and use one chain stitch for each petal, catching it down with a tiny stitch. Work in a circle to complete the flower.

Chain stitches
Cable chain stitch
Interlaced cable chain stitch
Lock stitch

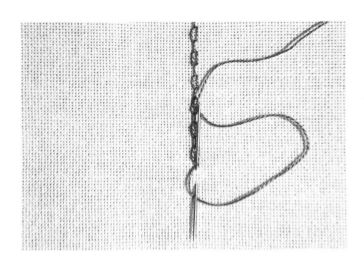

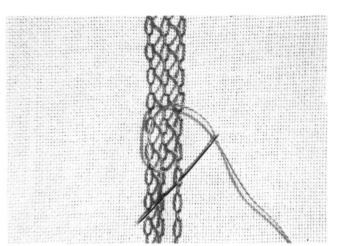

Cable chain stitch This stitch can be worked either as a straight line or in curves. Work vertically, from top to bottom. Bring the thread to the right side of the fabric and make a chain stitch. Place the thread in a left to right loop on the fabric. Pass the needle first under and then over the thread at the top of the loop, making a twist. Then insert the needle into the fabric to make the short linking stitch and bring it out again for the next chain stitch. Make the chain stitches double the length of the stitch in between.

Interlaced cable chain stitch This stitch can be used to cover an area of fabric. Work three or more rows of cable chain stitch, then decorate the rows with a thread of the same or a contrasting color by lacing through the corresponding loops of the first two rows. Repeat this process with the second and third rows etc, forming a network.

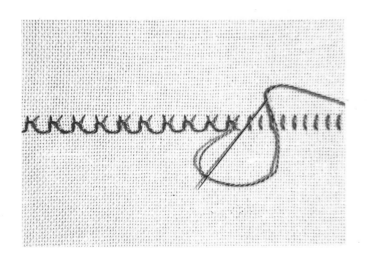

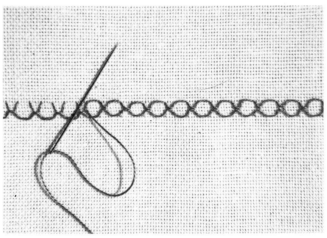

Lock stitch 1. This stitch is made in stages. The foundation, working from right to left, is to make a row of equally sized and spaced vertical stitches. The first stage is worked from left to right, starting at the base of the first stitch. Holding the thread in a loop below the sewing line, thread the needle under the vertical stitch from right to left and pull the thread taut. Work in the same way through the next vertical stitch, but with the thread held in a loop above the stitching. Continue to the end of the row.

2. Work from right to left in the second stage of the stitch. Repeat the previous stage in reverse, without turning the work.

133

Buttonhole and Blanket stitches

Blanket stitch   Cording
Buttonhole stitch   Padded scallop stitch
Scallop stitch

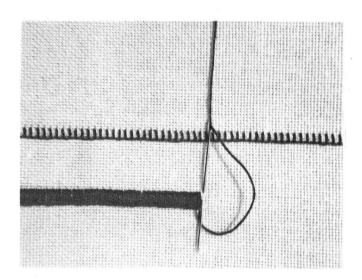

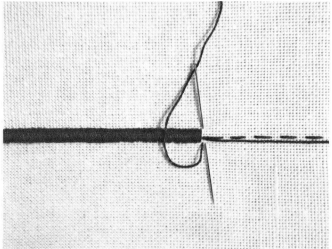

Blanket stitch and Buttonhole stitch These stitches are made in the same way, but blanket stitch is more widely spaced than buttonhole stitch. Working from left to right, bring the thread through to the right side of the fabric on the base line. Make a loop with the thread and hold it in position with the thumb. Stitch from above, and downward to the base line. Pull the thread through, tightening the loop.

Cording Working in two stages, first make a row of running stitches as a guide line and lay a thicker thread alongside as a filling. Then complete the cording by stitching over the running stitches and filling thread with small, very close, vertical stitches, so that they are completely covered.

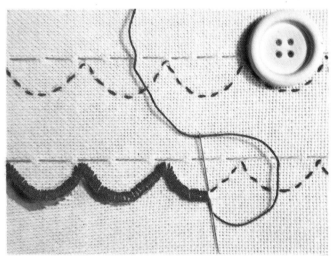

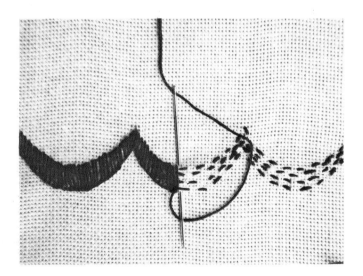

Scallop stitch This stitch is used to give a finishing touch to the edge of a piece of work. Make a straight line of running stitches, and placing a button on the line, mark around it to give regular scallop shapes. Working over this guide line, use short, close buttonhole stitches to outline the shapes. Cut off the excess fabric very carefully.

Padded scallop stitch This is used in scallop-shaped patterns. Mark out the scallops on the right side of the fabric and fill them with rows of running stitch to make a filling for the completed shape. With buttonhole stitches of varying lengths, cover the shapes exactly.

Buttonhole and Blanket stitches

Closed blanket stitch	Two colour blanket stitch
Boat stitch	Loop stitch
Crossed blanket stitch	Woven blanket stitch

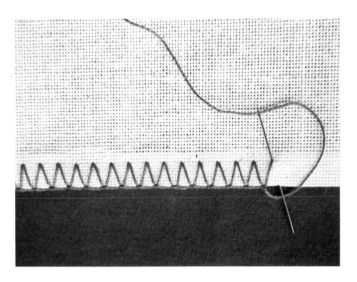

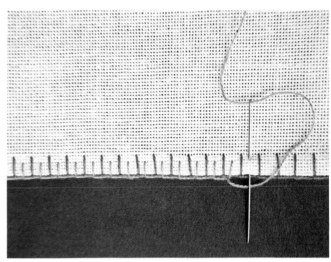

Closed blanket stitch Blanket stitches can add a decorative element to a ready folded and tacked hem, and can be used instead of ordinary hemming. Closed blanket stitch is worked from left to right. Bring the thread through to the right side of the fabric at the hem edge and stitch up to the right. Come out again down to the left. Go in at the top of the stitch again and stitch down to the right. Repeat these two stitches, keeping the thread under the needle.

Two color blanket stitch This is two rows of blanket stitch, one over the other. Sew the first row in one color keeping the stitches about $\frac{3}{16}$ in) apart. With the second color work along the same row between the existing stitches, but using shorter stitches. The same method can be used with more than two colors by making the distance between each color greater.

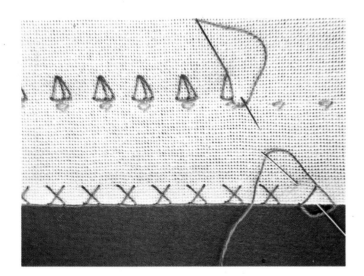

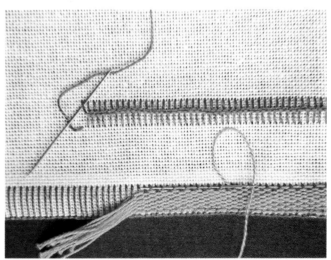

Boat stitch The sails of the boat are made by working three blanket stitches into the same starting point. The boat itself is made with straight stitches.

Crossed blanket stitch Bring the thread through to the right side of the work and stitch diagonally to the right. The next stitch, which is diagonally to the left, starts to the left of the first stitch with the needle emerging to the right. Keep the thread held under the needle.

Loop stitch Working from right to left, bring the needle up at the center line. Insert it up and to the left, and bring out vertically below. Pass the needle under the previous stitch as shown.

Woven blanket stitch Make a row of blanket stitch with closely-worked long stitches. Using the same color or a contrasting one, darn rows of threads over and under the blanket stitch to give a woven effect.

Feather stitches

Feather stitch   Straight feather stitch   Double feather stitch   Fly stitch
Single feather stitch   Closed feather stitch   Triple feather stitch   Arrow stitch

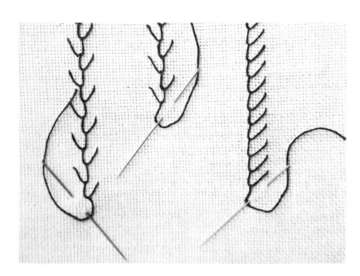

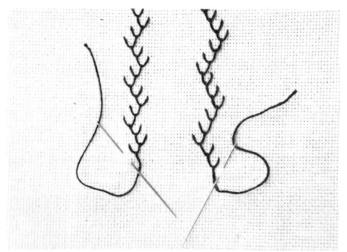

Feather stitch Working from top to bottom, pick up several threads of the fabric to the left, holding the needle obliquely and stitching toward the center with the thread under the needle. Repeat this to the right and continue in the same way.

Single feather stitch This is done in the same way as feather stitch, but working only to one side, left or right, holding the thread at the center. It gives the effect of sloping blanket stitch.

Double feather stitch Work as for feather stitch, making alternately two stitches to the left and two to the right, giving the effect of a sloping, alternating blanket stitch.

Triple feather stitch This is done in the same way as double feather stitch, but working three stitches to the left and three to the right, instead of two.

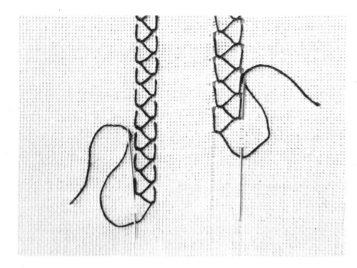

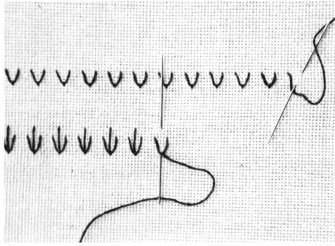

Straight feather stitch This is worked in the same way as feather stitch, but holding the needle vertically when making the left and right-hand stitches.

Closed feather stitch This is worked in the same way as straight feather stitch, but without leaving spaces between the stitches. It can be used on drawn thread work.

Fly stitch Working from left to right, bring the needle out at the left, insert again several threads to the right and out at the bottom center of the stitch, keeping the thread under the needle. Finish with a small stitch to hold.

Arrow stitch This is a variation of fly stitch. Make a fly stitch, catching the thread at the center, and stitching up and out again, finishing at bottom center.

Knotted stitches

Coral stitch	Zigzag coral stitch
French knots	Knotted buttonhole stitch
Scroll stitch	Bullion stitch

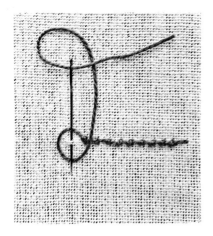

Coral stitch (left) This stitch is worked from right to left. Bring the thread through to the right side of the fabric, then make a small vertical stitch a little to the left, making sure that the thread passes under the point of the needle from left to right. Pull gently to the left to form a knot.

Zigzag coral stitch (right) Proceed as for the previous stitch, working the stitches one upward and one downward, making a zigzag pattern. When tightening the stitch, always hold the thread in the direction of the next stitch, alternately up and down.

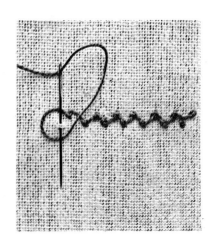

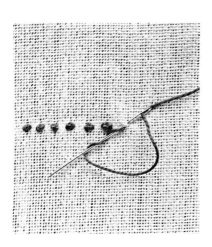

French knots (left) Bring the thread through to the right side of the fabric. Take a tiny diagonal stitch, without pulling the needle through. Wind the thread around the needle two or three times and draw the needle through the knot. Stitch back into the fabric near the starting point, pulling the knot tight.

Knotted buttonhole stitch (right) Work from left to right. Bring the needle through to the right side of the fabric and pick up one thread of the fabric to the right, passing the needle through the loop. Tighten the stitch. Make a second stitch over the first, picking up more threads.

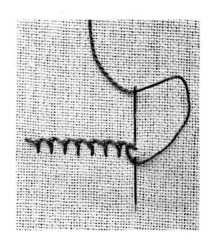

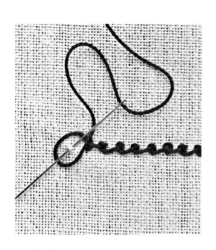

Scroll stitch (left) Work from right to left. Bring the needle through to the right side of the fabric, loop the thread as shown and stitch obliquely downward, picking up one or two threads inside the loop. Draw the thread through to the left, without making the stitches too tight.

Bullion stitch (right) Make a backstitch, the size of the bullion stitch required, and bring the needle point out where it first emerged, without pulling it right through. Wind the thread round the needle point as many times as required. Holding the left thumb on the coiled thread, pull the needle through. Still holding the coiled thread, turn the needle back to where it was inserted and insert in the same place. Pull the needle through.

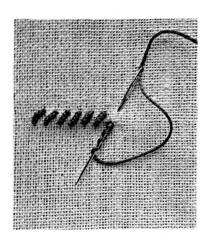

137

Herringbone stitches

Herringbone stitch   Double back stitch
Closed herringbone stitch   Right angles in closed herringbone stitch
Shadow work border   Shadow work with fringing

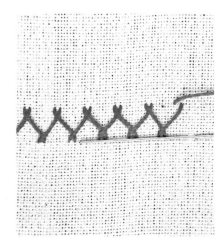

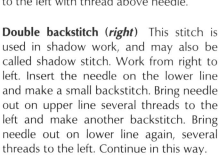

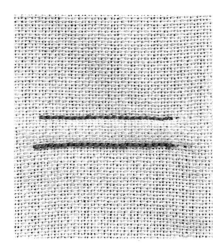

Herringbone stitch (left) Bring the needle out on the lower line at the left-hand side and insert on the upper line to the right, taking a stitch to the left with thread below needle. Next, insert the needle on the lower line to the right and take a stitch to the left with thread above needle.

Double backstitch (right) This stitch is used in shadow work, and may also be called shadow stitch. Work from right to left. Insert the needle on the lower line and make a small backstitch. Bring needle out on upper line several threads to the left and make another backstitch. Bring needle out on lower line again, several threads to the left. Continue in this way.

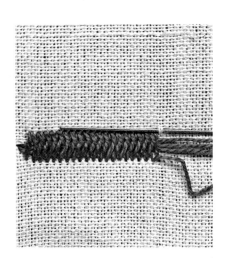

Closed herringbone stitch (left) This is the reverse side of double backstitch. Work on the back of the fabric as for herringbone stitch, but leaving no space between the stitches. If a more obvious result is required for the shadow work, work the herringbone stitch over several threads laid the length of the row.

Right angles in closed herringbone stitch (right) Work a horizontal row of closed herringbone stitch as usual. To turn the corner, at the right angle, reduce the size of the inner stitches, but not the outer ones. When the right angle is completed, continue to work normally.

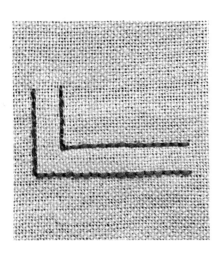

Fringed shadow work Shadow work may be used to form a border around a tablecloth or mat. To finish the edge attractively, fringing can be used. First work the border and corners in double backstitch (**left**). Trim the fabric leaving enough extra all around for the fringe. Next, pull the horizontal threads from around the edge. The vertical threads form the fringe (**right**).

Herringbone stitches
Double herringbone stitch
Interlaced herringbone stitch
Closed herringbone as filling stitch

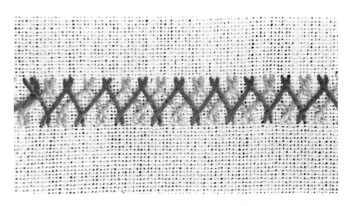

Double herringbone stitch Working from left to right, make a row of simple herringbone stitch. Then, with a different color, work a second row over the first so that the stitches alternate, using the free spaces.

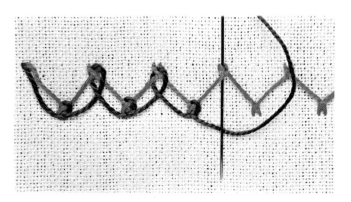

Interlaced herringbone stitch Working from left to right, make a row of simple herringbone stitch. Then, with a contrasting color, thread under the crossed stitch on the top line, and then on the bottom line, keeping the thread below the point of the needle. This stitch can be used in straight rows or to decorate a border.

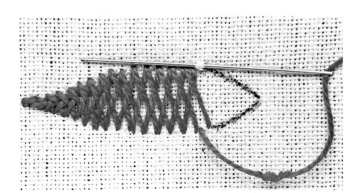

Closed herringbone as a filling stitch *1* This is used to fill shapes with a curved outline, such as flower petals, leaves etc. In order to cover the area of the shape well, the stitches must be worked very closely, so that each new stitch touches the previous one.

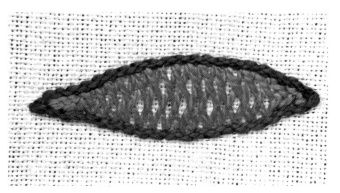

Closed herringbone as a filling stitch *2* Fill in the area of the shape with closed herringbone stitch, as before. Then for greater impact, outline it in stem stitch, either in the same or in a contrasting color.

Pekinese and Cretan stitches

Pekinese stitch   Interlaced Pekinese stitch
Cretan stitch   Open Cretan stitch

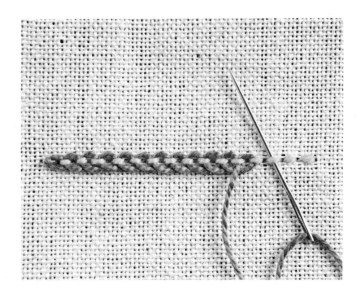

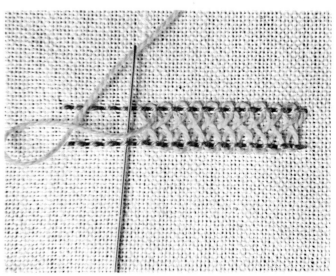

Pekinese stitch This is worked in two stages. First, make a row of fairly large backstitches. Then, working from left to right, loop a second thread through the bottom of the second stitch, back through the top of the first, up through the third and back down through the second, and so on. Pull the loops slightly to tighten them. Two colors or two thicknesses of thread can be used.

Interlaced Pekinese stitch Work two rows of fairly long back-stitches. Working from right to left, pass the needle under the first stitch in the bottom row, and up through the second stitch in the top row. Pass the needle back down through the first stitch on the top row and under the third stitch on the bottom row. Pass up through the second stitch on the bottom row and up through the third stitch on the top row, then back down and under the second stitch on the top row, and so on.

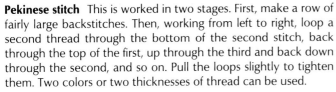

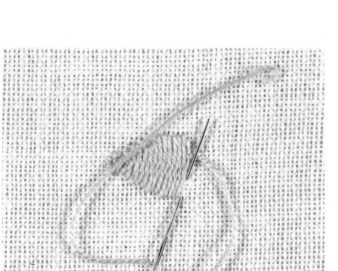

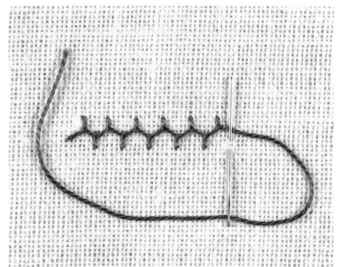

Cretan stitch This is useful for filling small shapes. Work from left to right. Bring the thread through at the bottom left of the shape and take the needle back through at the top of the shape, making a small stitch toward the center with the needle pointing inward and the thread under the needle. Then take the needle through at the bottom of the shape, making another small stitch toward the center with the needle pointing inward and the thread under the needle as shown above. Continue in this way until the shape is filled.

Open Cretan stitch This is a useful border stitch. It is worked in the same way as Cretan stitch but, whereas this stitch follows the outlines of a shape, Open Cretan stitches are all the same height and are spaced at regular intervals.

Straight stitches
Free straight stitching
Tied straight stitching
Interlaced back stitch

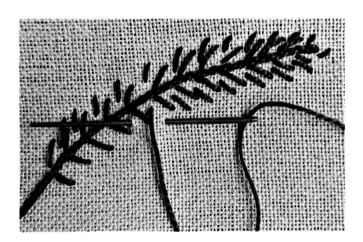

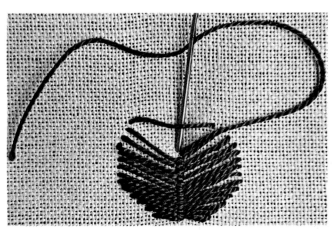

Free straight stitching This is frequently used in floral designs to create the effect of foliage, and can be used in conjunction with the other stitches, such as stem stitch. It can be worked regularly or randomly, and the stitches can vary in length.

Tied straight stitching This can be used to fill leaf and petal shapes. Make a long stitch from left to right, bringing the needle out in the center of the shape, one or two threads lower down. Then make a short couching stitch over the long one to hold it down, as shown. Bring the needle out at the left of the shape again, slightly higher up, and make another long stitch to the right. Hold this down with a short couching stitch and so on.

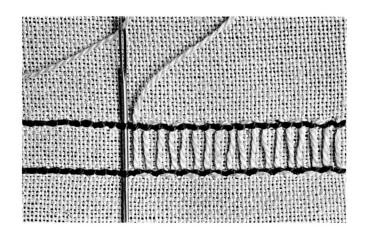

Interlaced backstitch Work two parallel lines of backstitch. With another thread of a contrasting color, pass the needle up and under, then down and under the stitches of alternate backstitch rows.

Motifs using interlaced backstitch This stitch can be used to fill in areas of embroidered motifs such as the wings and body of these decorative beetles. The lines of backstitch need not be parallel – they can curve, as here.

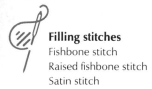
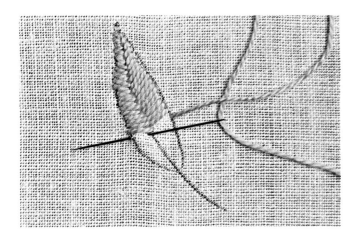

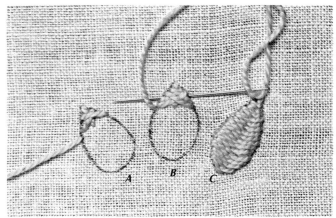

Fishbone stitch Bring the thread through at the top left of the shape. Make a sloping stitch across the central line. Bring the thread through opposite the first stitch, on the right of the shape, and make a similar sloping stitch to overlap the first stitch. Continue working alternately on each side until the shape is filled.

Raised fishbone stitch Bring the thread through just down from the top center of the shape. Stitch into the top point. Come out down to the left and go in on the right, very close to the top. Come out again on the left and stitch down to the right to form two crossed stitches. Come out again on the left (***A***). Stitch up to the right (***B***), and come out to the left. Continue until the shape is filled (***C***).

Satin stitch 1. Working from left to right, bring the thread through on the lower edge of the shape and stitch into the opposite edge. Come out to the right of the first stitch, at a distance equal to the thickness of the thread being used, and stitch into the top edge in the same way.

2. Cover the entire surface of the shape. To achieve the smooth satin effect characteristic of this stitch, take care that the stitches are very even. To cover a large area, use an embroidery frame or ring, to ensure an even tension.

Padded stitches
Padded satin stitch   Circular padding
Double padding   Crossed padding

Padded satin stitch This is often used when working flowers and leaves. The relief effect is created by first working a thick, regular running stitch around the outline of a shape and then filling the center with closely scattered stitches. Having worked this padding, cover it with satin stitch.

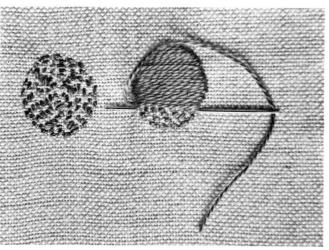

Circular padding When working circles with this method, the finished shape needs to be perfect, so it is necessary to use an embroidery frame. Outline the shape in running stitch and then fill the center, staggering the stitches in each row. Finally, cover the shape with satin stitch, following the outline.

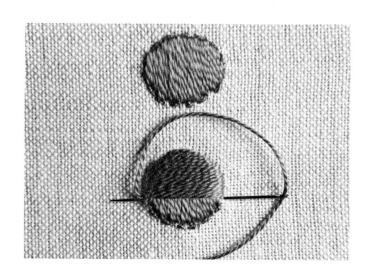

Double padding Use an embroidery frame when working circular shapes. Outline the shape with running stitch and then fill the center with vertical rows of satin stitch. Next, cover the padding with satin stitch worked horizontally, following the outline precisely.

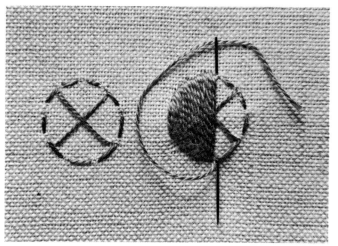

Crossed padding This is used when the circles to be covered are small. Outline the shape in running stitch, then pad the center by using straight stitches worked one over the other to form a cross. Cover the shape with satin stitch, carefully following the outline.

Shading stitches

Long and short satin stitch   Split satin stitch
Block shading   Outline satin stitch

Long and short satin stitch As with all filling stitches, it is best to use a frame. Bring the needle through on the upper edge of the motif and, following the outline, make a row of alternately long and short stitches in toward the center. Work the second row with stitches of equal length, fitting them into the stitches of the previous row. Continue working in this way until the motif is covered, combining various shades of color to give a pleasing natural effect.

Split satin stitch Bring the thread through a short distance from the top of the motif and stitch back into the top. Bring the needle out a little way below this stitch and take it back through the center of the first stitch, thus splitting it. Continue in this way. At the opposite edge of the motif, turn the work and proceed in the other direction.

Block shading When marking the design on the fabric, divide it into concentric or parallel sections. The sections are worked one after the other, either covering the surface of the design or leaving unstitched spaces between them. Start work in the outer section of the design, stitching inward. Work toward the center of the design on the following sections, interlocking the stitches very slightly with those of the previous row.

Outline satin stitch Work around the outline of the design, stitching inward with a series of straight stitches of varying lengths to give a delicate effect. Use a thread with a sheen and soft colors for the best results.

Filling stitch variations
Roumanian couching   Brocade stitch
Roumanian stitch   Double buttonhole stitch

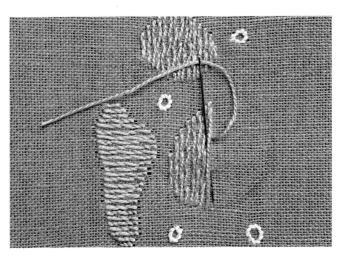

Roumanian couching Work from left to right. Bring the thread through at the bottom of the motif and stitch into the top, coming out on the right three or four threads below. Make a small oblique tying stitch over the laid thread, coming out four or five threads down. Continue like this, covering the laid thread with little stitches.

Brocade stitch This is a variation of the previous stitch. The method is the same; the laid thread is covered with small oblique tying stitches, but a small space is left between the laid threads so that each stitch is separate from the next. The finished effect is of old, worn brocade.

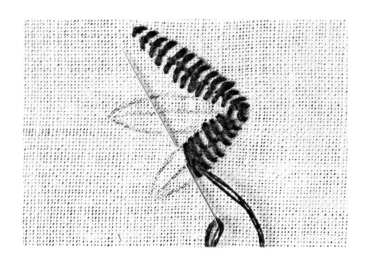

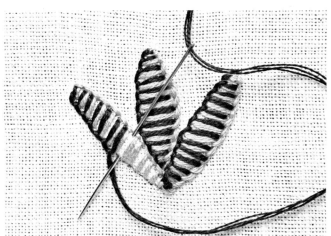

Roumanian stitch Bring the thread through at the top edge of the motif. Stitch to the opposite edge and come out on the center line to the right of the first stitch. Make a small tying stitch, bringing the needle out again at the top edge of the motif. Continue in this way.

Double buttonhole stitch This can be used as a covering stitch on small designs, such as leaves and petals. Work two rows of interlocking buttonhole stitch, one along the lower edge, and the second along the opposite edge, fitting into the spaces left by the first row. On the second row it is easier to turn the work so that the working edge is always the lower one.

Cross stitches

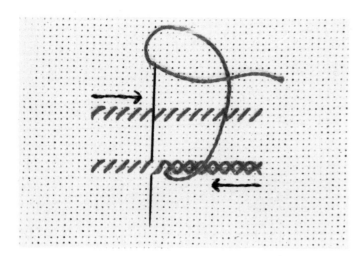

Cross stitch worked in two stages The first stage is worked from left to right and the second from right to left. Bring the thread through to the right side of the fabric, and make a diagonal stitch up to the right over the required number of threads. Stitch down over an equal number of threads and continue in this way until the row is completed. On the return row, repeat the process in reverse, completing the crosses.

Spaced cross stitch Work in two stages, spacing the crosses as required. Having decided how far apart the stitches should be, work a row of diagonal stitches of equal size from left to right. Complete the crosses on the return row from right to left, making sure that the stitches are the same size.

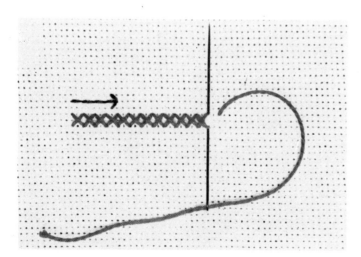

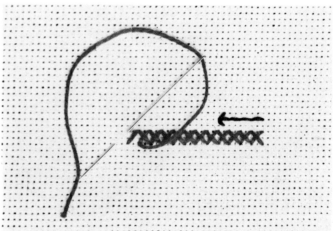

Cross stitch worked from the left Bring the thread through to the right side of the fabric. Stitch diagonally down to the left, coming out vertically, level with the top of the stitch. Stitch diagonally to the right into the lower stitching line, completing the cross. Next, stitch diagonally to the right to start the second cross.

Cross stitch worked from the right Bring the thread through to the right side of the fabric, and stitch diagonally up to the right. Come out vertically downward and complete the cross by stitching diagonally up to the left. Come out diagonally down to the left and start the second stitch.

Cross stitches
Two-sided insertion stitch   One-sided insertion stitch
Montenegrin cross stitch   Long-armed cross stitch

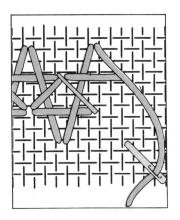 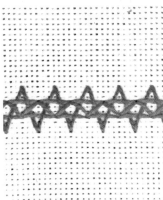

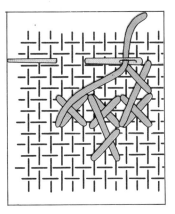 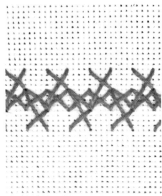

Two-sided insertion stitch Stitch diagonally up over nine threads and three to the right. Come out down to the right with a diagonal stitch on the reverse of the fabric, three threads in height and width. Stitch horizontally to the left over six threads. Come out at the top of the first long stitch. Go in again six threads to the right of the base of the first stitch and come out up to the left with a diagonal on the reverse of the fabric, three threads in height and width as shown above. Make a diagonal up to the left over three threads, coming out at the beginning of the same stitch. Make another diagonal to the right, again over three threads, coming out at the beginning of the same stitch. Then make a horizontal stitch over six threads to the right. Come out at the base of the second long diagonal. Starting from this point, make the next long diagonal to the right.

One-sided insertion stitch Make a diagonal stitch up to the right over three threads in height and width. Come out horizontally three threads to the left and stitch diagonally down to complete the simple cross. Come out horizontally three threads to the left, then make a long diagonal up to the right, three threads wide and six high. Come out horizontally three threads to the left. Complete the irregular cross down to the right, going in at the top of the first stitch. Come out six threads horizontally to the left. Make the second simple cross, coming out at the top left to make the long arm of the irregular cross, six threads down and three to the right. Come out horizontally left and stitch diagonally up to the right to complete the irregular cross. Come out six threads to the left to make the third simple cross and so on.

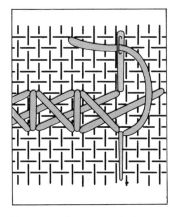 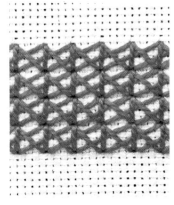

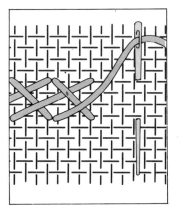 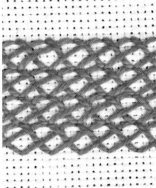

Montenegrin cross stitch Work in rows from left to right. Bring the needle through to the right side of the fabric and make a diagonal stitch to the right over eight vertical and four horizontal threads. Come out four threads to the right of the base of the first stitch and make a diagonal stitch up to the left over four threads. Come out at the beginning of the same stitch. Stitch vertically upward over four threads, again coming out at the same point as before. Start the next stitch by making a second long diagonal to the right.

Long-armed cross stitch Work in rows from left to right. Bring the needle through to the right side of the fabric and stitch up to the right over eight vertical and four horizontal threads. Come out four threads vertically downward. Stitch diagonally up to the left over four threads in height and width and come out four threads vertically downward. Begin the second stitch by making another long diagonal.

Holbein or Double running stitch
Holbein stitch border
Holbein stitch motifs
Holbein stitch variations

Holbein or Double running stitch border This is made up of a double line of running stitch worked in two stages. The finished effect is like backstitch. Work the first row from left to right. Following the pattern on a chart, make a line of equally spaced running stitches (the stitches must be the same length as the space between them). For the second row, work in the same way from right to left, filling in the spaces left in the first row until the starting point is reached.

Holbein or Double running stitch motifs This shows two completed motifs worked in Holbein stitch on evenweave fabric. Although they are made up of straight stitches, the flower petals look as though they have a curved outline. Use an embroidery frame for Holbein stitch and pull the thread up gently when working so as not to distort the fabric. Holbein stitch is used in the technique called Assisi work described on the opposite page.

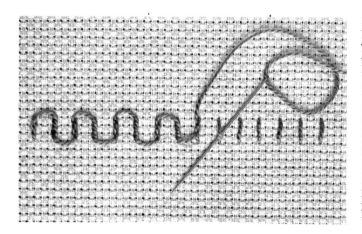

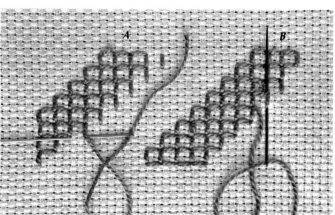

Holbein stitch variation 1 This can be worked in straight or curved lines. Working from right to left, bring the thread through to the right side of the work and, holding the needle pointing horizontally left, make a vertical stitch upward. Come out three fabric threads away to the left. Now make a vertical stitch downwards, again coming out three threads away to the left. Continue to the end of the row. Work the second row from left to right, passing the needle under the bars without picking up the fabric threads. Come out at the center right of the first bar and pass the needle under the bar from right to left and upward. Then pass the needle under the second bar from right to left and downward. Repeat to the end of the row.

Holbein stitch variation 2 This looks similar to four-sided stitch, but is worked in two diagonal stages, top to bottom, then bottom to top. Being double-sided, it is also useful on fine or transparent fabrics. In stage **A**, work a series of vertical stitches diagonally downward to the left as shown, bringing the needle out horizontally each time to begin the next stitch. At the end of the row, begin the second stage, **B**. This time work a series of horizontal stitches diagonally upward, bringing the needle out vertically each time to begin the next stitch. This completes the row of squares.

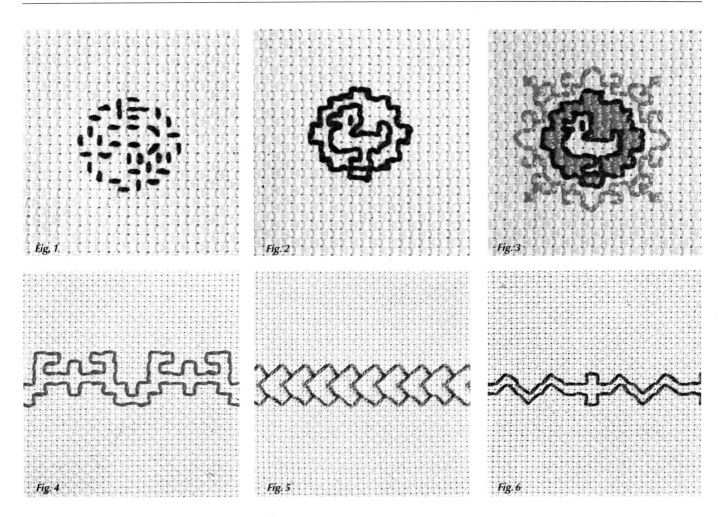

Fig. 1

Fig. 2

Fig. 3

Fig. 4

Fig. 5

Fig. 6

This distinctive form of embroidery takes its name from the town of Assisi in Italy where it has its origins. The stylized animals, birds and other motifs characteristic of this type of work are inspired by ancient embroideries which are still carefully preserved in the churches of the area, and also by designs found in other works of art such as mosaics, marble sculptures, wood carvings and inlay work. The method of embroidery used to produce these bold designs set inside geometric borders has remained unchanged over the centuries.

Materials The fabric used for this form of embroidery must have an even weave.

The thread used to work the filling around the shapes is traditionally blue or rust, and that for the outline is black.

Method The work is done in three stages; the outline, the filling and the finishing off. Following the design on a chart, work the first row of Holbein stitch (**Fig. 1**) as described on the opposite page.

Return along the row of stitching filling in the gaps, passing under the previous stitches and making sure that the outline of the design is continuous. The outline is worked in black to contrast with the filling (**Fig. 2**).

Having finished the outline, start the filling in cross stitch worked in two stages, first in one direction and then in the other (**Fig. 3**).

Make sure that the stitching on the reverse of the fabric is as perfect as that on the right side.

Figs. 4, 5 and 6 show examples of linear patterns used in Assisi work.

Finishing off the work with a decorative hem is important. The hem should be as narrow as possible, giving a corded effect. It is made by rolling the fabric between the thumb and forefinger of the left hand while work is in progress. The hems are often decorated with regular slanting oversewing stitches and the corners of the finished cloth are sometimes decorated with little tassels.

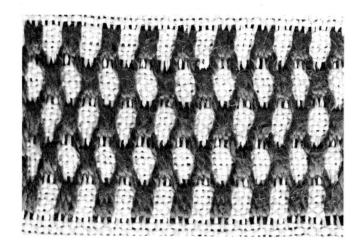

Threaded satin stitch This stitch is worked in two stages: the first makes the vertical satin stitch blocks and the second the zigzag lines. To begin with, work a row of satin stitch blocks, each made up of three bars worked over six threads of fabric. Leave four threads of fabric between each block. On the return row, work the blocks so they alternate with those in the first row. Continue until the surface of the work is covered in this way. Move on to the second stage. Bring the needle through on the right hand side of the work and pass it horizontally under the first satin stitch block from right to left without picking up the fabric. Then pass the needle under the next block in the row above, then under the next block in the first row and so on.

Zigzag filling stitch Work in two rows, one going from left to right and the other returning from right to left. Bring the needle through to the right side of the fabric and make a diagonal stitch five threads down and five to the left. Come out five threads to the right of the top of the first stitch. Stitch down again, five threads to the right of the base of the first stitch. Continue like this, making a row of small diagonal stitches. Work the following row below the first. Make the second part of the zigzag, stitching up and to the left, going in at the base of the stitches in the previous row.

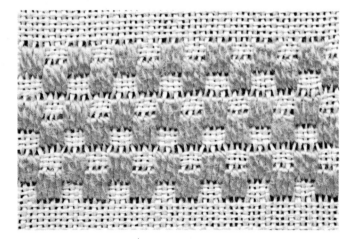

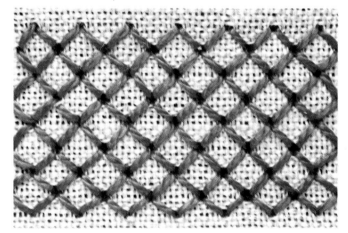

Basket filling stitch This is worked in two stages, each going from left to right. Bring the needle through to the right side of the fabric and stitch vertically up over six threads. Work another three stitches in this way on successive threads to make a block of four stitches. Move five threads to the right and work another block of stitches. Complete the row in this way. Turn the work and start the second stage, again moving from left to right. Work blocks of satin stitch as before, fitting them into the spaces left by the previous row and overlapping by three fabric threads. Work the third row the same as the first.

Squared filling stitch This stitch creates the effect of squares on the diagonal and is worked in rows from left to right and vice versa. Bring the needle through to the right side of the fabric and stitch diagonally up to the right, four threads up and four along. Come out on the lower line eight threads to the right. Now make a stitch up to the left, going in at the top of the preceding stitch. Bring the needle out at the base of the stitch just worked. Repeat the stitch to the right and then to the left to form a zigzag line. Work the return row below, so the zigzag points coincide to form the squares. The third row is started eight threads below, with another zigzag line.

Surface filling stitches
Reversing 'V' stitch   Eye stitch
Triangle filling stitch   Star squares

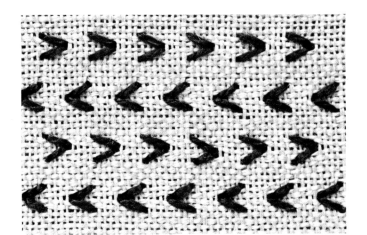

Reversing 'V' stitch Work each row in two stages. For the first row, begin working from left to right. Stitch diagonally down over two threads and over four to the right. Work a second stitch in the same way, beginning eight threads to the right, and so on to the end of the row. The return row from right to left completes the 'V' with the diagonal stitches sloping the other way. The third row is worked in the same way as the second from right to left, staggering the stitches as shown.

Eye stitch Work in horizontal rows. Bring the needle through to the right side of the fabric, stitch vertically up over three threads and come out again at the base of the same stitch. Stitch up to the left, over a diagonal of three threads and come out again at the same point; in the same way stitch horizontally to the left over three threads, diagonally down to the left, vertically down, diagonally down to the right, horizontally to the right, and diagonally up to the right, always over three threads. Having made the first eye, start a second, twelve threads to the right. On the return row, alternate the eyes with those in the first.

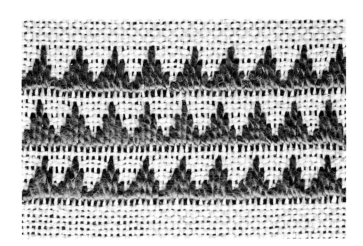

Triangle filling stitch Work in rows, from left to right and right to left. Bring the thread through to the right side of the fabric and make a vertical stitch up over two threads. Come out on the base line one thread to the right and stitch up again, this time over four threads and then over six and eight threads. Complete the triangle by stitching over six, four and two threads. Then work the next triangle as before. Work the return row from right to left in the same way.

Star squares Begin at top left of the motif. Bring the needle through to the right side of the fabric and stitch down over three threads, then diagonally left over three threads, and horizontally left over three threads, always stitching back into the same point. Come out three vertical threads down and stitch back into the same point. Come out diagonally down, three threads to the left to begin the second star. Stitch horizontally, diagonally, vertically and then horizontally again to make the second star, always working over three threads. Make the third and fourth stars in the same way. This completes one motif.

Surface filling stitches
Block and diamond filling stitch   Trellis filling stitch
Star network   Basketweave filling stitch

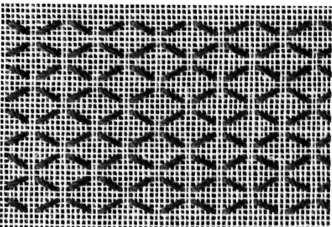

Block and diamond filling stitch First make a network of small, parallel, diagonal stitches over two threads of the fabric. These form small diamonds where the lines intersect. Inside the resulting spaces work satin stitch rectangles eight threads high and nine stitches wide.

Trellis filling stitch This background is very simple, and gives an effective result. One color only is used. Work horizontal rows, angling one stitch to the right and then one to the left, over two threads in height and four in width. In the following row alternate the slope of the stitches.

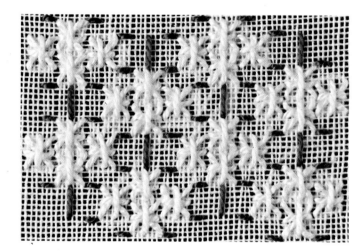

Star network First work the groups of stars, each group having four stars. Each star is made of two diagonal stitches, a horizontal stitch and a vertical stitch, one on top of the other. Link the groups of stars with short horizontal and longer vertical stitches.

Basketweave filling stitch The first stage is to work the checkered effect of the background. Each section is made up of blocks of four satin stitches worked horizontally over five threads, alternating on each row. The second stage completes the pattern with pairs of vertical stitches worked in the spaces left between the satin stitch blocks.

Surface filling stitches
Block and cross filling stitch   Diagonal block filling stitch
Double cross filling stitch   Grains of rice filling stitch

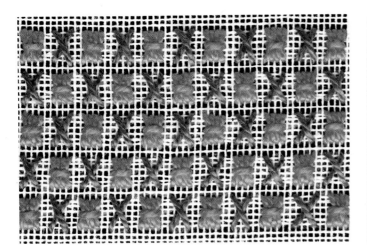

Block and cross filling stitch Work the tied satin stitch blocks first. These consist of four vertical stitches worked over six fabric threads. Having worked the last stitch, come out at the center left of the first stitch and work a horizontal stitch to the right. Work a second block seven threads to the right and so on. Alternate the position of the blocks in each row. Then fill the spaces with crossed diagonal stitches over the same number of threads as the satin stitch blocks.

Diagonal block filling stitch First work the diagonal stitches, three at a time, over four threads of the fabric. The blocks of stitches slope first to the right and then to the left. Leave two threads between each block. In the next row, the slope of the stitches alternates. The spaces left are filled with cross stitches over four threads of fabric.

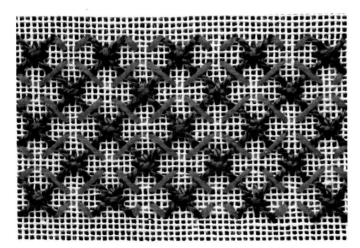

Double cross filling stitch First work cross stitch over six threads of the fabric, stitching diagonally from left to right and then from right to left. Next work a second cross with one vertical and one horizontal stitch, making a small cross over the first. Make a second large cross stitch six threads to the right of the first. On the second row alternate the crosses in the spaces left. To finish the pattern, work diagonal stitches over four threads at the point where the long diagonals meet.

Grains of rice filling stitch Bring the needle through to the right side of the fabric and work a horizontal stitch from left to right over six threads of the fabric. Repeat the stitch one thread lower. Then bring the needle up at the center of the first stitch and take down at the center of the second stitch, forming a small vertical tying stitch. Work the second group of stitches six threads to the right. The second row is worked one thread lower and the groups of stitches alternate with the spaces left in the first row.

153

Drawn thread work
Preparing the fabric
Cable stitch
Rhodes or Single faggot stitch

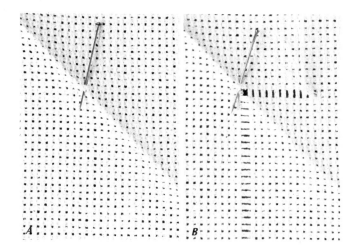

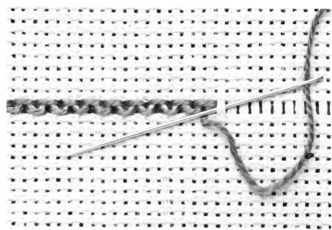

Preparing the fabric To draw a thread from either the warp or weft of the fabric, just lift the thread with the point of a needle and snip carefully with sharp scissors. Then gently pull it out. If several threads are to be drawn out, snip them in the middle of the row, draw out towards the edges and darn them in to prevent fraying. Care needs to be taken when the drawn thread turns a corner. First mark the diagonal with a crease. Work out the position of the corner and mark with a pin (**A**). At this point cut both the weft and warp threads and carefully pull them out as far as the next corner to be made (**B**).

Cable stitch 1. Make a drawn thread row, withdrawing two or three threads, depending on the thickness of the fabric and the thread. Bring the needle through to the right side, in the row of drawn threads. Holding the needle pointing horizontally to the left, make a stitch to the right over an even number of threads. Come out halfway along to the left, holding the thread below the needle.

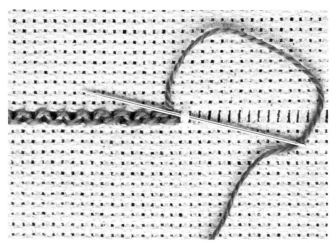

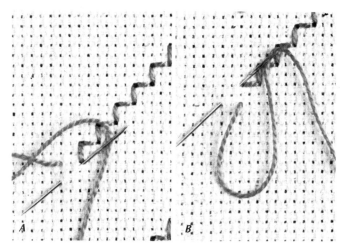

2. Make a second horizontal stitch to the right, over the same number of threads as the first stitch, coming out halfway along to the left but this time holding the thread above the needle. Continue in this way, pulling the thread slightly.

Rhodes stitch or Single faggot stitch This is a drawn fabric stitch, worked without withdrawing any threads, and can be used to decorate table linen with drawn thread borders. Pull the stitches firmly while working. It is worked on the diagonal. Bring the needle through to the right side of the fabric, and stitch horizontally to the right, joining the base of the previous vertical stitch and coming out diagonally down to the left (**A**). Make a vertical stitch upward, this time joining the previous horizontal stitch (**B**) and coming out diagonally to the left. Continue in this way.

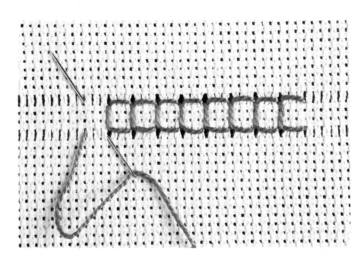

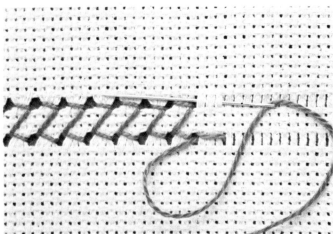

Italian squared ground Work on a double row of pulled threads, calculated so as to be able to divide the row into squares. Work from right to left, bringing the thread through to the right side of the fabric in the lower row. Make a horizontal stitch to the right over three (or the chosen number of) threads. Come out diagonally left in the upper row, as show above, forming a diagonal stitch on the reverse of the work. Stitch horizontally to the right, coming out at the beginning of the same stitch. Make a vertical stitch downward, then come out three threads to the left to begin another square.

Italian squared ground (reverse) Work from left to right on the wrong side of the fabric. Bring the thread through on the lower line of pulled threads and work a horizontal stitch over the chosen number of threads. Come out again at the beginning of the stitch. Stitch diagonally up to the right into the upper row of pulled threads, coming out horizontally to the left, as shown above. Make a stitch to the right to meet the diagonal stitch and come out vertically down. Continue as before. A row of squares is formed on the other side of the fabric.

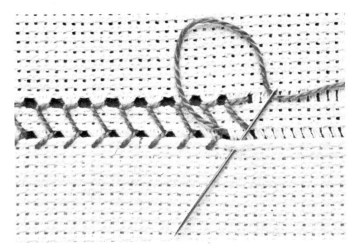

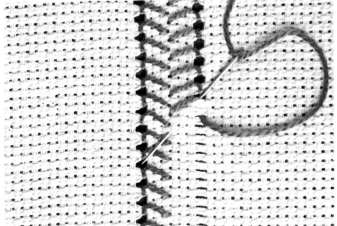

Sewing a hem with Italian squared ground Pull the first row of threads, then fold and tack the hem so that the fold lies along the row of drawn threads. Make a second row of pulled threads at the desired distance. Work on the reverse of the fabric. Bring the thread through from the inside of the folded hem to the right side of the fold. Make a diagonal stitch to the right into the drawn thread row and come out vertically up into the opposite row of drawn threads. Then make a horizontal stitch to the right, coming out again at the beginning of the stitch. Take the thread diagonally down to the lower drawn thread row, coming out horizontally to the left and reinserting the needle through the folded hem as shown.

Hemstitch worked in interlocking rows Work a fishbone pattern vertically from top to bottom in two stages, having made a double row of drawn threads. Work the first stage on the left. Pass the needle down behind several threads along the drawn thread line, come out, then insert the needle behind the same threads, coming out at the center of the two rows of drawn threads with a diagonal stitch. Stitch back into the bottom of the vertical stitch and continue in this way. Work the second row of stitches to interlock with the first.

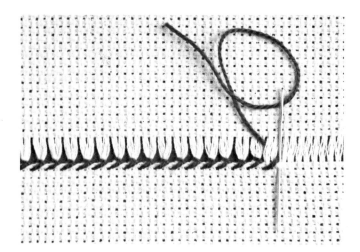

Hemstitch This is worked along a border of threads pulled from either the weft or the warp of the fabric. Bring the needle through one or two threads below the drawn thread border. Working from left to right, make a small diagonal stitch to the right, passing the needle horizontally to the left behind a number of the loose threads. Pull the needle through carefully, gathering the threads together. Stitch back behind the fabric, coming out below the drawn threads, as shown. Stitch again to the right, gathering the same number of loose threads and so on.

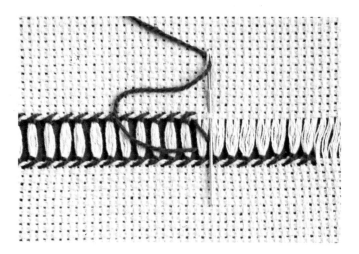

Ladder hemstitch First work a row of hemstitch at the base of a border of drawn threads. Turn the work around and work a second row along the opposite edge, picking up the same threads gathered into groups in the first row. The stitch can also be worked along the top edge without turning the work, as shown. Bring the needle through to the right side of the work to the left of the first group of threads, collect this group of threads by stitching horizontally to the left, pulling the thread through carefully. Then make a small diagonal stitch up and to the right. Bring the needle out in the drawn threads again with a small vertical stitch.

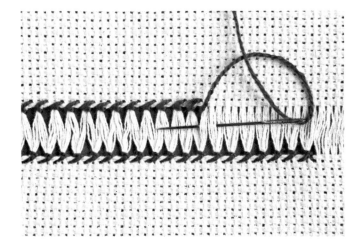

Zigzag hemstitch This is another double hemstitch, worked on both sides of a border of drawn threads. On either side of the border make a row of simple hemstitch, working from left to right. Gather up an even number of threads. On working the second row the stitches are made into the center of each of the groups of threads gathered in the first row. As in ladder hemstitch the second row can be made without turning the work, as shown.

Drawn thread work
Double knotted zigzag border
Wide double knotted border
Buttonhole stitch border

Double knotted zigzag border With this stitch it is not necessary to finish the edges of the drawn thread band, but this should not be too wide. Secure the sewing thread at the right-hand side. Make the first knot with the sewing thread looped into a coral knot stitch as shown, catching four threads together. Move up to the left, catching together two threads from the first group and two free ones. Continue in this way, always knotting together two threads from the previous group and two free ones, working up and down in a zigzag.

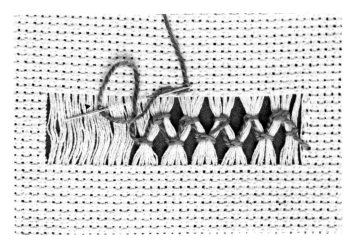

Wide double knotted border This needs a wide, hemstitched section of drawn threads, on which a double knotted effect is worked. Secure the sewing thread at the right-hand side. Always working over one third of the height, knot four groups of threads together. Take the sewing thread behind two of the threads, and moving down, knot together these two and two more, as shown. Continue in this way, zigzagging up and down.

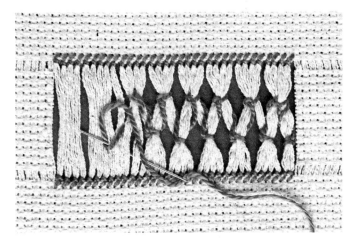

Buttonhole stitch border Work on a wide hemstitched section of drawn threads. The work requires accuracy. Secure the sewing thread at the right-hand side and start at the center of the drawn threads, working buttonhole stitch over three threads and finishing at about a quarter of their height. At this point make a stitch that takes in three new threads, and then continue working only on the new threads. Continue working zigzag fashion to the end of the first row. Work the return row over the incomplete section of work opposite the zigzag, completing the diamond shape in a symmetrical manner.

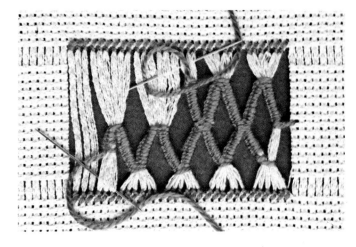

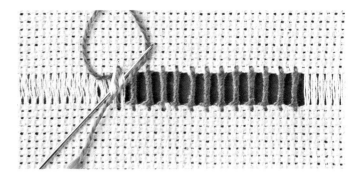

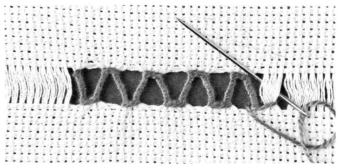

Vertical bars Bring the needle through to the right side of the work and take the thread across to the opposite side of the drawn thread border. This thread serves as a guide and is covered, along with a group of the vertical threads, by simply winding the sewing thread around them in an overcasting stitch. Having finished the bar, stitch through the back of the work and come out again ready to start the next one. The bars are worked from right to left.

Zigzag bars This uses the same method as the previous example, without the need for the guide thread. Overcast three drawn threads to the opposite edge of the drawn thread border. Then make a longer stitch over another three threads to the right as shown, and proceed to cover these three only. Continue in this way. The zigzag results from the longer stitch, which joins two groups of threads together each time.

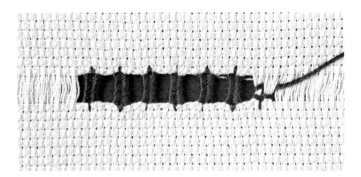

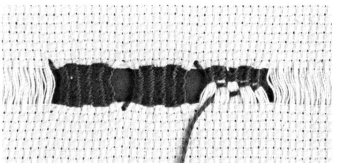

Double woven bars The illustration above shows how the sewing thread is woven in and out of the fabric threads. Work from left to right. To begin, lay the thread end along the first four fabric threads. Pass the needle over the first two fabric threads and under the second two. Then pass the needle back over the second two threads and under the first two, grouping the four threads and the thread end together in a figure-of-eight movement. Continue in this way until the bar is covered, and finish off by threading through the back of the worked bar.

Five column woven bars The method is identical to the previous example, weaving in and out of five threads instead of two. This method can also be used on larger numbers of threads, but in this case greater precision is required. The number of vertical threads in the drawn thread border should be worked out in multiples of the number of threads used for each bar.

Drawn thread work
Preparing drawn corners
Corners with web filling

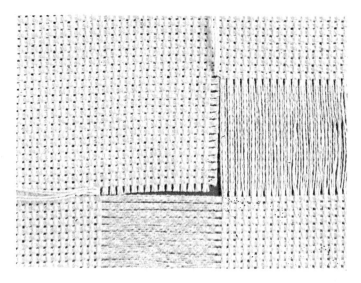

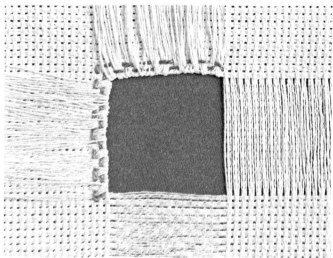

Preparing drawn corners 1. An empty square is left at the corners when the threads for a border have been withdrawn. These three stages illustrate how to work a perfect corner. Decide on the position of the corner and make two cuts at the inner right angle. Pull the weft and warp threads for the borders away from this angle.

2. Successively draw the threads of the square determined by the two border rows. Fold the freed threads to the reverse of the work and stitch them in place with a thread the same color as the fabric. In the illustration the thread is of a contrasting color for greater clarity.

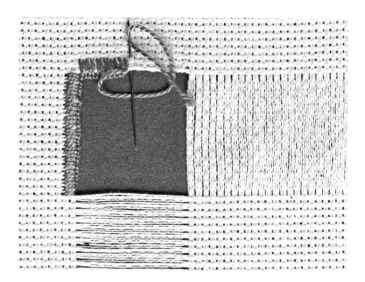

3. Work the edges of the square in buttonhole or satin stitch, so that they are completely covered and will not fray. Trim any excess threads from the edges on the reverse of the fabric, taking care not to damage the stitching.

Corners with web filling If the borders of drawn threads are fairly wide, the resulting corner will be correspondingly large and will need the support of diagonal, horizontal and vertical stitches, decorated in various ways, to help it keep its shape. In this example the center is covered with a web, made by passing the needle alternately over and under the threads.

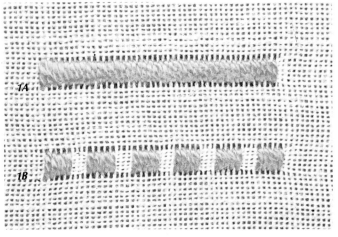

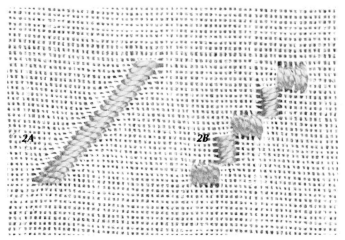

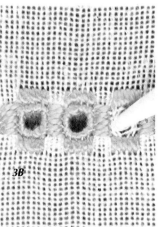

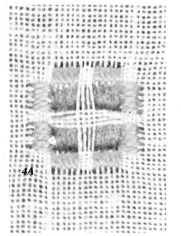

Hardanger embroidery takes its name from a district of Western Norway. It is based on stitches used in drawn thread and counted thread work and can have a very elaborate appearance. The fabric used should have a precise even weave and the thread should be chosen to suit the fabric. The basic blocks are worked in satin stitch which is used in conjunction with woven bars and various filling stitches.

Satin stitch This can be worked in a continuous manner to form bands of embroidery (*1A*). Alternatively it can be worked in blocks (*1B*) which form decorative patterns and can be arranged in a square formation with drawn threads at the center. It is best to use an embroidery frame for this.

Diagonal satin stitch Diagonal patterns are often used. With each stitch, move one thread up and sideways (*2A*) following the line of work. Satin stitch blocks can also be staggered, by stitching first vertically and then horizontally over a chosen number of threads, the corners meeting (*2B*).

Satin stitch blocks in square formation This border consists of a series of satin stitch blocks arranged in a square formation. While working each section, make sure that the fabric is kept taut. Complete the work by cutting away the center threads (*3A*) or by making the hole with the help of a bodkin (*3B*) in which case the threads are not cut but are oversewn with tight stitches.

Woven bars Work satin stitch blocks in a square formation, each side consisting of two blocks. When this is done, cut the threads as shown in *4A*. Then make woven bars (*4B*), weaving the threads two at a time as explained on page 158.

Hardanger embroidery
Diamond shapes   Web stitch
Weaving stitch   Triangular shapes

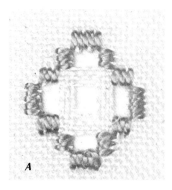
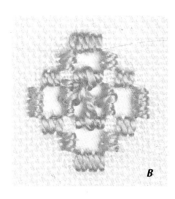

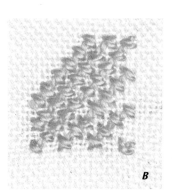

Diamond shapes First work the outline of the shape in satin stitch blocks over four threads of the fabric. The blocks are made of either three or five satin stitches. Withdraw the threads leaving a central rectangle (**A**). Outline the edges of the rectangle with an overcasting stitch and work loop stitch at the center (**B**).

Web stitch Make a long diagonal stitch upward and work back down over it, forming a row with a similar appearance to cross stitch (**A**). Work further rows to intermesh (**B**). The spacing of the diagonal lines and the length of the stitches can vary according to the effect required.

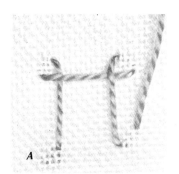
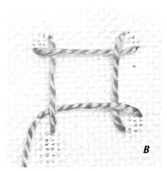
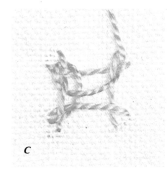
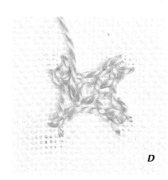

Weaving stitch 1. Work the base stitching, taking care to cross the threads as shown above (**A**). Having done this, return to the right side of the work with a small stitch, picking up a single thread of fabric (**B**).

2. Start to weave through the base threads without picking up any of the underlying fabric. The needle is passed under and over the base stitching in the order shown, starting at the bottom left-hand corner (**C**). Work right around clockwise (**D**).

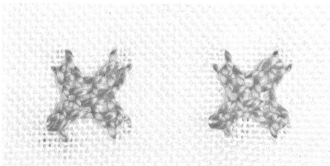

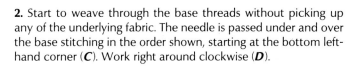

3. When the weaving is complete, finish off the thread at the back of the work.

Triangular shapes The outline is worked in satin stitch blocks consisting of three stitches worked either horizontally or vertically over four threads of the fabric. Withdraw threads from the inner area and decorate those remaining with overcasting and woven bars.

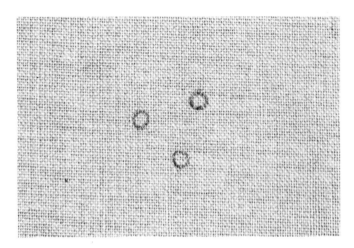

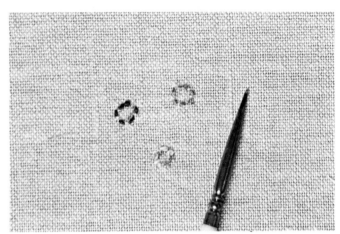

Broderie anglaise 1. This form of work falls into the category of cut work and is based on a design of round and oval eyelets. These are made either by piercing the fabric with a bodkin or, with larger eyelets, by cutting and turning back the fabric. The embroidery is worked entirely in white. Before starting the work, mark out the design on the fabric using dressmaker's carbon paper and a well sharpened pencil.

2. To keep the work as precise as possible, the fabric may be attached to a paper backing with basting stitches. This keeps the work firm. Work around the outlines of the patterns marked on the fabric with very small running stitches to strengthen them.

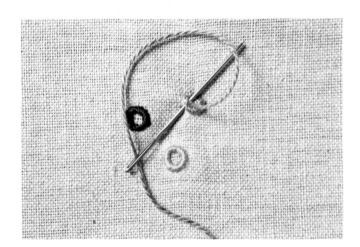

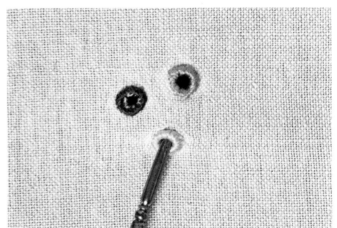

3. Cover the base stitches with very fine, close, regular over-sewing stitches so that the outlines of the patterns show up well. Remove the backing paper.

4. Pierce the center of the eyelets with a bodkin, pushing it first through from the right side and then through from the reverse of the fabric, so that the weave of the fabric is stretched well. If the holes in the pattern are larger, it is advisable to cut and turn back the fabric before the final stitching.

Pisa work This differs from broderie anglaise in that the cut areas are rather larger and need bars across them to hold the edges together. A firmly woven fabric is required, which is basted onto stiff paper while working the embroidery to prevent it stretching out of shape. Mark the design onto the fabric with dressmaker's carbon paper. Work a row of small running stitches around the edge of the design and at the first bar, cross it with a long stitch to the opposite side and then back again to continue with the running stitch. Do this each time a bar is reached (**A**). Complete the running stitch around the edge (**B**). Then returning over the same stitches, complete the bars without picking up any of the fabric beneath by working oversewing around them (**C**). Cut the fabric at the center of the design and fold it back around the edges (**D**). Oversew around the edges to secure them (**E**).

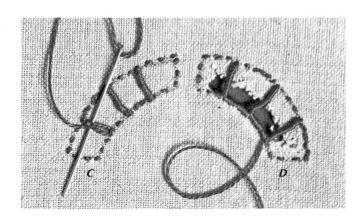

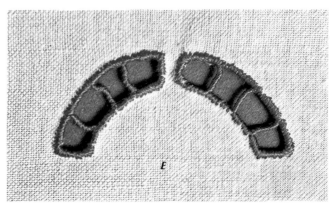

Richelieu embroidery Another way of covering the edges and bars of the design is with buttonhole stitch. Here, once the running stitch outline and bars have been worked, they are covered with buttonhole stitch. Begin the buttonhole stitch around the edge of the design. Then, on reaching a bar, take a third long stitch across to the opposite side and work back over the bar only with buttonhole stitch. Continue around the edge to the next bar. When the embroidery is complete, remove the backing paper and very carefully cut away the fabric right up to the edge of the buttonhole stitch.

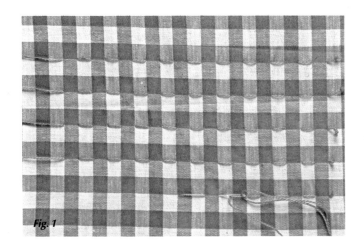

Fig. 1

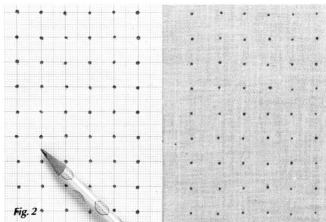

Fig. 2

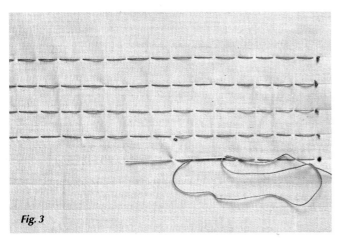

Fig. 3

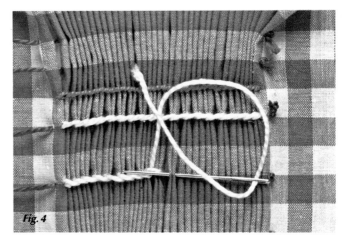

Fig. 4

Smocking was originally used to decorate the loose over-garments worn by farm workers in rural England. It spread from England and was soon in general use in many countries. The stitches used in smocking include stem stitch, chain stitch, cross stitch and any stitches that are slightly elastic.

Preparing the fabric The work is carried out in two stages: first the preparation, when the fabric is gathered into pleats, and second, by working the decorative embroidery stitches over the gathers. Once the gathers are regular, stroke them into even parallel lines with the head of a large needle. It is helpful to use a fabric with regular points of reference such as checks, small repeating designs or stripes (**Fig. 1**). With plain fabric, which has no points of reference, smocking dots must be marked first. Iron-on transfers with rows of smocking dots are available. Alternatively the fabric can be marked in other ways. The first method requires a sheet of graph paper and a pencil sharp enough to pierce the paper. Place the paper in position on the reverse side of the fabric and pierce it, forming a small dot on the fabric where the vertical and horizontal lines of the graph paper cross

(**Fig. 2**). Continue across the fabric, moving the paper along carefully if necessary, until the row is completed. The second method is to use a ruler and the point of a large needle. With the ruler as a guide, prick the fabric in a series of parallel equally-spaced lines which will indicate where to gather the fabric. If the fabric has vertical stripes, just the horizontal lines need to be pricked, but if the fabric is plain, prick both horizontal and vertical lines, using the intersections as the dots. Using a long thread with a large knot in the end, start gathering from right to left. With the point of the needle, pick up several threads of the fabric at each dot (**Fig. 3**). At the end of each row, unthread the needle and leave the thread hanging. When all the rows are completed, pull the hanging threads, two at a time, to the required width, then fasten the threads with a firm knot. For the best results, the width of the fabric to be gathered should be three times the required finished width.

Outline stitch This basic stitch (**Fig. 4**) is similar to stem stitch and is usually worked from left to right. Each pleat, or group of pleats, corresponds to one stitch. The thread must be held either always above or always below the needle.

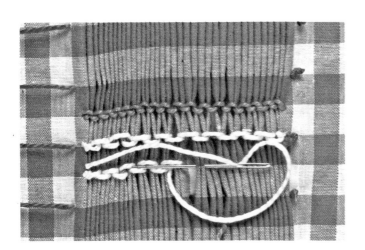

Cable stitch Cable stitch is a firm control stitch. Hold the needle horizontally, with the thread alternately above and below the needle, working through two pleats at a time.

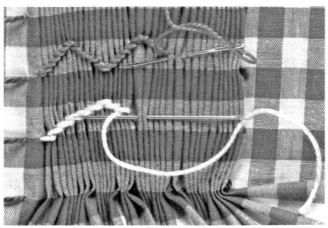

Wave stitch Make a row of ascending horizontal stitches, and using the top stitch as a joining stitch, make a descending row of stitches, changing the position of the thread. On the ascending row the thread is below the needle, and on the descending row it is above. This stitch can be made less elastic by using one new pleat and one previous one (as in the top row), instead of two new ones (as in the bottom row).

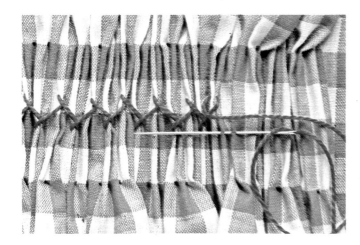

Herringbone stitch This smocking stitch is similar to ordinary herringbone stitch. Working from left to right, sew through the first pleat on the left. The first stitch is made diagonally up and to the right, picking up the pleats horizontally from right to left. The next stitch is made diagonally down and to the right, again picking up the pleats from right to left. Each stitch picks up two or more pleats and the thread is pulled through gently. Continue working to the right, making one stitch on the top sewing line, and one on the bottom.

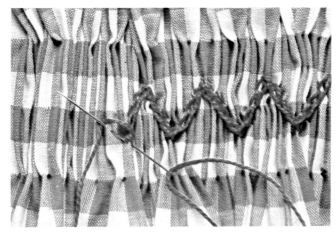

Chain stitch The elasticity of this stitch depends on the firmness of the smocking. If maximum elasticity is required, work in zigzags. Moving from right to left, sew through the first pleat on the right and work the first chain, picking up the first and second pleats. Work the second chain by picking up the second and third pleats, and so on. Continue along the row in a zigzag fashion.

Smocking

Feather stitch   Double feather stitch
Diamond stitch   Vandyke stitch

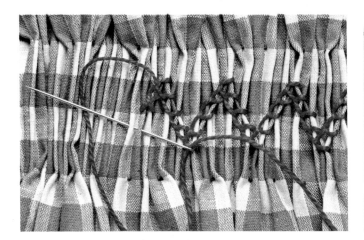

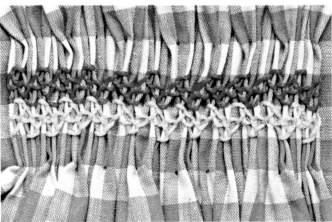

Feather stitch This stitch can be made in various ways, as with ordinary feather stitch. Hold the smocking so that the thread is always toward you and then work from right to left and vice-versa to form the zigzags. Start at the first pleat on the right. To make the first stitch, pick up the first and second pleats catching the thread under the point of the needle. Work the second stitch, picking up the second and third pleats, and so on, according to the number of stitches planned. Turn the work and start the next row from left to right. Continue in a zigzag manner.

Double feather stitch Work two rows of double feather stitch in opposite directions. Turn the work for each row so that the work proceeds in the right direction. Double feather stitch is quite tight and can be used to firm the smocking, at the same time producing a pretty decorative effect.

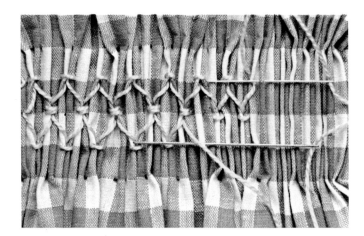

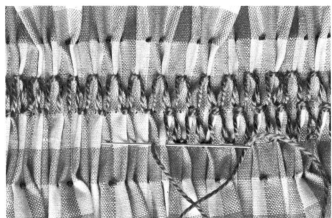

Diamond stitch This stitch is completed in two rows. Work from left to right. Start at the first pleat on the left. Take the thread up and to the right and pick up the next pleat, passing the needle from right to left. Now make a horizontal stitch, passing the needle through the following pleat from right to left. Take the thread down and to the right, and pick up the following pleat from right to left. Make another horizontal stitch, passing the needle from right to left through the next pleat. Complete the first row in this way. Work the second row so that the horizontal stitches coincide and the characteristic shape of the stitch is formed.

Vandyke stitch This stitch is worked from right to left. Bring the needle through to the right side of the work at the second pleat from the right. Make a backstitch over the first two pleats. Take the needle down to the row below. Pick up the second and third pleats and make a backstitch over them. Take the needle back up to the row above. Pick up the third and fourth pleats and make a backstitch over them. Return to the row below and continue in this way to the end of the row. The next line of stitching is worked in the same manner, beginning on the third row down and taking the needle up to the second row where the backstitches will coincide.

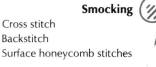

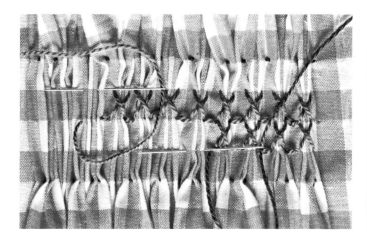

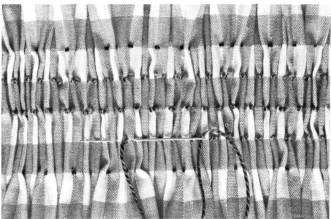

Cross stitch A single row of cross stitch can be used to arrange the gathers in the smocking. Plan out the area of smocking on which you wish to work, and the height of the stitches. Working from right to left, take the needle through four pleats to the left, make a diagonal stitch up to the right and then stitch through the same four pleats to the left. Complete the cross by stitching to the bottom right and out at the starting point. Repeat this to form a continuous row of small, joined crosses. Working on a checked fabric, such as gingham, makes the work easier. This stitch gives only a slight elasticity.

Backstitch This is a simple stitch used to firm the gathers. The result is only slightly elastic. To make the stitch, pick up one pleat with the needle and stitch through three pleats to the left. Backstitch over one pleat and again stitch through three to the left. Continue in this way to the end of the row. The result will be a succession of free pleats and pleats held by the backstitch. Stagger the rows so that the backstitches hold the free pleats in alternate rows.

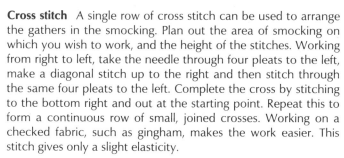

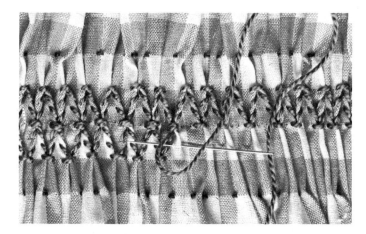

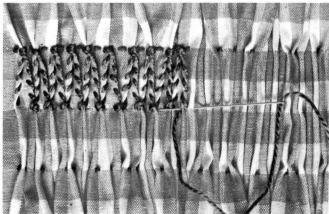

Surface honeycomb stitch 1 Work from left to right. Stitch through the first pleat on the left and make an upward slanting stitch around the pleat with the needle pointing from right to left. Make a second stitch in the same way. Then make a horizontal stitch to the right, picking up the second pleat to the right and coming out between the two pleats. Repeat the two slanting stitches downward, make another horizontal stitch picking up the third pleat, then start the upward slanting stitches again. Continue in a zigzag manner. A second row beneath the first completes the diamond pattern.

Surface honeycomb stitch 2 This is an extended version of the previous stitch, the diagonals being longer and held firmly by two horizontal stitches at top and bottom in order to strengthen the stitch at these points. Complete the diamond pattern with a second row below.

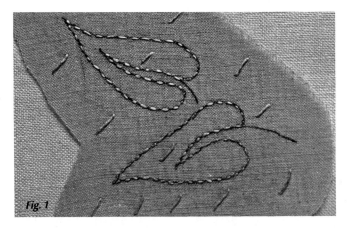

Fig. 1

Fig. 2

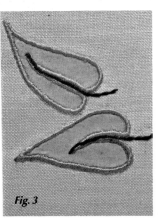

Fig. 3

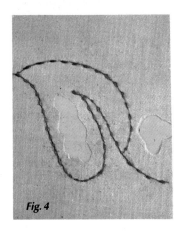

Fig. 4

Fig. 5

Appliqué is the technique of arranging pieces of fabric on a contrasting background and securing them with decorative embroidery stitches. The applied fabric can be in the form of leaves, flowers or other small decorative designs. The stitches used for securing the shapes can be divided into two main groups: those which border an unhemmed edge which is later trimmed and those which are worked over a small single hem to prevent fraying. The first group includes buttonhole stitch and oversewing and the second straight stitch, stem stitch, chain stitch and cross stitch.

Stitch and cut appliqué With this method, the shapes are applied with a border of fabric left around them. This is cut off when the embroidery is complete. Prepare the work by carefully marking out the design on the right side of the background fabric. Also mark the shapes on the appliqué fabric, leaving a margin of fabric all around. Place the appliqué pieces on the corresponding outlines on the background fabric and stitch the two fabrics together with a small running stitch around the edge of the shapes (**Fig. 1**). Baste the outer margin of the appliqué fabric to the background fabric away from the design outlines. Iron thoroughly, then work around the design with the chosen stitch. Trim the excess fabric as below.

Buttonhole stitch Secure the appliqué pieces with buttonhole stitch so that the base line of the stitching is at the outer edge of the shape (**Fig. 2**). Stitch firmly and continuously, following the line of the design. When the stitching is complete, remove the basting and press with a warm iron on the reverse side. Finally cut away any excess fabric with a pair of very sharp scissors, taking care not to damage the stitching thread. If there are a lot of shapes to be applied, make sure that the threads of both the shapes and the background fabric run the same way.

Oversewing stitch Prepare the work and then edge the appliqué shape in close oversewing stitch (**Fig. 3**). Cut away the excess fabric, leaving only the narrowest of margins. This stitch is most commonly used to apply lightweight fabrics, such as fine linen or organza.

Reverse appliqué In this method, two layers of fabric are placed together, one on top of the other. Mark the outline of the motif on the top layer, then work small running stitches around it through both layers. Cut away the top layer of fabric from inside the motif (**Fig. 4**). Finish the edges with close oversewing stitch worked through both layers (**Fig. 5**). This method can be used as a border on a wide hem or on tablecloths and other household linen. It it not suitable for use over a wide surface area.

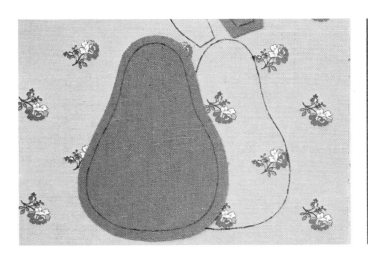

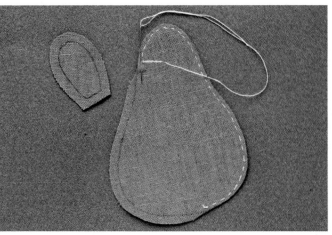

Preparing the hemmed appliqué 1. Mark out the design on both the background fabric and on the fabric to be applied. Cut out the appliqué shape, allowing an extra $\frac{3}{16}$ in all round to turn under.

2. Baste this hem to the wrong side with small stitches, folding it under carefully so as not to spoil the shape. With a curved shape, tiny folds can be made at right angles to the edge to make the hemming easier and neater.

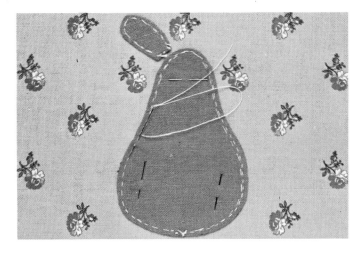

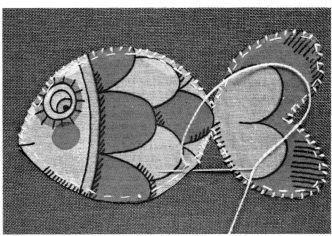

3. Now baste the hemmed shape to the background fabric to match the previously marked out design. To prevent the shape from moving, pin it at various places. Baste the shape into place with even stitches along the edge, finishing off with a couple of small firm stitches. Work the chosen embroidery stitch around the shape, then remove the basting thread and press lightly on both sides.

Securing with slipstitch Having prepared and tacked the appliqué shape in place, sew it into position with small, even stitches. Work from right to left, picking up first a thread of the background fabric and then of the appliqué shape to make a line of neat, slanting stitches.

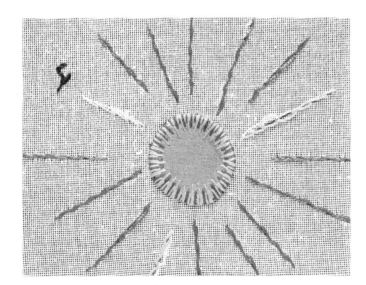

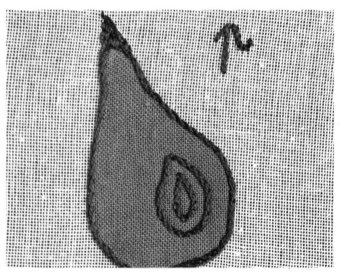

Straight stitch This is used to create a textured, irregular edging. First make a border of stitches of the same length, then, in a second row, intersperse these with longer or overlapping stitches.

Stem stitch Using short, close stitches, work around the folded edge of an appliqué shape. Further rows can be added around the edge at varying distances apart, either on the appliqué shape itself or on the background fabric.

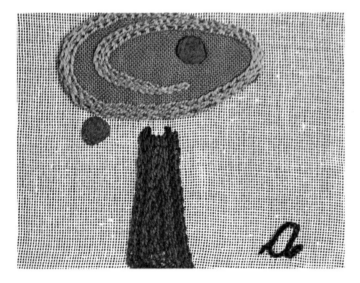

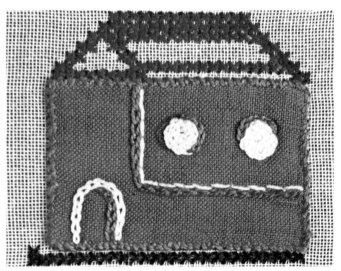

Chain stitch This stitch is particularly useful on curving shapes such as trees, clouds or petals. The first row is stitched all around the edge of the shape and then spirals toward the center two or more times.

Cross stitch This is best used on motifs with straight edges. To make sure that the appliqué shape is accurate, first rule a line on the appliqué fabric, then fold the hem under and baste the shape to the background fabric. With evenweave fabrics, the stitches can be worked as in counted thread work. Work the cross stitch in two stages, counting the threads to ensure that the stitches are of uniform size.

Applying lace
Making a lace-edged border
Paris stitch
Three-sided stitch

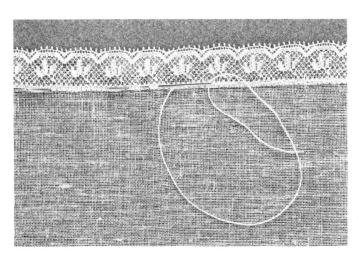

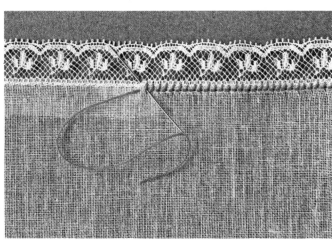

Making a lace-edged border This can be done in two ways. The first is for medium thickness fabric. Baste the lace $\frac{3}{8}$ in from the edge of the fabric. Stitch it with the chosen embroidery stitch, then cut off the excess fabric. The second method is for finer fabrics. Place the lace $\frac{3}{8}$ in from the edge of the fabric, baste it and oversew it with a fine thread. Remove the basting and fold down the edge of the fabric. Finish off the lace with the chosen stitch, sewing through the folded edge. Finally, cut away the surplus fabric.

Paris stitch This is an excellent stitch to use when applying fine fabric, as well as for lace as in this example. Work from right to left. Bring the needle through the fabric and make a small backstitch, bringing the needle out diagonally through the lace, above the beginning of the backstitch. Make a vertical stitch back down to this point, then bring the needle out through the fabric one stitch to the left. Continue as before. The thread used in the illustration for clarity should, in fact, be of the same color and weight as the fabric.

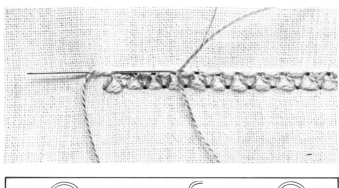

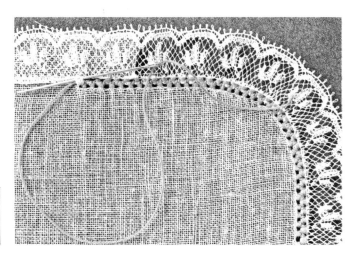

Three-sided stitch This is a useful appliqué stitch, and can also be used in straight rows in drawn fabric design. Working from right to left, follow the above diagram. The resulting stitches are double.

Using three-sided stitch Three-sided stitch is a firm and attractive way of joining two fabrics and adding a lace edging. The thread used should be of a similar thickness to the fabric.

Embroidery on tulle
Preparing the tulle
Running stitch
Staggered running stitch

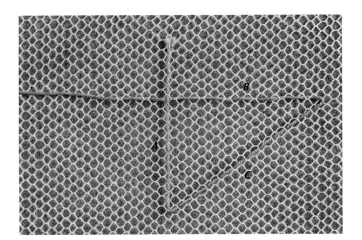

Fig. 1

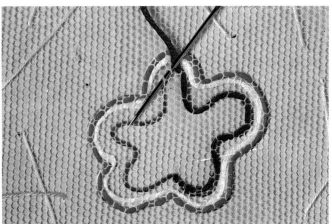

Fig. 2

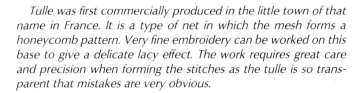

Running stitch

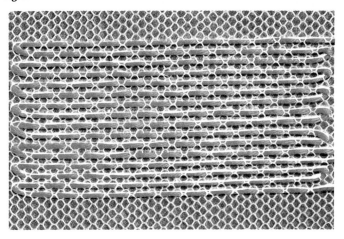

Staggered running stitch

Tulle was first commercially produced in the little town of that name in France. It is a type of net in which the mesh forms a honeycomb pattern. Very fine embroidery can be worked on this base to give a delicate lacy effect. The work requires great care and precision when forming the stitches as the tulle is so transparent that mistakes are very obvious.

Preparing the tulle 1. There are many types of tulle (cotton, silk, nylon) with small, medium or large mesh. Use only fine tulle of the highest quality – to check this, insert a bodkin into the weave which should enlarge without stretching. Use a needle with a rounded tip. The embroidery can be worked over counted threads or by following a pattern drawn on paper, either as an all-over design or as a border. Work is carried out in the three directions shown in *Fig. 1*: *A* is vertical, *B* is horizontal and *C* is diagonal.

2. Draw the pattern with permanent ink on paper or firm cloth. To avoid making the tulle dirty, turn the paper over. The pattern will show through on the reverse side and can still be easily followed. Attach the paper or firm cloth to the tulle with basting stitches of the correct tension. Start the work by stitching around the outline of the design with running stitch, then complete it with the chosen stitches. *Fig. 2* shows how the needle slides over the paper without stitching into it. Remove the paper when the work is finished.

Running stitch Running stitch is used for outlining a design, but is also the simplest way of covering a background. In the example it is worked in rows back and forth. The stitches are worked in columns, one above the other, giving a soft, regular relief pattern.

Staggered running stitch This stitch is also worked horizontally. In this case, however, stagger the stitches in each row to give a different effect from the previous stitch.

172

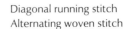

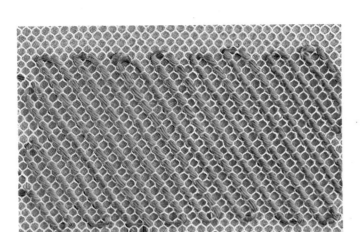

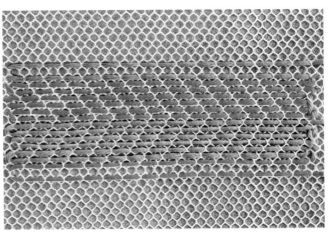

Diagonal running stitch Work diagonally, on every other row of threads. In each row the running stitch is worked over one thread and under one thread of the tulle. In the example two colors have been used, going through alternate holes, but only one may be used if preferred. This produces a firm border.

Simple woven stitch This is worked in running stitch, staggering each row by one thread. Covering all the holes in the tulle in this way gives the fabric a woven appearance. It is especially useful for borders and bolder areas of work.

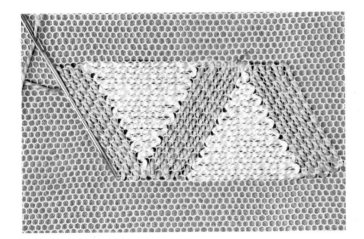

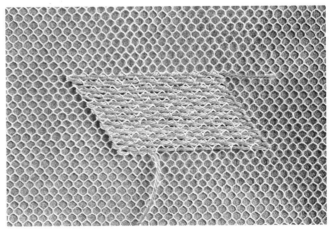

Alternating woven stitch This is a classic border stitch. Work the diagonal lines first. Start at the right of the work, and in rows back and forth, work the first section. Then continue with the second diagonal section without a break and so on. Use the weave of the tulle alternately to stagger the stitches. Next, fill the gaps, changing to horizontal running stitch and pulling the thread through gently. The final result is a contrast of light and shade, which can also be worked in a single color.

Darning stitch This is a stitch which creates a good relief effect, using a soft, colorful thread. It can be worked in three directions, vertical, horizontal and diagonal. Work the first row in running stitch, then return along the same row of holes but alternating the stitches. In this stitch it is important not to pull the thread too tightly.

Embroidery with beads and sequins

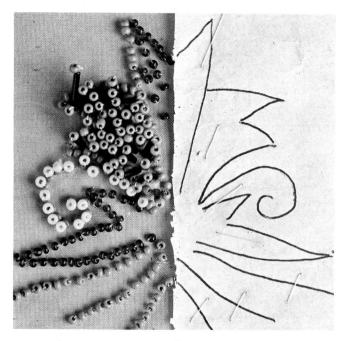

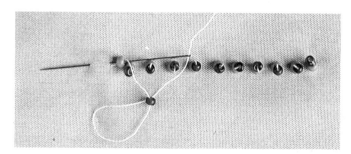

Superimposed beads 1 For maximum effect the beads can be superimposed, one on top of another. Bring the needle through to the right side of the work, thread one bead and then another. Thread through the first bead again and secure with a backstitch. Come out at a chosen distance and stitch another pair of beads.

Preparing the work This is a method of embroidery in which small beads or sequins are sewn onto fabric following a traced design. In some cases, especially if the fabric is very delicate, it is best to trace the design onto tissue paper and baste this to the fabric with small stitches. Start the bead work along the outer lines. Carefully tear away the paper from the finished section, and then begin another area. This is because it would be difficult to remove all the paper when the work is finished.

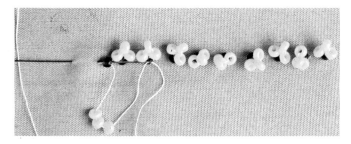

Superimposed beads 2 Using the method described above, an even greater effect can be achieved by superimposing three beads on top of the first. A small trefoil can be made using beads of various colors.

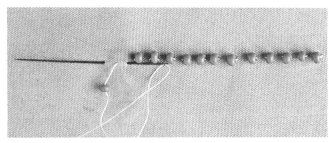

Attaching beads with backstitch This is the most traditional and widely used method. Choose a needle and thread fine enough to thread through the selected beads. The thread should be as strong as possible. Bring the thread through to the right side of the fabric, thread the bead and secure it with a backstitch. Thread another bead and so on, following the traced line. The beads can be closely spaced or further apart, depending on the length of the stitch.

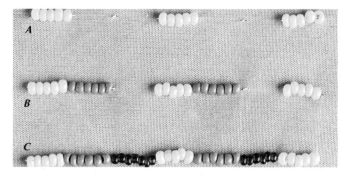

Grouped beads The beads can also be attached in a row of various colors and groupings. Work a series of beads so that gaps are left for beads of another color (**A**). Fill in the second section (**B**) and then the third (**C**). For a balanced result, calculate in advance the size of the gaps and the number of beads required.

Embroidery with beads and sequins

Bugle beads	Spaced sequins
Superimposed sequins	Sequins with beads
Fringes of beads and sequins	Sequin flowers

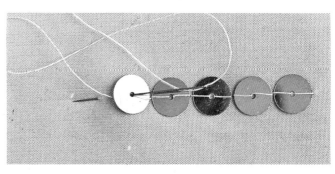

Bugle beads There is no particular method of stitching bugle beads to fabric. Simply thread the beads onto the needle and stitch them into place, carefully judging the length of the stitches. Using bugle beads, it is possible to make zigzag patterns.

Spaced sequins Bring the thread through to the right side of the fabric, thread the sequin and stitch to the right, coming out on the left of the sequin. Stitch back into the center and out again to the left, ready to stitch the second sequin.

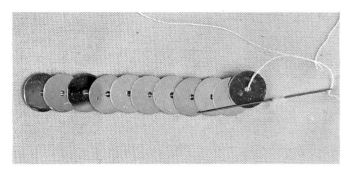

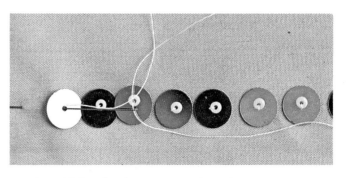

Superimposed sequins Bring the thread through to the right side of the work, thread a sequin onto the needle and make a small backstitch in the fabric to the right as shown. Thread a second sequin onto the needle and make another small backstitch through the fabric to the right. Continue in this way, so that the sequins overlap.

Sequins with beads This is a way of attaching a sequin with a bead at the center. Bring the thread through to the right side of the work. Pass the thread through the hole in the center of the sequin and then add a bead. Pass the needle back through the sequin. Stitch through the fabric to the left, to the position of the next sequin.

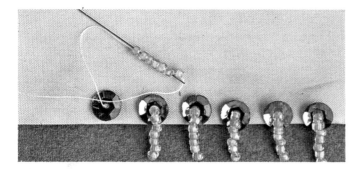

Fringes of beads and sequins Thread the sequin onto the thread, followed by a number of beads (in this case seven). Pass the thread back through six beads and the sequin and secure them all with a small stitch.

Sequin flowers To achieve this decorative effect, choose sequins which are slightly concave. Thread in order 1 sequin, 1 bead, 1 sequin, 1 bead, 1 sequin, 1 bead, and secure them all with a small stitch. Work around in a circle.

Basic needlepoint stitches

Half cross stitch
Continental (tent) stitch

Half cross stitch over tramming
Backing pattern of continental (tent) stitch

Half cross stitch Working from left to right, bring the needle up through the canvas and make a small diagonal stitch, going in one hole up and to the right. Come out again one hole vertically downward. Continue to the end of the row. Turn the work completely upside down for the return row, again working from left to right.

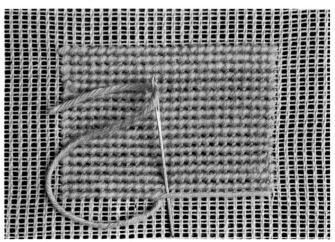

Half cross stitch over tramming Here the half cross stitch is worked over lines of tramming threads which are stitched along the horizontal canvas threads, overlapping about every 4¾ in. This pads out the stitches to achieve good coverage of the canvas.

Continental (tent) stitch Working from right to left, bring the needle through to the right side and make a diagonal stitch, going in one hole up and to the right. Come out again on the bottom row one hole further to the left. Continue to the end of the row. Turn the canvas completely upside down and work the next row in the same way, again from right to left.

Backing pattern of Continental (tent) stitch Long slanting stitches are formed on the back of the canvas with Continental (tent) stitch. This makes a more durable finish than half cross stitch. However, compared with basketweave (diagonal tent) stitch (see opposite page), this stitch pulls the canvas out of shape more.

Basic needlepoint stitches
Basketweave (diagonal tent) stitch
Backing pattern of Basketweave (diagonal tent) stitch
Web stitch

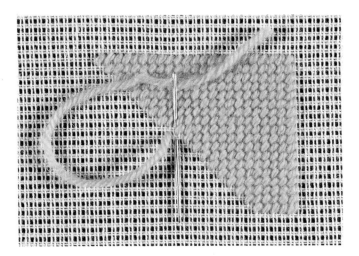

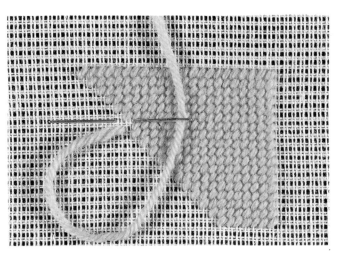

Basketweave (diagonal tent) stitch 1. This method of working continental stitch is in diagonal lines. When working from top to bottom, the needle is held vertically. Make a diagonal stitch over one intersection of canvas, then bring the needle out two holes vertically downward to begin the next diagonal stitch.

2. When working the next row from bottom to top, the needle is held horizontally. Make a diagonal stitch over one intersection of canvas, then bring the needle out two holes to the left to begin the next stitch. The rows of diagonal stitches interlock.

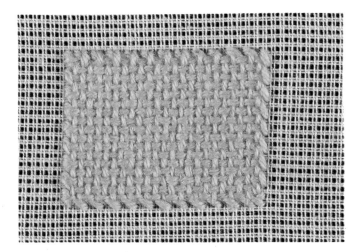

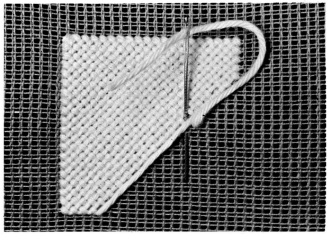

Backing pattern of Basketweave (diagonal tent) stitch This stitch produces a firm backing pattern which looks woven and is more durable than half cross and continental stitch. It has the added advantage of pulling the canvas out of shape less.

Web stitch Lay a tramming thread diagonally from bottom left to top right, then work back down it with diagonal stitches over one canvas intersection. On the next row, work the diagonal stitches so they alternate with those in the previous row, leaving the tramming thread showing in between.

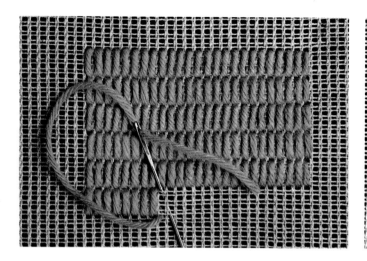

Upright Gobelin stitch This is a classic stitch with infinite variations. It is stitched over two or three threads. Work from left to right and vice-versa. Make a vertical stitch upward over three threads of the canvas, coming out on the slant and one thread to the right (or to the left on the return row). Continue in this way until the work is completed.

Brick stitch Work from left to right and vice-versa. Make a vertical stitch upward over three threads of the canvas. Come out three threads down and two to the right. Continue to the end of the row. On the return row, fill in the gaps between the stitches of the previous row with more vertical stitches over three threads, but overlapping the row above by one thread. Repeat the first and second rows until the work is completed.

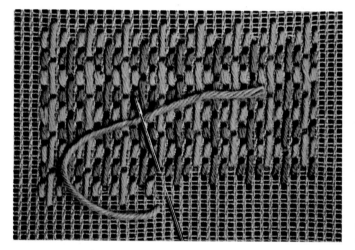

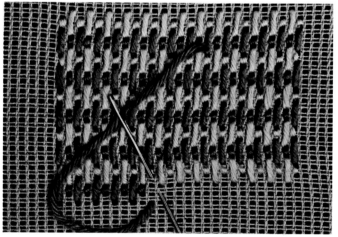

Hungarian stitch Work from left to right and vice-versa. Bring the thread through to the right side of the canvas and stitch up over two threads. Move one thread to the right and one down, and make a vertical stitch over four threads. Move one thread to the right and one thread higher than the previous stitch, and make another vertical stitch over two threads. Move two threads to the right and repeat these stitches to the end of the row. The following row is worked in a contrasting color to interlock with the row above.

Parisian stitch Work in horizontal rows from left to right, and vice-versa. The first row is worked with alternately one vertical stitch over one thread of the canvas and one over three threads, leaving one thread between each stitch. In the following rows the long stitches coincide with the short stitches and vice-versa. Use a contrasting color on alternate rows.

Vertical needlepoint stitches

Parisian stitch variation   Chevron stitch   Mosaic diamond stitch
Diagonal straight stitch   Gobelin variation   Vertical bands

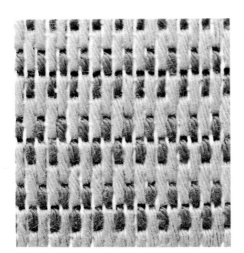

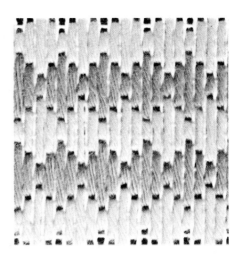

Parisian stitch variation Work the first row by stitching over four threads, and then over another four, two threads lower. Work the second line of stitches to correspond, but a whole row lower. These two rows form bands, leaving spaces between them. In the second stage, these are filled with small straight stitches over two threads in a contrasting color.

Chevron stitch The long vertical stitches are worked over four threads in a zigzag pattern, ascending or descending one thread at a time. The spaces between the rows are filled with short vertical stitches worked over two threads in a contrasting color.

Mosaic diamond stitch This pattern is worked over two, four and six threads to form small diamond shapes. The stitch shows up well if the color changes with each row.

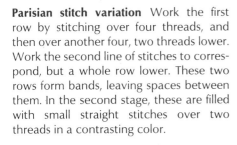

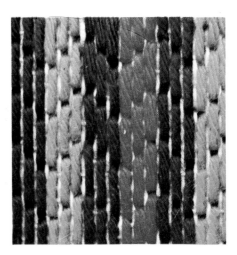

Diagonal straight stitch The stitches are worked vertically and staggered by one thread every stitch. Start the work at the top left-hand corner and work diagonally down to the right, finishing at the end of the area to be covered. This diagonal serves as a guide for further rows. Work these rows from right to left and vice-versa.

Gobelin variation Work from left to right and vice-versa. Make vertical stitches upward over one or two threads, coming out one thread to the right (or one to the left on the return row). Blocks of contrasting colors form a chevron pattern.

Vertical bands This is worked in groups of three vertical stitches, each staggered by one thread as shown. Each band changes color. The bands can be made wider by working more than three stitches across.

179

Slanting needlepoint stitches

Oblique Gobelin stitch   Alternating slanting Gobelin stitch
Stem stitch   Fern stitch

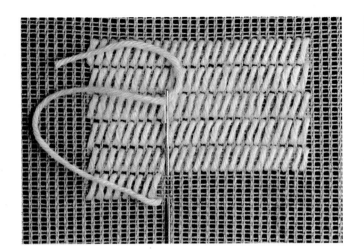

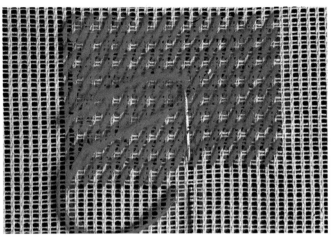

Oblique Gobelin stitch This is a classic tapestry stitch, worked over two or three threads in height. Work only from left to right, turning the work at the end of each row. Work each stitch slanting one thread to the right, then stitch vertically down, picking up two or three threads of the canvas as shown.

Alternating slanting Gobelin stitch Work in rows from left to right, turning the work on the return row. Work each slanting stitch over three threads of the canvas in height and two threads to the right. On the return row, alternate the stitches to interlock with those of the previous row.

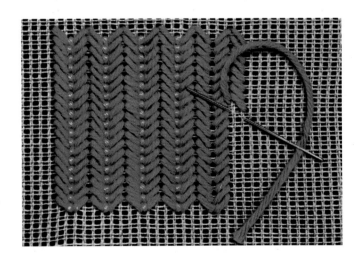

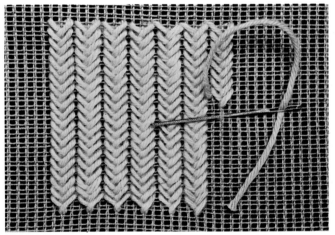

Stem stitch Work from top to bottom and vice-versa. Bring the thread through at the top left-hand corner and make a diagonal stitch down over two threads of the canvas, coming out one thread below the start of the first stitch. Finish the row in this way. On the return row, work from bottom to top, making the stitches symmetrical with those in the first row. When this stage of the work is finished, work small backstitches between the rows, using a finer thread in a contrasting color.

Fern stitch Work from top to bottom, starting at the top left-hand corner of the work. Stitch diagonally down to the right over two threads, coming out one thread horizontally to the left as shown. Now make an upward diagonal stitch to the right over two threads of the canvas, coming out one thread below the first stitch. Continue in this way to the end of the row, finish off and restart the successive rows.

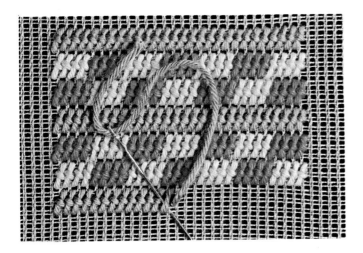

Knotted stitch Work from left to right. Bring the needle through at the bottom left of the work, make a slanting stitch to the right over three threads up and one to the right. Come out two threads of the canvas vertically down. Make a small diagonal tying stitch one thread up to the left and come out one thread to the right of the initial stitch.

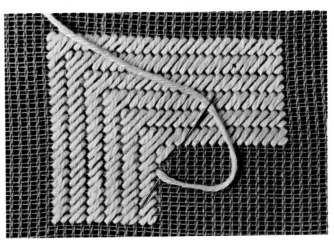

Oriental stitch variation Work diagonally from top to bottom, starting at the top left-hand corner of the work. Stitch diagonally over one thread, then over two, three and four threads, making a small triangle. Now make a series of slanting stitches over two threads of the canvas, first from top to bottom and then from left to right from the triangle in the corner. Fill in the angle made in this way with another small triangle and so on.

Diagonal stitch Work diagonally in rows from left to right and from bottom to top and vice-versa. The first and the fifth stitches in each pattern cover one thread, the second and the fourth cover two threads, while the third, central stitch covers three. On the return row work the stitch covering three threads below the stitch covering only one thread, and so on.

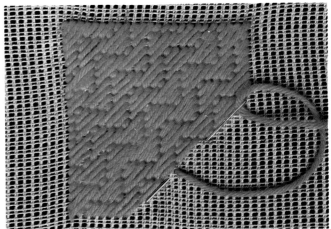

Milanese stitch Start work in the top left-hand corner, working in rows of back stitch back and forth. Having filled in the corner with a diagonal triangle, work a row of diagonal stitches, alternating first over one thread, then over four. In the second row, under each stitch covering one thread, work one which covers two threads, and under each stitch covering four threads, work one which covers three. In the third row, under each stitch covering two threads, work one which covers three threads, and under each stitch covering three threads, work one which covers two. Repeat these rows to produce a series of interlocking triangles.

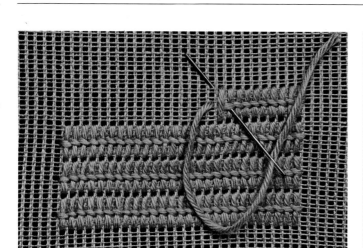

Renaissance stitch Work rows back and forth from left to right and vice-versa. Bring the thread through to the right side of the canvas and stitch vertically down over four threads. Bring the needle back out two threads up and one to the left. Make a horizontal tying stitch to the right over one thread and come out one thread to the left of the first stitch as shown.

Alternating Renaissance stitch This is a simple variation of Renaissance stitch. Leave a space between each vertical stitch which is filled in successive rows. The horizontal tying stitch is worked over two threads. Work in two colors to show the alternating rows.

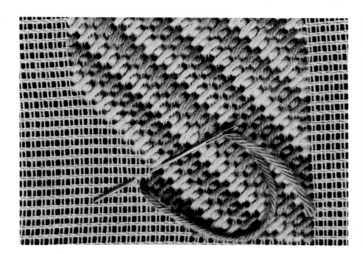

Florentine or Diagonal mosaic stitch This is worked in diagonal rows from left to right and from top to bottom and vice-versa. The first diagonal stitch covers a single thread of canvas and the second stitch covers two. On the return row, the long stitch meets the short one in the previous row. Using two colors on alternate rows gives a diagonal striped effect.

Rococo stitch The vertical stitches are worked over four threads of canvas, the horizontal tying stitches over two. Bring the needle through at the starting point and make a vertical stitch. Make another vertical stitch, re-entering at the top of the stitch just made, and coming out two threads down to the right. Make a horizontal stitch two threads to the left, coming out at the bottom of the vertical stitch. Work the other two sides of the diamond symmetrically and slightly looser. The centers of the diamonds are spaced at six-thread intervals. Make the next row of diamonds interlock with the first.

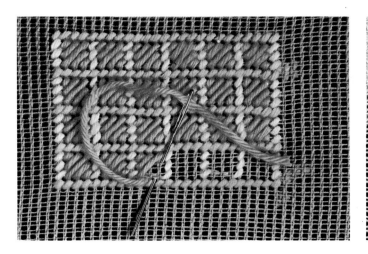

Scottish stitch This is worked in two stages. First make a series of squares using continental stitch and then fill in the squares with blocks of flat stitch worked over one, two and three threads of canvas.

Jacquard stitch This stitch is made up of two different diagonal stitches. The first stage is in continental stitch. Work six horizontal and five vertical stitches, making a series of steps diagonally across the canvas. Leave at least two threads of canvas between each row. The intervening spaces are filled with diagonal straight stitches over two canvas threads.

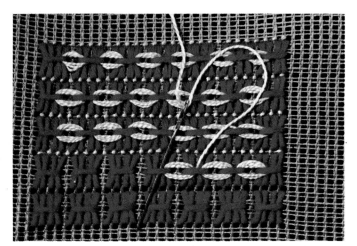

Shell stitch Work four vertical stitches over four threads of the canvas. Make a horizontal stitch from left to right over the four stitches, gathering them together. Come out at the bottom right and start the next group of stitches. For the second stage, using a finer thread in a contrasting color, work a row of backstitches between the rows, over one thread of canvas. Finally, using the same thread as for the backstitch, thread through the center of each group of stitches, making spirals.

Chain stitch Bring the thread through to the right side of the fabric and stitch back into the same point, holding the loop made by the thread with the thumb of the left hand. Bring the point of the needle through several threads away into the center of the loop and pull up. Stitch back each time into the exit point of the stitch just made.

Crossed needlepoint stitches
Simple cross stitch   Alternating cross stitch
Oblong cross stitch   Oblong cross stitch with back stitch

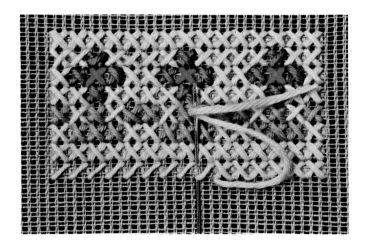

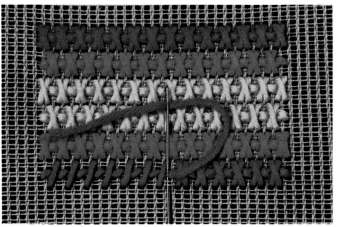

Simple cross stitch This stitch is worked in two rows. In the first row make diagonal stitches from left to right over a chosen number of canvas threads. In the second row, keeping the stitches symmetrical, stitch over those already worked, forming a cross. On canvas this is the ideal stitch for working large motifs from a chart.

Alternating cross stitch This example shows oblong cross stitch over three horizontal threads of canvas and one vertical, and simple cross stitch over one horizontal thread and one vertical. Work in rows from left to right and return from right to left, using the same method as for simple cross stitch. Alternate the position of the crosses in following rows.

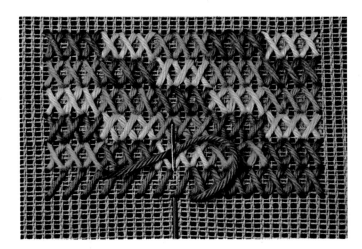

Oblong cross stitch Use the same method as for simple cross stitch, but stitch over a greater number of horizontal canvas threads than vertical canvas threads. In this example, the crosses are worked over three horizontal and two vertical threads. Work from left to right for the first stage and from right to left on the return row.

Oblong cross stitch with backstitch Work a row of oblong cross stitch. Next work a row of backstitch so that the stitches cover the intersections of the crosses. Change the colors of the rows to give a bold striped effect.

184

Smyrna or Double cross stitch Each cross is completed before starting the next, working in rows from left to right. Having made an ordinary cross stitch, the needle is brought through to the right side of the canvas at the center bottom of the stitch. Make a vertical stitch and come out at the center right for the horizontal stitch. Stitch up to the right to the starting point of the next stitch.

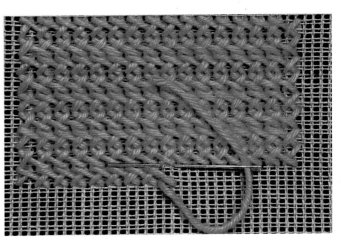

Greek cross stitch Work from left to right. Start on the left of the work and stitch diagonally up to the right over two threads of canvas. Come out two threads to the left. Stitch down to the right over four vertical threads, and two horizontal. Come out two threads to the left. Continue in this way to the end of the row.

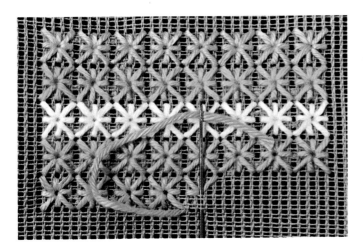

Star or Algerian eye stitch Work in horizontal rows from left to right and vice-versa. The star is worked over four threads of the canvas each way. Bring the needle through at the top left and stitch diagonally down into the center over two threads. Come out vertically two threads to the right and stitch down into the center. Work the other six stitches also down into the center, alternating a diagonal with a horizontal or a vertical.

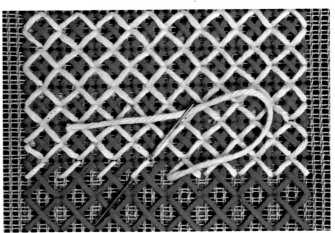

Rice stitch or Crossed corners Work fairly large cross stitches to cover the surface of the canvas. This example uses four threads of the canvas each way. Then, with a contrasting color, tie down the diagonals with a row of smaller diagonal stitches over two threads. First make a row from left to right. On the return row, work from right to left, filling the gaps left in the first row. It is usual to use a light color on a dark background.

Florentine work
Symmetrical flame stitch
Modern flame stitch

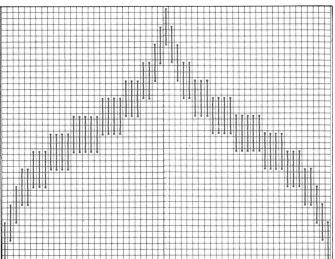

Symmetrical flame stitch 1. This decorative stitch, which takes its name from the pattern formed by the stepped blocks of vertical stitches, resembles tongues of flame. The first row of stitching follows an undulating line and must be counted out carefully from a chart. The successive rows all follow this first line.

2. Symmetrical flame stitch is worked from left to right and vice-versa, following the pattern on the chart (see above). The pattern is continuous and the stitches are all the same height. The stitches are worked from top to bottom with the needle held on a slant, and moving one thread to the left (or right) with each stitch. The stitches are vertical on the right side of the work and slanting on the reverse. In the second and following rows, the stitches fit into the top or bottom of the stitches of the foundation row.

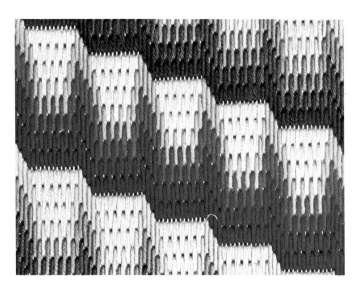

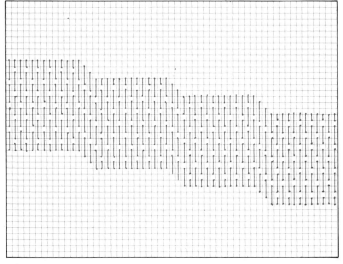

Modern flame stitch 1. Use the same method as described for symmetrical flame stitch. If a regular effect is desired, start at the centre of the work, and work to the left and right of this point. In this example the stitches are spaced so that they intersect one another as in brick stitch.

2. Working in rows from left to right and vice-versa, follow the pattern from the chart above. To achieve a good result, choose a selection of contrasting colors. The best effects are achieved by shading the colors from light to dark and vice-versa. Flame stitch needlepoint, either traditional or modern, can be used to cover stools, period chairs, small objects such as boxes etc, and pillow covers.

Florentine work
Irregular flame stitch
Asymmetrical flame stitch

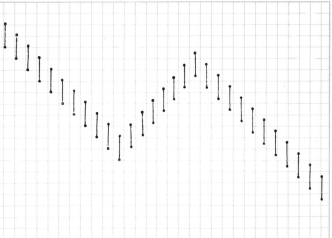

Irregular flame stitch 1. Flame stitch usually follows a symmetrical pattern, but the following example is for an irregular zigzag. The pattern is repeated but the zigzag line drops down to the right. This method is used in modern work, in place of the traditional versions of flame stitch.

2. Work the first row from left to right over two threads of canvas, following the chart shown above. This pattern is most pleasing when each color is used in several tones.

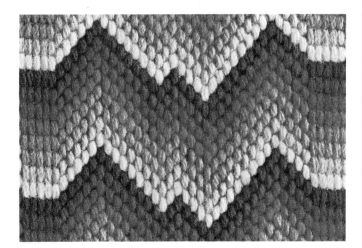

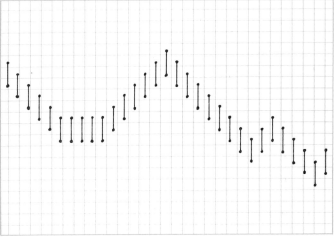

Asymmetrical flame stitch 1. This sequence of stitches, as in the previous example, follows a zigzag line. The stitches are worked over two threads of canvas.

2. Follow the pattern on the chart above, and repeat it across the work, making an asymmetrical but continuous design. Having worked the first row, the following rows fit in above and below.

Decorative needlepoint patterns

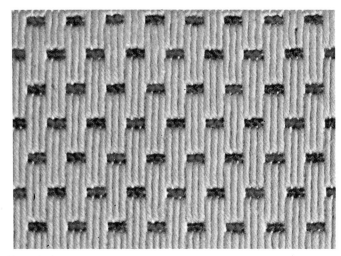

Dot stitch

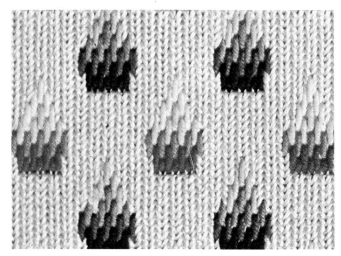

Swiss stitch

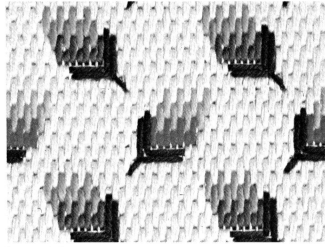

Flower stitch

Zigzag stitch

Basket stitch

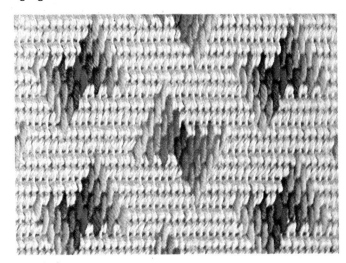

Bow stitch

Decorative needlepoint patterns

Arrow stitch   Wave stitch   Flame stitch variation
Step stitch   Lightning stitch   Pine stitch
                 Diamond stitch   Beehive stitch

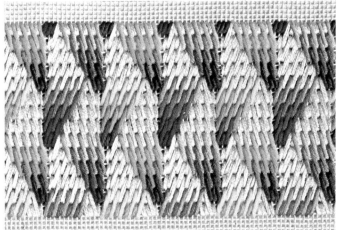

Arrow stitch

Flame stitch variation

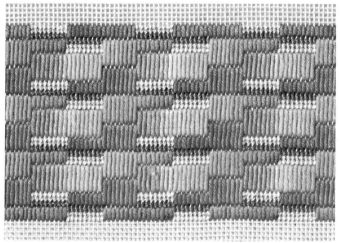

Step stitch

Pine stitch

Wave stitch

Lightning stitch

Diamond stitch

Beehive stitch

189

INDEX

CREDITS

Endpapers, p. 66 and p. 128 – Robert Harding Picture Library
p. 8 – Jacqui Hurst

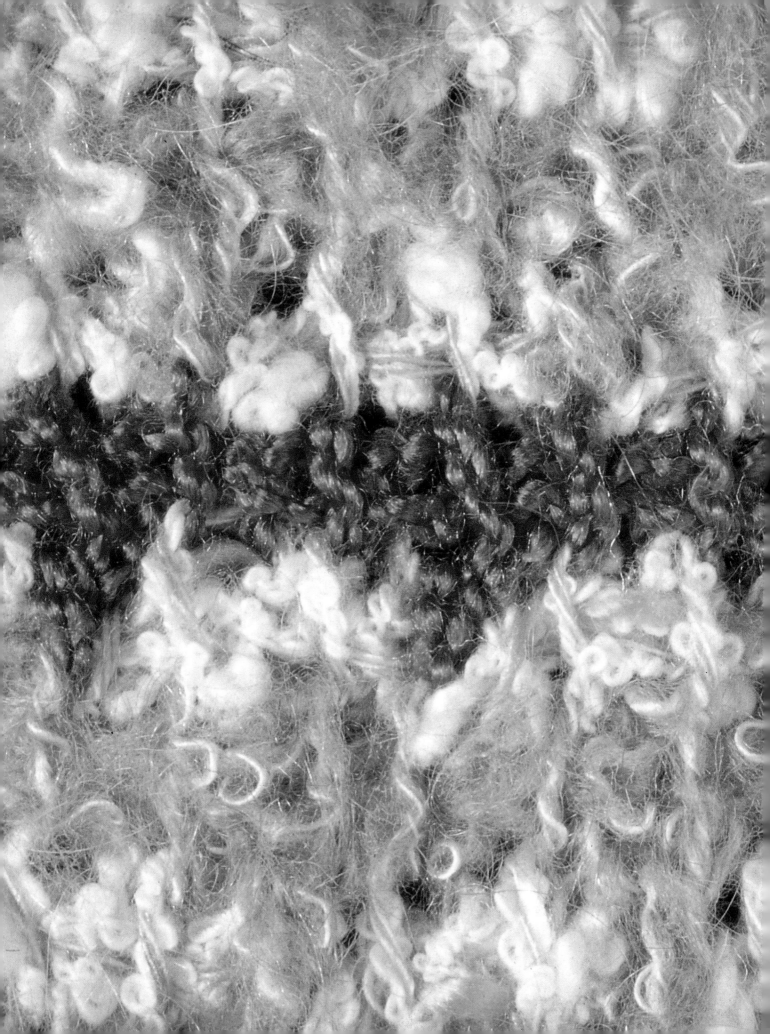